FILM NOIR

Traditions in American Cinema

Series Editors Linda Badley and R. Barton Palmer

Titles in the series include:

The 'War on Terror' and American Film: 9/11 Frames Per Second
by Terence McSweeney

American Postfeminist Cinema: Women, Romance and Contemporary Culture
by Michele Schreiber

Film Noir
by Homer B. Pettey and R. Barton Palmer (eds)

www.euppublishing.com/series/tiac

FILM NOIR

Edited by Homer B. Pettey and R. Barton Palmer

EDINBURGH
University Press

For Jennifer Jenkins
and
To Betty Pettey

Edinburgh University Press is one of the leading university presses in the UK. We publish academic books and journals in our selected subject areas across the humanities and social sciences, combining cutting-edge scholarship with high editorial and production values to produce academic works of lasting importance. For more information visit our website: www.edinburghuniversitypress.com

© editorial matter and organisation Homer B. Pettey and R. Barton Palmer, 2014, 2016
© the chapters their several authors, 2014, 2016

Edinburgh University Press Ltd
The Tun – Holyrood Road
12 (2f) Jackson's Entry
Edinburgh EH8 8PJ

First published in hardback by Edinburgh University Press 2014

Typeset in 10/12.5pt Sabon by
Servis Filmsetting Ltd, Stockport, Cheshire

A CIP record for this book is available from the British Library

ISBN 978 0 7486 9107 4 (hardback)
ISBN 978 1 4744 1307 7 (paperback)
ISBN 978 0 7486 9108 1 (webready PDF)
ISBN 978 0 7486 9109 8 (epub)

The right of the contributors to be identified as authors of this work has been asserted in accordance with the Copyright, Designs and Patents Act 1988 and the Copyright and Related Rights Regulations 2003 (SI No. 2498).

CONTENTS

List of Illustrations — vii
Acknowledgements — ix
Notes on the Contributors — xi

Introduction: The Noir Turn — 1
Homer B. Pettey

1. The Cinema of Uncertainty and the Opacity of Information from Louis Feuillade's Crime Serials to Film Noir — 16
   Vicki Callahan

2. Warning Shadows: German Expressionism and American Film Noir — 38
   Janet Bergstrom

3. Hard-boiled Tradition and Early Film Noir — 58
   Homer B. Pettey

4. Cold War Noir — 80
   R. Barton Palmer

5. Noiring the Pitch: The Conflicted Soundtracks of *Out of the Past*, *The Blue Gardenia* and *The Long Goodbye* — 103
   Krin Gabbard

6. Split Screen: Sound/Music in *The Stranger/Criss Cross* — 122
   Robert Miklitsch

7. Gender and Noir 143
   Elisabeth Bronfen

8. The Subversive Shade of Black in Film Noir 164
   Charles Scruggs

   Postscript: A History of Our Writing about Film Noir 182
   Alain Silver and James Ursini

Selected Book Chapters on Film Noir 192
Selected Film Noir Books 196
Selected Guide to Film Noir 200
Index 216

LIST OF ILLUSTRATIONS

Figure I.1	Honoré Daumier, *Rue Transnonain, April 15, 1834*	3
Figure I.2	Marlowe (Dick Powell) blinded by gun blast, *Murder, My Sweet*	5
Figure 1.1	Diana Monti and Moralés arrange their kidnapping, *Judex*	30
Figure 1.2	Phyllis Dietrichson (Barbara Stanwyck) as Diana Monti's direct descendant, *Double Indemnity*	31
Figure 2.1	*Dr. Mabuse, the Gambler*: the party at Count Told's home	43
Figure 2.2	Cover of the 1965 reprint of Kurtz's *Expressionismus und Film*	44
Figure 2.3	*Criss Cross*: close-up of Anna (Yvonne De Carlo)	52
Figure 2.4	Reverse close-up of Steve (Burt Lancaster), with anxious hope	53
Figure 2.5	Return to Anna's close-up	53
Figure 2.6	Orson Welles' *Lady from Shanghai*	54
Figure 3.1	Brigid (Mary Astor), the caged bird, *The Maltese Falcon*	66
Figure 3.2	Marlowe's (Dick Powell) hallucination, *Murder, My Sweet*	70
Figure 3.3	Girl with bat in front of Dietrichson house, *Double Indemnity*	73
Figure 4.1	American communist meeting, *I Was a Communist for the FBI*	96
Figure 4.2	Seductive communist appears, *The Woman on Pier 13*	99

Figure 5.1	Jeff (Robert Mitchum) and Kathie (Jane Greer) in conflicted embrace as 'The First Time I Saw You' plays, *Out of the Past*	110
Figure 5.2	Nat King Cole, *The Blue Gardenia*	112
Figure 6.1	Konrad Meinike (Konstanin Shayne) captured in the lens, *The Stranger*	124
Figure 6.2	Mary (Loretta Young) watches concentration camp footage, *The Stranger*	127
Figure 6.3	Yvonne De Carlo seductively dances with Tony Curtis, *Criss Cross*	134
Figure 7.1	Vince (Lee Marvin) brutalises Debbie (Gloria Graham) before throwing scalding coffee into her face, *The Big Heat*	156
Figure 7.2	Phyllis (Barbara Stanwyck) experiences the joy of her husband's strangulation, *Double Indemnity*	159
Figure 8.1	Eunice Leonard (Theresa Harris) suspicious of Markham (Robert Mitchum) in the nightclub scene, *Out of the Past*	166
Figure 8.2	Lotte (Butterfly McQueen) and Mildred (Joan Crawford) making home-made pies, *Mildred Pierce*	168
Figure 8.3	Stoker (Robert Ryan) cornered like a rat in *The Set-Up*	178

ACKNOWLEDGEMENTS

First of all, considerable gratitude must be proffered to the contributors of this volume on film noir. Vicki Callahan wrote a fascinating examination of Feuillade's proto-noir from a vantage of her insightful category for film studies, cinema of uncertainty, which will soon be coined throughout the academy for noir studies. Moreover, her exemplary eye for the noir aesthetic details in early French cinema also reveals itself in her persuasive comparisons to classic American noir. Janet Bergstrom provided profound insights that re-evaluate German Expressionist influences on film noir. Krin Gabbard initially underscores the musical consistency for most film noir scores, only to pitch in a new key the concept of otherness and its fundamental relationship to noir music. He re-analysed essential films noirs and revealed, through his sharply attuned ear, not what was there, but rather what was left out and why a love theme went missing. Robert Miklitsch extended his previous groundbreaking work on musical and sonic dimensions and theories to film noir, in the process providing new approaches for discussing the complex noir aesthetic. He opens up a new critical field for aesthetic consideration of the movements of silence and ambient sound, along with music, in the complex sonic landscape of film noir, one as pervasive and essential as its visual experiments. Elisabeth Bronfen gave an expansive reading of gender in film noir that will demand re-evaluations of the genre for some time to come. Once again, she forces critics to re-examine the most foundational noirs and provides readings that not only open up those texts, but also make them appear utterly modern. With his typically discerning eye for literary and film connections, Charles Scruggs revealed yet another side to film noir with his poetics of racial concerns within the genre. As usual, Charlie opens our eyes to racial issues that so often escape even the most perceptive of film scholars. Without doubt, we owe considerable debts to these internationally renowned scholars.

To Alain Silver and James Ursini, a tribute needs to be offered for their generous and frank history of their exceptional work for many decades on film noir. Moreover, it is altogether fitting that their work be recognised alongside that of academicians, since all of the contributors to this volume, as well as film historians, critics and scholars, know all too well the immense debt owed to them for providing such essential, useful and comprehensive texts on film noir. For those books on film noir and this fine essay, my co-editor and I wish to offer to them a highly appreciative, sincere thank-you.

Of course, admiration needs to be extended to my co-editor, R. Barton Palmer, who saw this project from its inception through to this final production. His support for the new directions taken by the contributors in this volume has made its publication possible. Moreover, his insights in his chapter on Cold War noirs will remain a standard for the genre for many years to come. That he took on the indexing of this volume will remain a generous gesture I will not long forget.

Most definitely, gratitude has to be offered to Professor Susan White, who, with an expansive view and a startling and always impressive knowledge of film history, provided such valuable insights into my initial concepts about film noir. Clearly, this book would not have come to fruition without numerous conversations with her over the course of a year. For her generous spirit, I offer my thanks.

So often, friends outside the academy do not realise how much they contribute over time to one's interests and intellectual development. In terms of film noir, the workings of the Hollywood film industry and being partners in numerous crimes, I would like to express my profound thanks to Chip Johannessen, exceptional television producer, and to Carter Burwell, film composer extraordinaire. For sharing an interest in hard-boiled detective fiction, particularly Raymond Chandler, I would like to thank Allan Arffa, attorney-at-law, especially for conversations dating back to my blurry, yet enjoyable college days. For enhancing my comic world-view and teaching me that the right kind of cynicism always has a tinge of humour, my heartfelt appreciation goes to the men and women who haunt the *Harvard Lampoon* Castle.

Finally, much of this work could not have been accomplished without the love of Jennifer, Jo Anne, Melissa, Olympia and Josephine. To them, most likely I owe everything.

Homer B. Pettey
Tucson, Arizona

NOTES ON THE CONTRIBUTORS

Janet Bergstrom, Professor of Cinema & Media Studies, University of California, Los Angeles, specialises in archive-based, cross-national studies of émigré directors such as Murnau, Renoir, Lang and Sternberg. She pursues the same approach in 'visual essays' she has published on DVD – *Murnau's 4 Devils: Traces of a Lost Film* (Twentieth Century-Fox, released internationally with *Sunrise*), *Introduction to* Phantom (Flicker Alley), *Murnau and Borzage at Fox: The Expressionist Heritage* (Edition Filmmuseum, with Borzage's *The River*) and *Sternberg's* Underworld: *How It Came to Be* (Criterion). She is currently working on a monograph on *Sunrise* and a book on 'Murnau in America'.

Elisabeth Bronfen is Professor of English and American Studies at the University of Zurich. She has published on a wide range of literary and visual culture topics. Her most recent books are *Home in Hollywood. The Imaginary Geography of Cinema* (2001), *Specters of War. Hollywood's Engagement with Military Conflicts* (2012) and *Night Passages. Philosophy, Literature and Film* (2013).

Vicki Callahan is an Associate Professor in the University of Southern California's School of Cinematic Arts. She is the author of *Zones of Anxiety: Movement, Musidora, and the Crime Serials of Louis Feuillade* (2005) and editor for the collection *Reclaiming the Archive: Feminism and Film History* (2010). Her publications range from silent cinema and experimental film to remix strategies with a special focus on disruptive narrative forms.

Krin Gabbard is Professor of Comparative Literature and Cultural Studies at Stony Brook University. He is the author of *Hotter than That: The Trumpet, Jazz, and American Culture* (2009), *Black Magic: White Hollywood and African American Culture* (2004), *Jammin' at the Margins: Jazz and the American Cinema* (1996) and *Psychiatry and the Cinema* (2nd edition, 1999). He is currently writing an interpretive biography of jazz artist Charles Mingus.

Robert Miklitsch is a Professor in the Department of English Language and Literature at Ohio University. His essays have appeared in numerous collections, including, most recently, *Lowering the Boom: Critical Studies in Film Sound* (2008) and *Neo-Noir* (2009). He is the editor of *Psycho-Marxism* (1998) and the author of *From Hegel to Madonna: Towards a General Economy of 'Commodity Fetishism'* (1998), *Roll Over Adorno: Critical Theory, Popular Culture, Audiovisual Media* (2006) and *Siren City: Sound and Source Music in Classic American Noir* (2011). He is currently writing a book on film noir in the 'atomic age'.

R. Barton Palmer is Calhoun Lemon Professor of Literature at Clemson University, South Carolina, where he also directs the film studies programme. Palmer is the author, editor or co-editor of more than fifty books and a hundred book chapters and journal articles, including two volumes on film noir.

Homer B. Pettey, Associate Professor of English, University of Arizona, has forthcoming chapters on Hitchcock's American noirs (Cambridge University Press), Wyatt Earp biopics (State University of New York Press) and violence in noir (Praeger). He has also written essays on Melville and Faulkner, as well as working as a script consultant for several television series.

Charles Scruggs is a Professor of American Literature at the University of Arizona. In addition to writing books and articles on African-American literature and film, he is a co-author (with Gary Holcomb) of a recent book on Hemingway's influence on African-American writers.

Alain Silver's articles have appeared in *Film Comment, Movie, Wide Angle* and the online magazines *Images* and *Senses of Cinema*. Among his other books are studies of the samurai film, Raymond Chandler and cinematographer James Wong Howe. His produced screenplays include *White Nights* (from Dostoyevsky), the Showtime movie *Time at the Top* and *Nightcomer* (which he also directed). He has also produced a score of independent feature films (including *Cyborg 2, Beat* and *Crashing*) and forty soundtrack albums. His commentaries may be heard and seen on numerous DVDs, where he discusses Chandler, the gangster film, sci-fi, horror and the classic period of noir. His PhD in Theater Arts/Motion Pictures, Critical Studies is from the University of California, Los Angeles.

NOTES ON THE CONTRIBUTORS

James Ursini provided text for the Taschen Icon series on Bogart, Dietrich, Elizabeth Taylor, Mae West and De Niro. His early study of Preston Sturges was reprinted in a bilingual edition by the San Sebastián Film Festival. With Alain Silver, he has also written on the vampire film, the zombie film and directors David Lean, Robert Aldrich and Roger Corman. He has been a producer on features and documentaries, and lectured on filmmaking at UCLA and other colleges in the Los Angeles area where he works as an educator.

INTRODUCTION: THE NOIR TURN

Homer B. Pettey

> Without question, you try to learn from everybody you possibly can. You look at everything; you research everything. You know how I started 'film noir'? – of course I didn't know it was 'film noir' until the French told me but you know how I started it? I wanted to get a high-key-low-key lighting and looked through a copy of Daumier's works. Those of you who know Daumier know the kind of paintings he did. I showed it to my photographer and I said, 'This is the kind of effect I want in this picture: very deep shadows and very hot lights'. That's how it started. It was our version of Daumier. It wasn't an original version at all and it wasn't exactly the same; but it was close, and I've done the same thing with other situations.
>
> Edward Dmytryk, 'On influences'

So Dmytryk informed his audience in 1980 at the University of Texas about the original moment of inspiration for his evolving noir aesthetic.[1] That Dmytryk chose Honoré Daumier as the basis for film noir is hardly surprising, since Daumier's works not only exhibit what would become the noir visual style, but also contribute to the noir sensibility, its *Weltanschauung* and its social commentary. Moreover, Dmytryk and Daumier found themselves at odds with their governments for their sardonic critiques of economic repression and political hypocrisy. By referring to Daumier's style, Dmytryk also invokes Honoré de Balzac's sardonic realism in *La Comédie humaine*, since Daumier illustrated Balzac's works and both he and Balzac contributed to *La*

Caricature in the 1830s.² Not surprising, then, that aesthetic experiments of modernism in the nineteenth century would attract the critical and cinematic eye of film noir directors and be the basis for the evolution of the art form. As evidenced by French cinema from the 1930s, film noir was already a term applied to films with subversive accounts of the 'black despair of a hopeless life',³ as Georges Altman concluded of *Le Jour se lève* in 1939: 'Actors, theme, and words are cast and bathed in images which are never common, banal, or pernicious. A *film noir*, but that's as it should be'.⁴ That concept of a noir vision, as Dmytryk admits, depended upon the transmutation of style and content from antecedent artistic movements and texts, an evolutionary process both imitative and original. Dmytryk discovered in Daumier's aesthetic both a noir visual sensibility and realism.

Henry James saw the ironic, satiric and reactionary elements of Daumier's caricatures and offered a naturalistic, evolutionary analogy for Daumier that could apply as well to film noir:

> Irony, skepticism, pessimism are, in any particular soil, plants of gradual growth, and it is in the art of caricature that they flower most aggressively. Furthermore, they must be watered by education – I mean by the education of the eye and hand– all of which takes time. The soil must be rich, too; the incongruities must swarm. It is open to doubt whether a pure democracy is very liable to make this particular satiric return upon itself; for which it would seem that certain complications must not be wanting. These complications are supplied from the moment a democracy becomes, as we may say, from its own point of view; from the moment variations and heresies, deviations, or perhaps simple affirmations of taste and temper begin to multiply within it. Such things afford a *point d'appui*; for it is evidently of the essence of caricature to be reactionary.⁵

So much of James's remarks correspond to the development of film noir, especially its relationship to the American dream turned into a nightmare, the corruption within the political and economic system, and the venal nature of modern society. James also hit upon the very problem of caricature within democracy: that inability to perceive the harsh reality of social conditions. Film noir, then, functions as a new type of caricature, *à la* Daumier of the *Charivari*, as a reaction to Depression-era economic conditions, the spread of anti-democratic ideology, the emotional cataclysm of World War II, its subsequent psychological and social malaise, and the paranoia of the Cold War. James was impressed by Daumier's ability to provide his caricatures 'with their abnormal blackness as well as with their grotesque, magnifying movement'.⁶ Daumier's representations of society, for James, are reflections in 'a big cracked mirror'.⁷ Film noir's mirror is equally cracked in its reflections of mid-twentieth-century culture.

INTRODUCTION: THE NOIR TURN

Rue Transnonain, le 15 avril 1834 is Daumier's most political and most poignant work (see Figure I.1).[8] On 14 April 1834, it appears that an infantry captain was wounded on the barricade of the rue Transnonain (actually rue Beaubourg) by a shot fired from a neighbouring building. The officer's detachment received orders to massacre all of the inhabitants of that building, an event to be remembered as the most scandalous intrusion by the army upon the citizenry, especially since it had been done without a magistrate's mandate and clearly violated the Constitution. Daumier relied upon the graphic, vivid depiction of the aftermath, which he found in a pamphlet by the radical Ledru-Rollin: 'In one single house on the rue Transnonain, a dozen cadavers were horribly mutilated; four people had been dangerously wounded: women, infants, and the elderly were not spared'.[9] Baudelaire, in *Quelques caricaturistes français*, praised Daumier's work: 'It is not exactly a caricature; it is a story of vulgar and terrible reality'.[10] Early praise for Daumier's ability to render a reality to 'this cruel scene in its horrifying details' that exceeds even the most graphic verbal descriptions of historians, thus placing Daumier's disturbing political commentary alongside Goya's realistic and allegorical sequence, *The Disasters of War*.[11]

Roger Passeron comments that the use of light in and composition of *Rue Transnonain* are cinematic qualities:

> The quality of light is fantastic. It is the terrible light of dawn shining through one window and highlighting the central character of the tragedy, while the rest of the apartment is in a half-light in which further crimes seem to be lurking. The border between light and shade falls tragically on the bolster of the bed, while the sheets were pulled down

Figure I.1 Honoré Daumier, *Rue Transnonain, April 15, 1834*.

by the man who had slept and had dragged them with him into death. The quality of the composition is prodigious. It is a century ahead of its time, anticipating techniques discovered by the great film-makers of the twentieth century, who used similar effect for their shots and close-ups. With our experience of the cinema we can easily imagine the camera lens placed a little above floor level, recording the scene.[12]

The figures in *Rue Transnonain* are also situated along axes of two oblique angles, the abscissa demarcating shadow to shadow, while the ordinate follows the harsh lighting of the open doorway. In the line of shadows can be discerned two bodies, the lower right merely the head, upturned face and shoulders of an elderly man, the upper left the feet and torso exposed, but no view of the head and face of a woman. The light streaming in not only depicts the man fallen from his bed, but also the dead infant beneath his body. The scene is a tragedy cast in chiaroscuro.

Murder, My Sweet often offers scenes of visual parody of Daumier's *Rue Transnonain*. The first scene with the Grayles in their mansion is nearly the obverse of Daumier's lithograph, with bright, artificial light saturating the luxurious mise-en-scène. The final scene at the beach cottage, however, almost repeats *Rue Transnonain*, with the bodies, death-like on the floor, fragmented and nearly disembodied by the frame, and captured in severe axes of harsh light and deep darkness. Marlowe (Dick Powell) tries to stop the mayhem, but his movement along the floor towards the semi-automatic places him in danger of receiving the gun's cast-off powder explosion, which blinds him. The oblique camera angle, the chiaroscuro lighting upon Marlowe's face and his hand, the disembodied hand with the pistol cut by the frame – all mimic Daumier's technique in *Rue Transnonain*. Marlowe's blindness becomes a classic theme and visual aesthetic for film noir, those moments in which the protagonist's figure is entrapped within shadows or tries to perceive through an adumbrated world only to discover his own lack of perception. Dmytryk plays upon Daumier's style in order to suggest a world in which the intersections of light and shadow, metaphors for moral, social, psychological and ethic polarities, only produce tragic consequences. Moreover, like the signature noir effects of lines, bars and striations produced by the junction of light and shade, this chiaroscuro effect reveals the dilemma of the contemporary society in which blindness dominates over insight and whose self-constructed entrapment offers no escape.

For historical comparison, it is worth noting that both Daumier and Dmytryk land in jail for their political art at the tyrannical, oppressive whims of governmental authorities. Daumier protested at his trial that *Gargantua* represented not the King, but the Budget, and to the court 'pictures were . . . more dangerous than words . . . not only because of widespread illiteracy but also because images were relatively easy to disseminate among various classes

INTRODUCTION: THE NOIR TURN

Figure I.2 Marlowe (Dick Powell) blinded by gun blast, *Murder, My Sweet* (1944).

and regions'.[13] Of course, jail did not stop Daumier from lampooning the King with a large, very recognisable drawing of Gargantua on the prison wall. *Rue Transnonain* reveals Daumier's more pointed attack upon Louis-Philippe's government, one that has evolved from cartoonish, scatological sketches to a new realism. Daumier's work has served political causes and interpretations for nearly a century and three-quarters, often making Daumier an ideological figure of social rebellion, as evidenced during the fiftieth anniversary of his death in 1929 and the later fascination with his work in the Soviet Union.[14] Daumier's influence on fin-de-siècle graphic arts in France was tremendous, as can be observed in the chiaroscuro techniques of Théophile Alexandre Steinlen's *La Rue Caulaincourt* that reveals 'poverty exists at both ends of the street'.[15]

Edward Dmytryk would face the harsh realities of the House Un-American Activities Committee (HUAC) and McCarthyism for his political affiliations and his social commentary in his noirs. Both Adrian Scott and Dmytryk were called before HUAC with the 'pink subpoena' on 23 September 1947. Scott and Dmytryk were linked throughout the HUAC proceedings, so much so that the Committee's chief investigator, Robert E. Stripling, confused their names at times. It was assumed that Scott and Dmytryk were facing HUAC's scrutiny due to *Crossfire*, as Scott argued openly to the Committee that he and Dmytryk were being persecuted for making *Crossfire* and for its message against racial hatred. *Murder, My Sweet* also provided Scott and Dmytryk with a frank depiction of class politics in Los Angeles, with its collision between the lower-class mean streets and the faux aristocracy of life among the wealthy in their ostentatious mansions. For Scott and Dmytryk, this film combined 'the realism of wartime noir and the idealism of the Popular Front progressives'.[16] After the separate trials of John Howard Lawson and Dalton Trumbo resulted in guilty verdicts, both Scott and Dmytryk were also found guilty of contempt of Congress. After serving his time in a Federal prison in West Virginia, and with no prospects for directing, Dmytryk realised that he was going to have to talk. Dmytryk, in *Odd Man Out*, compares his decision to talk to Philip Marlowe's in *Murder, My Sweet*:

> In *Murder, My Sweet*, Philip Marlowe is pistol-whipped, carried away to a phony sanitarium, and drugged to the gills. After two days of DTs, he awakens to find himself literally befogged. As he struggles to dispel his hallucinations, his progress is monitored, metaphorically, by the gradual attenuation of the web of smoke that overlays the scene. When it has disappeared entirely, we know that his mind is finally clear. And so does he. 'I was ready to talk to somebody!' he narrates.
>
> After a measurable amount of self-examination, situational analysis, and discussion with Jean, the sensible member of the family, the fog had lifted. I was no longer angry. Instead, I, too, 'was ready to talk to somebody!'[17]

In April of 1951, Dmytryk was again before HUAC, but this time, he was there willingly. Dmytryk makes clear that being on a 'greylist' was far worse than being blacklisted, since at least one knew that one was blacklisted. The greylists were numerous in Hollywood, even though George Murphy and Ronald Reagan, two actors who profited from HUAC politically, 'have denied the existence of such protective measures, but that is like neo-Nazis denying Hitler's concentration camps'.[18] Dmytryk, reflecting some forty years later, viewed the main source of his problems not so much as the HUAC members or the Reagans of Hollywood, although they were certainly to be blamed. The real source of his rancour was 'the liberal chic' and its 'hypocrites who rated snitching a higher crime than treason and who, from no-risk positions, kept the conflict alive into the present decade'.[19] For Dmytryk, both right and left political factions in America ruthlessly sought power, money and status, as though little had changed since politics of greed represented by Daumier and especially Balzac.

As Peter Brooks so eloquently expressed it, Balzac invented the nineteenth century. Balzac's works comment on capitalist economy and the desire for and denial of access not only to market successes, but also to stable class definition:

> The linguistic sign, money, the accessory things purchased by money, and the desire that subtends things, money, and signs, appear to belong to an overheated libidinal economy that is ever on the verge of crash. It is the paradox of Balzac's realism that the world he describes in such

impassioned detail seems, like the inflationary economy, menaced with collapse, mined from within by the threat of non-meaning.[20]

Brooks's trenchant analysis of the paradox of nineteenth-century realism certainly applies to the systematic expression of both macro- and microcosms of mid-twentieth-century American culture in film noir. In so many ways, nineteenth-century Paris serves as the primogenitor for the noir city, as T. J. Clark describes its more venial traits:

> Here was ostentation, not luxury; frippery, not fashion; consumption, not trade. And here above all was *uncertainty* – a pantomime of false rich and false poor, in which anyone could pretend to be anything if he or she had money for clothes.[21]

Unlike other American genres, film noir explores money and economies (market, domestic, gendered, racial and class) as fundamental to its expression. Nineteenth-century Paris, London and even New York serve as examples of the unreal city, that sick, venal metropolis of deadly night. Certainly, Realism is always first and foremost a literary and artistic expression of the nineteenth century urban scene as film noir is the visual, nearly voyeuristic if not prurient, scopic analysis of the modern cityscape, especially at its most visceral level. So much of film noir relies upon urban landscapes, from location shooting of run-down tenements and lower-class street scenes to expansive Bel Air mansions, from low-life lounges to high-brow cabarets, from skid row alleys to Park Avenue. Balzac creates a sense of the physical environment with his verbal reconstruction of senses, including touch and smell; that kind of synaesthesia became a hallmark of the cinematic details of Edward Dmytryk, Fritz Lang, Joseph H. Lewis, Samuel Fuller, John Huston, Robert Siodmak, Anthony Mann and Stanley Kubrick, among others.

In *Père Goriot*, Balzac provides an exacting description of the *Maison Vauquer* that stimulates, often with disgust, the reader's senses in a shock of primal recognition:

> An odor rises from the *salon* for which, alas, the language has no word, so we must call it 'the *pension* smell'. It is a stale, musty, mouldy scent, rancid, and it makes you freezing cold, it makes your nose water, it bores into your clothes; it has the flavor of a room where people have eaten; it stinks of kitchens and servants and the poorhouse. You might be able to describe it, if someone had invented a technique for analyzing all the tiny, nauseating particles that each and every one of the lodgers, old and young alike, dumped into the air with their nasal effluvia, and all their other highly personalized bodily exhalations.[22]

Both Balzac and Dmytryk developed new styles, narrative strategies and social critiques *avant le déluge* of scholarly classifications of literary Realism and film noir. Not only Daumier's exacting eye for detail, but also Honoré de Balzac's literary analysis of class antagonism, economic obsessions and moral corruption in his contemporary French society would influence twentieth-century realist depictions of culture. In a sense, then, that literary and artistic dimension of Realism constitutes the noir turn, the shift in style, aesthetics and social, political and economic commentary.

The kinds of details proffered by Balzac in order to disarm and repulse his reader find their heir in Raymond Chandler, who also attempts a Balzacian depiction of the Florian residence in *Farewell, My Lovely*, the novel adapted for Dmytryk's *Murder, My Sweet*:

> I stepped through the door and hooked the screen again. A large handsome cabinet radio droned to the left of the door in the corner of the room. It was the only decent piece of furniture the place had. It looked brand new. Everything else was junk – dirty overstuffed pieces, a wooden rocker that matched the one on the porch, a square arch into a dining room with a stained table, finger marks all over the swing door to the kitchen beyond. A couple of frayed lamps with once gaudy shades that were now as gay as superannuated streetwalkers.[23]

What characterises both depictions of the underclass is the author's insistence upon making the reality of scenes as sensory and physical as possible. The original script for *Murder, My Sweet* combines Balzac and Chandler in the description of Mrs. Florian:

> **39. INT. Mrs. FLORIAN'S PARLOR – Night**
> CLOSE SHOT – of Mrs. Florian with the name superimposed, as she blows her nose. Her face is grey, puffy. The CAMERA PULLS BACK SLOWLY. She is wearing a shapeless outing flannel robe, sitting in a rocker.
> **MARLOWE'S VOICE**
> She was a charming, middle-aged lady with a face like a bucket of mud
> . . .
> The ANGLE WIDENS to include Marlowe's back as he leans forward, refilling a glass in her hand.
> **MARLOWE'S VOICE**
> I gave her a drink – and she was girl who'd take a drink – if she had to knock you down to get to the bottle . . .[24]

In the film adaptation, Mrs Florian reflects her surroundings, even if she does not influence their tawdry, sleazy and neglected conditions. There is a tactile realism to Dmytryk's camerawork and Marlowe's voiceover exacerbates the disturbing assault upon the senses, creating a all-too-real Balzacian depiction of this lower-class world. Ultimately, Daumier, Balzac and Dmytryk pose the vexing question of what is film noir – a reactionary caricature of society, a synaesthetic art form of modernity or an extension of nineteenth-century Realism?

Stanley Corkin's approach to American Realism is to ground it historically to show that literary and cinematic texts are not simply theoretically hegemonic and ideological, but 'what these works meant *within* a culture where specific activities to reorder social and economic activity from the top down were coalescing in business, politics, and social life'.[25] For cinema, Corkin investigates Thomas Edison, Edwin S. Porter and D. W. Griffith in order to reveal that these texts reproduce 'the political and cultural agenda of corporate liberalism'[26] and 'naturalize the objectification and fragmentation of modern life'.[27] Realism in early cinema, as well as in literature, not only expressed the complex politics and economics of the period aesthetically, but also had a social impact upon prevailing capitalist views. By mid-century, American cinema questioned ethical and political acceptance of a dominant view of modern industrial existence. Film noir comments upon this type of early cinematic Realism, since its narratives do not reveal a coherent social landscape but a fragmented, dissociative world.

Amy Kaplan's inquiry into Realism focuses upon social change, class difference and mass culture in order to reveal the 'unreality at the heart of middle-class life' caused by 'intense and often violent class conflicts which produced fragmented and completing social realities, and the simultaneous development of a mass culture which dictated an equally threatening homogeneous reality'.[28] While Kaplan's work deals with literary texts of the Realist period, she does offer insights into narrative patterns adopted by film noir, especially for the construction of the modern, noir metropolis. Artistic metaphors in Kaplan's argument define the boundaries of urban class and social forces, as she describes for William Dean Howells' *A Hazard of New Fortunes*: 'Throughout the novel, narrative excess strains the boundaries of the urban representation and forces their realignment. Fragments threaten to intrude into the foreground, and the background threatens to engulf the characters'.[29] That shifting of fore- and background elements exemplifies oblique camera work and alienating mise-en-scène associated with the depiction of the noir city. The worlds of criminality and law enforcement, between ethnic and white neighbourhoods, between middle-class verities and bourgeois vices, between domestic sphere and urbanisation – these worlds exist in the noir city as shifting margins in conflict, not unlike capitalist and working-class populations within the *fin-de-siècle* city in America. In film noir, there is little attempt to neutralise these boundaries into a coherent social landscape; instead, the framed world is always already perceptible and hidden simultaneously by means of the intense shifting patterns of light and shadow. The very aesthetic of film noir exposes the radical separations among social, political, racial, gender and economic spheres in modern life. This noir aesthetic, then, functions as a signifying system for representing binary oppositions and dialectical poles that question the unifying mythology of the American Dream.

In *Symbolic Economies*, Jean-Joseph Goux includes a discussion on the development of writing in relation to social formation. There exists a corresponding development between two types of exchange – economic and signifying – that also includes other social modes of production and exchange: patriarchal systems, religion, kinship, sexuality, laws and contractual relationships:

> From barter to coins and to paper money, from the pictographic signifier to alphabetic and algebraic notation, from mental image to conceptualization, from the dyadic intersubjective relation to the complex relations under the aegis of the internalized law of the father, from primitive law to institutionalized law (developed on the basis of the contradictory equivalence relation between crime and punishment), from the polymorphous libidinal economy to so-called phallic centralization of drives – all these various developments, whether ontogenetic or essentially phylogenetic, obey the logic of the symbolization process. The successive modes of symbolizing deployed by this logic correspond to the historical sequence of social modes of production and exchange, including relations of production.[30]

Hence, there is a 'monetary metaphor that haunts discussions of language' and that can be extended to art, specifically the development from the realist through the sensualist to the modernist abstract modes of painterly representation. These signifying stages also correspond to the development of film, which, oddly enough, Goux omits from his argument, falling into the high–low art division. Still, Goux provides a conceptual framework for discussion of the development of film noir from its nineteenth-century complex intersection of influences to its appearance in Dmytryk's *Murder, My Sweet*. Moreover, ontogenetic or phylogenetic developments open up the question of film noir as a genre.

When addressing film noir as a genre, debates immediately arise as to whether it is a genre, a style, a movement, a response to a *Zeitgeist*, a narrative strategy, a psycho-social reaction to modernity or some combination of all of these essential elements. The problem, then, is not with film noir, but with the concept of genre. Homology, topology, taxonomy – all relate to the process of imposing systematic, often rigid categories upon art. The case of Dmytryk poses questions for the many approaches to defining film noir.

INTRODUCTION: THE NOIR TURN

The issue of genre has plagued studies of film noir for decades, since its inception by French critics. Discussions of film noir fall prey to several divisive problems; in short, whether film noir can be defined as a genre or as a style. Of course, scholars and critics have used these initial categories to distinguish more precisely the nature of film noir as a cycle, an aesthetic movement, a psycho-emotional mood, a sceptical modernist tone, an existential narrative or some combination of these elements. Most studies of film noir view the 'cycle' beginning in 1940 with Boris Ingster's *Stranger on the Third Floor* and concluding with Robert Wise's 'film gris', *Odds Against Tomorrow*, in 1959.

Falling just outside the supposed film noir cycle's end (1940–59), *Girl of the Night* (1960) focuses upon the emotional struggles of Bobbie Williams (Anne Francis), a love-lorn, love-torn call girl with an unhealthy dependency on inverted plays of power dominance with her pimp boyfriend Larry (John Kerr). Based upon Harold Greenwald's scholarly work, *The Call Girl: A Social and Psychological Study* (1958), the film traces Bobbie's cycles of doubt and belief in her ability to love through lengthy sessions of analysis with an avuncular psychologist (Lloyd Nolan). The highly stylised opening title sequence has Bobbie desperately running through the urban nightscape, rendered in harsh chiaroscuro effects, shot in low and oblique angles, with occasional freeze-frames to accentuate her silhouette against blurred commercial storefronts as female mannequins stare blindly at this living mannequin. The credit sequence concludes with an extreme close-up of Bobbie's partially illuminated face against a foreboding blackdrop. *Girl of the Night* also relies upon flashbacks and montage sequences, employs venetian blind shadow techniques to suggest entrapment, moves through the transient world of smoked-filled lounges and claustrophobic hotel rooms, and depicts realistic moments of physical and emotional violence in order to convey the brooding, unrelenting world of high-class urban prostitution. The film concludes quite ambiguously with Bobbie rejecting her pimp and heading out with her suitcase, significantly reversing the film's opening with a high-angle crane shot that makes her figure recede into afternoon city light. Such an ending, however, is not a resolution, since Bobbie has left and returned to the demi-monde life before. Yet for all of these visual and narrative elements, scholars, critics, encyclopedias and studies devoted to film noir do not place *Girl of the Night* within that genre.

Of course, the theoretical problem begins with the dire need for scholars to construct a homogeneous schema for a collection of seemingly heterogeneous elements comprising film noir. In many respects, then, the problem is not with film noir, but with the concept of genre itself.

Constructing an historical evolution for film noir often incurs similar problems as in biological taxonomies. There are relevant analogies to the biological approaches to species definition for film genre studies, so long as the analogous elements retain the features of a theoretical method. Basic observable conditions and patterns of the natural world relate to inherent, developmental and environmental constraints that determine species; for example, organisms appear to be suited to their environment; diversity of organisms can be organised by a homogeneity of morphology within a hierarchical structure; and, finally, the distribution of organisms through space and time. Translating these observable traits to the visual medium of film reveals the initial attempts at genre categorisation for film noir, and presents a somewhat homogeneous aesthetic and narrative, well suited to the postwar *milieu*, and distributed during that certain 'cycle' in the United States. Of course, Darwinian natural selection, based upon inherited, shared traits within a struggle for existence, can be read as the homogeneous noir style faced with changing studio and audience fads, tastes and budgetary constraints during the Cold War period into the 1960s. This systematic historical approach, however, does not account for the recurrence of film noir after the cycle's conclusion (read: aesthetic extinction). The Modern Synthesis for genetics expanded Darwinian evolution by accounting for mutation and genetic drift, but did not account for environmental influence on inherited phenotypes. In film terms, such a model allows for the sub-genre mutations of film noir, from the police procedurals to the anti-communist propaganda vehicles, but it does not address how film noir suddenly reappears in form, narrative and adaptations beyond the closed dates of the cycle theory. Game theorists have entered the evolutionary scene to construct a classical game theory based upon the players as opposed to the evolutionary model, which is based upon inherited strategies and occasional 'novel strategy' 'as a mutation'.[31] This modelling brings into relief patterns at the micro level and also at the macro level, and also takes into account species archetypes and the dynamic theatre of their environment. Such an approach lends itself to a method of viewing the inherited nineteenth-century influences from art and literature, the development of filmic archetypical aesthetic and narrative strategies, and the inevitable transformation, mutation and adaptation of the genre over time. Such a model offers more viable historical, sociological and economic assessments for defining both the apparently heterogeneous collection of films first observed as film noir and their subsequent influence upon new film experiments with visual and narrative designs.

As W. G. Runciman asserts, most attempts by 'selectionist explanations' to account for influence and outcomes resemble little more than 'just-so stories'; by dint of critical accumulations, such explanations do provide patterns that

> combine theoretically grounded accounts of the mechanisms of transfer of information affecting behavior in the phenotype with narratives of path-dependent sequence of historical events in which the relatively higher probability of reproduction and diffusion of one rather than

another item or package of heritably variable information explains the outcome observed.[32]

Genre theorists have a tendency toward a Grand Unified Theory for cinema studies, so that nomenclature for generic categories occurs as foundational and fixed taxonomies. Even genre theorists who desire a phylogenetic or evolutionary tree as representative of sub-genres for film noir, such as police procedurals branching away from hard-boiled detective narrative, still limit the scope of and possible permutations for the noir aesthetic. Often genre theorists searching for a root for film noir so that a bifurcating tree can be produced, when multifurcating, unrooted expansion more accurately describes the process for artistic evolution. Tracing backward common lines of cinematic narrative and stylistic modes to a common set of sources or a given cycle for film noir has been an admirable beginning for scholarship, but such a gesture has also delimited investigation of related arts and social constructs that clearly influenced film noir.

Genre, then, defines a nexus of common aesthetic and narrative elements recurring in a number of films that are recognisable for formulaic features or violations of expected stylistic and plot constructions, all in order to distinguish these films from other cinematic forms. Additionally, genre involves a unique yet developing combination of patterns, frameworks and contextual relationships with other modes of artistic expression, among them theatrical, literary and early cinematic styles. Attempts to designate, to restrict and to isolate film noir too often end up restricting and isolating noir itself, as though artistic movements emerge without individual imagination and remain static. Cycles and periods of cinema movements arbitrarily demarcate and delimit film noir in particular to categorical stasis. Moreover, the classification of a work of cinema as film noir requires two oppositional strategies, one that extracts from within the text those elements that fit the genre, and the other that imposes upon the work of cinema conditions that the genre proscribes. A film genre must be created from a collection of cinematic works that differ in terms of auteur, studio, year of production, actors and actresses, mood, stylistic and narrative strategies, and spectator reaction and recognition, none of which are exactly the same. In this sense, then, film noir identifies itself as a genre that has recognisable properties that are paradoxically variable. Defining film noir categorically defies the very nature of the experimentation within the cycle of films delimited by the imposition of a field for the genre. Dynamism, experimentation and variation are essential to the life of any film genre, probably most true for film noir. Scholars who constrain film noir by style, cycle and historical ideology ironically rely upon defining that confinement in terms of pre-, post- and neo-noir, which betrays the paucity of their static systems. While film noir can be viewed as a group of stylistic and narrative correspondences among a variety of films in the 1940s and 1950s, its aesthetic did not emerge only then and did not cease to exist as a genre after that period.

The cinematic elements that define film noir in traditional generic designations – chiaroscuro lighting, voiceover narration, flashback narrative, the femme fatale and homme fatal, location shooting, oblique angles – are not the only characteristics of the genre. Aural experiments, especially the creation of sound-image, in film noir offer new and fertile ground for recognising new aesthetic experimentation, as well as expanding the genre's membership. The same is true for musical experimentation and the function of scores emotionally, psychologically and narratively, as well as music editing in film noir. Revisiting film noir through the lenses of economic, political, gender, class and racial content expands upon the concepts of the noir angst, the noir protagonist's world-view, noir urban malaise and the conditions that permeate the noir world. Again, these new views of film noir open up the genre before, during and after the World War II and postwar eras.

Aesthetic, thematic and interpretative strategies for opening up, expanding upon, revisiting and re-evaluating film noir will emerge in the insightful essays in this volume. This volume also serves as a companion volume to *International Noir* in the Edinburgh University Press series of *Traditions in World Cinema*. Viewing film noir as a global cinematic expression and aesthetic expands the boundaries for this most influential twentieth-century art form.

NOTES

1. Edward Dmytryk, 'Dmytryk on film', ed. William McRae, *Journal of the University Film and Video Association* 34(2) (spring 1982), 17.
2. Bruce Tolley, 'Balzac et "*La Caricature*"', *Revue d'Histoire littéraire de la France* 61e année 1 (Jan–Mar 1961), 23.
3. Georges Altman, '*Le Jour se lève*: A pure *film noir*', in Richard Abel (ed.), *French Film Theory and Criticism: A History/Anthology, 1907–1939, Volume II 1929–1939* (Princeton, NJ: Princeton University Press, 1988), p. 267.
4. Ibid., p. 269.
5. Henry James, *Daumier, Caricaturist* (Emmaus, PA: The Rodale Press, 1954), pp. 3–4.
6. Ibid., p. 8.
7. Ibid., p. 30.
8. Honoré Daumier published *Rue Transnonain* in *L'Association Mensuelle*, September 1834.
9. Robert Fohr, *Daumier: Sculpteur et Peinture* (Paris: Société Nouvelle Adam Biro, 1999), p. 41, translation mine.
10. Ibid., p. 43, translation mine.
11. Champfleury, *Histoire de la Caricature moderne* (1865), as quoted in Honoré Daumier, *Daumier: Raconté par lui-même et par ses amis* (Geneva: Pierre Cailler, 1945), p. 40, translation mine.
12. Roger Passeron, *Daumier*, trans. Helga Harrison (Oxford: Phaidon Press, 1981), p. 106.

13. Elizabeth C. Childs, 'The body impolitic: Censorship and the caricature of Honoré Daumier', in Elizabeth C. Childs (ed.), *Suspended License: Censorship and the Visual Arts* (Seattle: University of Washington Press, 1997), p. 159.
14. Michel Melot, 'Aesthetic judgement/political judgement', trans. Neil McWilliams, *Art Journal* 11(1) (1988), 13–15.
15. Phillip Dennis Cate, 'Paris seen through artists' eyes', in Phillip Dennis Cate (ed.), *The Graphic Arts and French Society, 1871–1914* (New Brunswick, NJ: Rutgers University Press, 1988), pp. 17–18.
16. Frank Krutnik, Steve Neale, Brian Neve and Peter Stanfield (eds), *'Un-American Hollywood': Politics and Film in the Blacklist Era* (New Brunswick, NJ: Rutgers University Press, 2007), p. 154.
17. Edward Dmytryk, *Odd Man Out: A Memoir of the Hollywood Ten* (Carbondale, IL: Southern Illinois University Press, 1996), p. 152.
18. Ibid., p. 179.
19. Ibid., p. 202.
20. Peter Brooks, *Realist Vision* (New Haven, CT: Yale University Press, 2005), p. 33.
21. T. J. Clark, *The Painting of Modern Life: Paris in the Art of Monet and His Followers* (Princeton, NJ: Princeton University Press, 1984), p. 47.
22. Honoré de Balzac, *Père Goriot*, trans. Burton Raffel, ed. Peter Brooks (New York: W. W. Norton Critical Edition, 1994), pp. 8–9.
23. Raymond Chandler, *Farewell, My Lovely* (New York: Vintage Crime, 1992), p. 27 [1940].
24. John Paxton, *Murder, My Sweet (1944): Shooting Script*, p. 15.
25. Stanley Corkin, *Realism and the Birth of the Modern United States: Cinema, Literature, and Culture* (Athens, GA: University of Georgia Press, 1996), p. 4.
26. Ibid., p. 17.
27. Ibid., p. 106.
28. Amy Kaplan, *The Social Construction of American Realism* (Chicago, IL: University of Chicago Press, 1988), p. 9.
29. Ibid., p. 54.
30. Jean-Joseph Goux, *Symbolic Economies – After Marx and Freud*, trans. Jennifer Curtiss Gage (Ithaca, NY: Cornell University Press, 1990), p. 69. The monetary example for Goux is an operational model, whereby pictography is equivalent to 'barter' substitution between signifying object and signified object; ideography, such as hieroglyphics, corresponds to 'extended form of value' in order to avoid an 'unmanageable increase in the number of signs' by different kinds of equivalence; and phonographic with consonantal notation attains a value that appears universal, so that all *'meaning* is condensed in a few graphic signs of phonetic value, just as economic exchange-value appears to be reified in official currency' (pp. 69–71). Goux places both modes – economic and signifying – within the mode of *'symbolizing'*, which means that 'economic exchange as realized in the primitive mode of production belongs to the same moment of the symbolization process as signifying exchange, realized in pictographic writing' (p. 73).
31. Thomas L. Vincent and Joel S. Brown, *Evolutionary Game Theory, Natural Selection, and Darwinian Dynamics* (Cambridge: Cambridge University Press, 2005), pp. 74–5. The authors offer a systematic mathematical game theory, the G-function approach, which can account for micro- and macro-evolutionary dynamics.
32. W. G. Runciman, *The Theory of Cultural and Social Selection* (Cambridge: Cambridge University Press, 2009), pp. 30–1. While Runciman employs the terms evoked for biological conditions and acquired for cultural, imposed for social, this model of distinctions among arguments, or better critical strategies, affords genre theorists a method for articulating the characteristics of their own methods.

1. THE CINEMA OF UNCERTAINTY AND THE OPACITY OF INFORMATION FROM LOUIS FEUILLADE'S CRIME SERIALS TO FILM NOIR

Vicki Callahan

> The more you see, the less you know.
> *The Man Who Wasn't There* (Joel and Ethan Coen, 2001)

As we try to define the cinematic origins of, and influences on, film noir, we inevitably find ourselves faced with the bigger problem of defining noir itself. Following stories that take the divergent paths of hard-boiled detectives, police investigations and romantic deadly triangles, and traverse across urban cityscapes, suburban households and remote wastelands, we realise the 'centre' of noir cannot be located. Critics have argued equally persuasively on behalf of German Expressionism or Poetic Realism as the true progenitor of the genre, but here I want to argue that the path to finding the antecedents to noir lies not in mapping out specific visual motifs or narrative elements, such as the 'rain-slicked highway', high-contrast lighting or even the 'hard-boiled detective', since each of these components is frustratingly variable from film to film. Rather, we are better off approaching noir from the question of its epistemological and ideological missions, which are much more consistent across the many films we identify as noir, despite the dissimilar styles, narrative lines and character types we are likely to cross in our investigation.

If we start with the kind of knowledge produced and the status of evidence, especially the role of visual evidence in defining what we know in noir, then I would argue that Louis Feuillade's crime films in the silent era are a productive venue to explore as the genre's predecessor. These films, as I have argued elsewhere, offer neither a strategy of 'showing' nor one of 'telling', but rather a third path in film history, one preoccupied with the limits of knowledge, the 'cinema of uncertainty'.[1] As Allan Sekula notes in his seminal essay, 'The Traffic in Photographs', the photographic image has long been at the centre of the crisis of bourgeois culture, which simultaneously claims that the world is a collection of visible, 'knowable and possessable objects' but also maintains that the creative artist/spirit can transcend and transform the alienating machine of science/rationality and its economic handmaiden, capitalism.[2] While the photographic image and most of narrative cinema have worked to erase this crisis through a reification of the truth of appearances, Feuillade's crime films operate right at the centre of the crisis and destabilise this belief. As such, these films operate as a form of counter-cinema, but one where we might assume its later historical markers only lead through non-narrative or avant-garde paths. Here, I will argue that what makes noir both 'recognisable' as a genre and also so erratic in terms of markers of the 'genre' is that the form cannot be reduced to a series of narrative or stylistic traits, but rather must be explored in terms of the relationship of key formal elements – space, character, narrative – to evidence and knowledge. Examined in this way, noir then becomes a continuation of the 'cinema of uncertainty' but existing within, or perhaps rather existing 'underground', Classical Hollywood film.

A Troubled Realistic Aesthetic – Space

While many have argued for the influence of German Expressionism on noir style or a consistency of 'visual motifs' that utilise many of these dramatic stylistic elements, in looking across the range of films that are typically labelled as noir, the visual style is a bit more complicated and diverse.[3] Ginette Vincendeau acknowledges the significance of Expressionism on the genre, but reminds us about the international collaboration and hybrid styles throughout national cinemas that shaped both French and Hollywood films.[4] Vincendeau points to noir's strong realist tradition and, considering its attention to urban space and the shadowy elements surrounding characters, links the genre to aesthetic and thematic components found in 1930s poetic realism.[5] Marc Vernet goes a step further, expressing considerable scepticism about the Expressionist connection, seeing the low-key and dramatic lighting in noir as consistent with Hollywood film traditions as early as DeMille and Griffith in the 1910s as well as common in an array of international contexts.[6] James Naremore also doubts the Expressionist heritage and sees little stylistic consistency in noir, tracing the visual patterns more to a cultural style (or series of 'fashions', from lighting to design).[7]

Like the above authors, I too think the Expressionist sensibility is overstated in the critical literature on noir and following Naremore's point as inspiration I would offer another 'visual pattern' that accounts for our 'recognition' of noir, which is that the 'essence' of noir is more abstract, an epistemological condition which is: what we see is rarely what we know. Noir is closely connected to a visual 'style' of uncertainty and in this sense is following a cinematic trajectory directly from Feuillade. There is not a particular device consistently employed as much as a series of visual strategies utilised to construct what we might label a 'troubled realist aesthetic'. Feuillade achieves uncertainty through a variety of mechanisms: the long take, deep space, bright and even lighting, and extreme depth of field put in combination with edits for 'clues' or shock and placed in settings that resonate with (mis)information. There are shadowy moments and presences throughout the Feuillade crime films, but these are made more forceful by their context to a world that seems fairly mundane – much like we will see later in noir.

In *Fantômas à l'ombre de la guillotine* (1913), the film opens with Princess Danidoff robbed by an unknown character shortly after returning to her hotel room late one night. She crosses over a shadowy area to enter the hotel but once inside the space and upstairs in her room all is open and brightly lit. The scene in her room is remarkable for the deep space and extreme depth of field so that we, like the Princess, have a sense of security in the place. As Danidoff goes off screen briefly, suddenly from behind a side curtain Fantômas emerges and then just as quickly hides again as she re-enters. Fantômas swiftly returns and robs the Princess of her money and jewels, a seeming polite gentleman thief who gives her a calling card when she inquires who he is. The card, shown through a close-up via a cut-in from a medium long shot, is blank (his criminal name will magically appear on the card later). As Fantômas exits, more false or conflicting information emerges on his identity. The now unreliable gentleman at first bows, then relays a menacing gesture of violence, walking her to the back of the deep frame where he kisses her farewell on her hand before viciously pushing her away. As the police inspector Juve enters Danidoff's room to investigate the crime, he retraces the criminal path through the deep space, giving us detail via a shot of extreme depth of field and in a long take such that the hazardous space now appears safe and clear. Of course the irony is that the room appeared this way right before the robbery.

Juve confronts a similar visual field as he goes to investigate the next mystery, the disappearance of Lord Beltham. The Beltham home is presented in deep space with extreme depth of field, and nothing seems obscured. Juve quickly sees another man's hat in the room and through another cut-in from medium long shot to extreme close-up, we have the information that another man (with the initial G) is visiting Lady Beltham. The hat belongs to a character named Gurn (really Fantômas, just offscreen) who is responsible for the murder of Lady Beltham's husband. In both cases, Danidoff and Beltham, Juve gains what he thinks is valuable information from his search of the open and clear space, filled with detail. But what has he learned precisely? In each case, these are phantom identities as the first identity card has so aptly relayed and there is nothing in one instance to link one crime to the other. Juve does indeed capture the criminal but that only occurs accidentally, as in tracking Gurn he finds Lord Beltham's body and also discovers, unexpectedly while at the murder site, Fantômas's card; there is no direct and rational line that connects these two events, rather a card with magical ink. Moreover, the larger message of the film is brought home to us as the capture and punishment of Fantômas is short-lived when the criminal exchanges his place in prison with an actor, who is almost executed through a misrecognition; thus the identity of Fantômas is perpetually unstable and unrecognisable throughout the series.

David Bordwell has a detailed analysis of how Feuillade's careful staging and choreography manipulate the relay of information, providing an elaborate hide and seek for the viewer.[8] This is undoubtedly true, but what I want to underline with Feuillade's aesthetic, and by extension noir's, is that we know disproportionally little given how much visual 'clarity' we seem to have, especially with regard to matters of identity, an element that carries over into noir. By comparison to Feuillade, consider Kathie in *Out of the Past* (1947), who appears to be a tragic victim of domestic violence as the evidence piles up that her boyfriend, Whit, is a thug who has caused her flight. Jeff, a detective sent to retrieve Kathie, promptly falls for her and they both run away from Whit and his henchman. Jeff and Kathie are in blissful co-habitation when suddenly Jeff's former partner, Fisher, turns up to blackmail them, threatening to reveal their location to Whit. A brawl between Jeff and Fisher ensues, when suddenly, unnecessarily and quite shockingly, Kathie shoots the partner. Nothing we know of Kathie up to that moment prepares us for the shooting (or even for a gun in her hand), but from this point the story relays a series of duplicitous acts from the heretofore innocent victim and romantic lead.

Or similarly, Brigid O'Shaughnessy, in *The Maltese Falcon* (1941), tells a series of conflicting stories until finally in a shocking ending we finally hear her confess – a surprise that is further magnified by the revelation that the detective, Sam Spade, has been equally duplicitous throughout the film. In both of these films, there is a gap between what we know and expect from the chain of narrative events and then what suddenly transpires, and with this opening or breach in the story, a shock, or disruption of order occurs. In addition, the visual style in both these films is realistic with mostly high key lighting and few shadows to obscure our view of events – nothing seems to be hidden from us, and yet . . .[9]

The setting of criminal activity in Feuillade's crime films, and that of film noir, provides further clues as to what may be at stake. In both cases, we imagine the urban zone as the centre from which all trouble collects and emanates, a product of the rise of the metropolis and the technological and cultural upheavals of late-nineteenth- and twentieth-century modernity. Ed

Dimendberg's fine examination of noir and the city space reminds us of the complex and ambivalent responses to the evolving urban space we see in these films, from a cohesive but alienating core to a dispersive and sprawling wasteland.[10] Moreover, Dimendberg's study points out the diversity of the noir landscape beyond the urban core that we often associate with the genre. As James Naremore notes, perhaps most overlooked in this discussion is the abstract relation between the city and border or 'marginal' spaces, a setting for exploring liminal zones across an array of social and cultural categories: race, ethnicity, gender, sexuality, class.[11]

It is precisely these troubled zones at the margins of our experience of daily life that Feuillade – and noir – attempt to map out for us, physically charting this for us as a geographical problem. In short order, these 'zones of anxiety' morph from an external to an internal dilemma, initiated from a crisis of vision, but landing at a crisis of self. In *Juve contre Fantômas* (1913), Juve has tracked the criminal to the wine warehouses of Bercy. As he sees a figure in the distance, Juve begins shooting and the person he has spotted returns fire. Both individuals keep firing and pursuing the other until they are face to face and are at the precipice of shooting in close quarters, when they suddenly recognise each other. Juve and his friend and fellow crime fighter, the journalist Fandor, have almost shot each other before they each exclaim: 'Juve, I thought you were Fantômas!' 'Me too, Fandor, I thought you were Fantômas!' They have little time to celebrate before Fantômas and his gang pop up from behind the wine barrels with guns blazing before setting the area on fire. Juve and Fandor escape but only to be trapped in a fiery explosion triggered by Fantômas with their fate unknown at the conclusion of the episode. The next episode, *Le Mort qui tue* (1913), picks up this problem of vision and recognition, as I will explain shortly.

The Opacity of Information – Character

One area of uncertainty recurrent from Feuillade serials to Hollywood noir resides within the motivation and identity of characters. While there is some critical back and forth over whether noir is better understood through the male lead (for example, the doomed romantic sap, the hard-boiled detective, the underachieving drifter) or the 'femme fatale', what is more useful is to explore the clarity of the lens through which we see the key characters. In noir, as in Feuillade's crime films, our understanding of what drives the characters and the boundaries of their moral universe is often obscure, and even more frequently deceptive. Neither *amour fou*, sheer greed, nor bloodthirsty homicidal tendencies quite serve as adequate explanations for the crimes that play out on screen; rather we are faced with deciphering if random events, inexplicable stupidity or hidden motivations are in play given what we see transpire does not fit into rational behaviour or indeed logical consequences of actions.

Perhaps the most classic example from noir we might refer to here is Walter Neff in *Double Indemnity* (1944). As Neff notes in his well-known over-narration detailing his crime spree in the opening of the film: 'Yes, I killed him. I killed him for money and for a woman. I didn't get the money, and I didn't get the woman'. At first glance, this does seem to counter directly my dismissal of the love and financial angles as primary character motivations. However, a closer look at Neff's likely romantic and financial gain, and his knowledge of this as a probability, are almost from the beginning of the film fairly remote. As soon as Neff realises that Phyllis Dietrichson's flirtation is motivated more by a desire to find a co-conspirator for her murder insurance plot against her husband, he recoils and points out the certain futility of the crime. In short order, he changes his mind, starts an adulterous affair with the obviously deceitful Phyllis, comes up with the hare-brained death-by-train 'accident' for Mr Dietrichson and then immediately declares a moratorium on any meetings for the couple outside of the grocery store. The surface motivations for Neff's actions of sex and money are undermined by the absolute unlikelihood that these goals can be achieved – as Neff himself predicted from the beginning.[12]

A similar phenomenon appears to be at play in *The Postman Always Rings Twice* (1946), whereby Frank Chambers repeatedly sets himself up for disaster with little to no payoff. Whether taking the grill cook/handyman job at the opening of the film even after finding out his lust is inconveniently directed at the boss's wife or returning to the diner after the trial with little hope of financial gain or romantic interest from Cora, Frank seems only to be courting failure. Or, let us consider Al Roberts in *Detour* (1945), where a litany of obviously bad choices are on display from the time of Haskell's death to Vera's demise. Even the hard-boiled detective Sam Spade in *The Maltese Falcon* seems to team up with Brigid O'Shaughnessy, romantically and in pursuit of the elusive bird, despite Brigid's recurrent and obvious lies, which Spade himself mocks along with the phantom nature of the object and its reward. In each of these instances, and in many other noir scenarios, the lead characters seem to defy logic with their choices – these are not just ill-fated and poor, but are also strikingly irrational decisions.

Contrast this with Jean Gabin's characters in poetic realist films such as Jacques Lantier in *La Bête humaine* (1938) or François from *Le Jour se lève* (1939), which are often seen as cinematic antecedents to noir. In both cases, Jacques' and François's motivations are very clear, their dire circumstances have been shaped by a romantic if at times misguided vision. These characters are in love, and we understand the intensity of their feelings through the context and depth of their stories, and while fate might not have been kind to either, these characters arrived at their choices with a consistency and logic missing from their noir male counterparts.

Le Jour se lève is a useful counterpoint since it appears to have many of the harbingers of noir, the use of dramatic shadows, a non-linear, flashback structure and, of course, the doomed lead character. But we listen in as François carries out his internal monologue throughout the film; the story is organised as his mournful memories during an extended stand-off with police. François's voice and memory are pathways into his subjectivity and quite distinct from the often heard external voiceover of noir that conveys objective information (*The Naked City*, 1948) or recounts a story or series of events to another person (as in the case of Neff to Keyes in *Double Indemnity* or in other noir voiceovers such as *Murder, My Sweet* (1944) and *The Lady from Shanghai*). The audio situates François's subjectivity in the foreground, which is repeatedly visualised with dramatic shadows that highlight the character's eyes and underline his emotions and humanity. François is not an abstraction but an individual and as his on-off lover, Clara, notes: 'He's not a criminal, he's an ordinary man'. The specificity of the man and his circumstances conveyed through the detail of his story and through the visualisation of him and his surroundings turn this into an existential crisis. It is no accident that François repeatedly returns to the room's mirror to study himself and finally concludes: 'François, he does not exist any more'. But this commentary is pointing to a loss and change in status, brought on by the impossible continuation of his love affair with Françoise. Unlike noir, the moral centre holds in *Le Jour se lève* and in many other poetic realist films. It is a clarity regarding values that is repeated in terms of information and knowledge. Unlike noir, with poetic realism we are not confused where we stand or in what we know.

Such character depth is not unusual for narrative filmmaking and has been key to the Hollywood classical tradition from the time of D. W. Griffith. Indeed, Dudley Andrew has noted the crucial impact of Griffith's *Broken Blossoms* (1919) on French film more generally and on poetic realism specifically.[13] Like the Griffith film, objects, settings, lighting and gesture all take on heightened significance toward an understanding of a character's subjective state, a sensibility that poetic realist filmmaker Jean Grémillon singled out as enabling the audience to 'feel intensely the presence of a living thought, of a human heart'.[14] For noir and for Feuillade, we could not be further from this 'presence' and uniquely disconnected from the human heart and mind.

The operative term that one might use to describe the void of motivation in the noir characters might well be 'loser' – a particularly apt piece of slang once we look more closely at the opacity and irrationality of their actions. If we look at the occupations of some of the key characters from noir, we notice an important continuity of 'failure'. Neff in *Double Indemnity* turns down the 'desk job' that promises less but surely assures a more steady income than his sales gig, not to mention the opportunity to work his way up the managerial class. Frank Chambers has likely hit a career peak with his grill cook/handyman employment. Sam Spade, while self-employed, makes it clear he cannot be bought and income beyond that required for his office's maintenance and spartan lifestyle does not seem a priority. Michael in *The Lady from Shanghai* and Al Roberts in *Detour* both have skills but, like Frank Chambers, are underemployed and essentially 'drifters' during the stories we follow. Even Jeff in *Out of the Past* is a former gumshoe, now small business owner, but never seems to work or even manage the books of his gas station located in the back of beyond.

Here again, the useful point of contrast is Gabin's poetic realist characters, who are specifically defined as working class in terms not just of atmosphere, the simple unglamorous settings of daily life, but of the detail of their work. We see Gabin/François at work in the dusty spaces of the factory where the sand destroys his lungs in *Le Jour se lève*. Or we see Jacques' face and clothes covered in grime from the coal that fuels the train he drives in *La Bête humaine*, and he breaks to eat a spare dinner from canned goods with his fellow railroad workers. Gabin's characters are not only clearly working class, they are defiantly so, taking an often explicit tack against the ruling sector.

The noir characters are markedly different from their poetic realist counterparts, and in case after case we see examples of figures who are outside the economic and political system or not aligned on either side of the vested interests. Neither workers nor managers nor owners, the men of noir are at best entrepreneurs, at worst apathetic and lazy, but in the main they stand outside the capitalist system as neither wilful participants nor ideological critics of the hegemonic system of exchange. Walter Neff's resistance to the office job offer by Keyes as well as his plot with Phyllis to defraud his employer speaks to this outsider status. Moreover, his vociferous insistence against the 'promotion' locates Neff as someone completely uninterested in 'moving up' in respectability, stability or career possibilities within the firm. Indeed, the very murder/fraud plot itself as noted above seems less inclined for romance and fortune than for an opportunity to see if he can defeat Keyes's rigorous logical analysis of insurance claims and thereby con the system.

The opacity of the noir male lead characters follows closely along the path set out for them by an equally opaque figure, visually and subjectively, Feuillade's paramount crime villain, Fantômas. A master of disguise, Fantômas is most recognisable by his black bodysuit and mask, which cast a shadowy presence across the five films that detail his exploits. But nothing is stable in Fantômas from his appearance, aliases or occupations, and even his calling cards of 'identity' begin as blanks that then fade in with his name (*Fantômas à l'ombre de la guillotine*). Prosthetic arms and trap doors repeatedly prevent the master criminal's certain police capture, and misrecognition enables his escape from the guillotine and almost generates an innocent man's state execution. But for Fantômas even the supposedly telltale costume of the bodysuit is a false sign, and *Fantômas contre Fantômas* features not one but three black-clad figures in an undecipherable chase sequence. Fantômas is everywhere and nowhere so that at one point, the police inspector Juve is reduced to grasping at his imagined phantom of the criminal, whose ghostly presence appears in his office and mocks the detective's failed efforts to capture him (*Fantômas à l'ombre de la guillotine*). A later episode, *Fantômas contre Fantômas*, finds Fantômas's identity so murky that any sign is latched upon as authentic which, unfortunately for a time, 'unmasks' Juve as the real criminal through a telltale scar on his arm (a scar that was in effect impossible to attain since he was locked in a cell away from a party where the injury occurred).

Any occupation taken up by the mastermind is simply a passing pretence for another criminal act, with the cover persona usually being one of bourgeois respectability and order; he poses at different points in the series as a doctor, judge, banker and even as an American private detective (Tom Bob). At first glance, his motivations seem in the main financially driven, but the ruthless calculation, bloodthirsty elements and intricate plotting against a consistent segment of society – the well-to-do and titled – place his acts as spectacular rejections of the ruling financial, legal and social order. Moreover, like Walter Neff, his noir successor, the driving mechanism for his actions appears to be less about the money than about the pleasure of the crime and the con itself. At one point in *Le Mort qui tue*, Fantômas, in disguise as a banker for a high-society engagement party, stops to smirk over the body of a woman he has just drugged and robbed in her boudoir. Given the crowd downstairs anticipating the quick return of one of the betrothed to the celebration, Fantômas's lingering pleasure over his accomplishment is particularly bold and speaks to the disdain he holds both for the law and for the social order.

Like the men of noir that he precedes, Fantômas is an outsider and essentially a loner. Unlike in the novel, in the film series he has no family or friends, and all relationships seem to be fleeting and instrumental. Joséphine, his criminal cohort and likely paramour in *Juve contre Fantômas*, turns over information on his whereabouts to the police inspector at the first sign of pressure (and Fantômas, in turn, quickly escapes). Even Lady Beltham, who does seem under the spell of Gurn/Fantômas, given her role in hiding him and in facilitating his exploits (including possibly murdering her husband), is hardly a soulmate. When she balks at participating in an extortion set-up (and likely murder), Fantômas reminds her he can kill her any time he wants (*Le Mort qui tue*). But all have only a utilitarian relationship to the criminal; his 'moral universe' is obscure at best and lacking even the minimal 'honour among thieves' code. In *Fantômas contre Fantômas*, posing as the detective Tom Bob he leads the police to his own gang so that he can keep all the stolen loot for himself. He has stalled the gang's payoff while disguised yet again as Fantômas's middle man, Père Moche, who explains to the criminal's cohorts that the mastermind will arrive soon with their cut of the goods.

Fantômas's shifting physical presence, ongoing exchange of identities and obscure motivation renders him an ambiguous character, but it is the series' larger assault on visual evidence which leaves the character unknowable and, more troublingly, leaves our ground for certainty destabilised. *Le Mort qui tue* offers an exemplary instance of this process. In at times painstaking documentary detail, the film shows the failures of a scientific method predicated on the reliability of visible and physical evidence, particularly as it is relayed, archived and measured through the photographic image. The irony, or perhaps the larger philosophical point, is made through an aesthetic that on the surface might be characterised as realistic: deep space, extreme depth of field, even lighting (with dramatic exceptions) and brightly lit outdoor location shooting. Yet despite such ostensive visual clarity, nothing is recognisable, nothing is foreseeable and nothing is as it appears; it is a contradiction that allows Fantômas to hide in plain sight throughout the five films in the series.

In *Le Mort qui tue* the problem of recognition is compounded by our faith in the visible. Jacques Dollon is an artist who is framed for a murder solely through appearance. He is chloroformed by Fantômas and while he is unconscious a young women who has been murdered is left in the room with him. A note of invitation from the artist to the woman to visit him, and her placement in the room are all that is required for the police to lead to Dollon's arrest and most significantly his entry into the police scientific archive. For almost two minutes of screen time we watch the measurements and imprints of Dollon being taken in the Police Scientifique area, with the fingerprinting segment taking up a full minute of time, mostly in close-up. The data collection from Dollon quickly appears inconsequential when Dollon turns up murdered in his cell. But in short order another crime is committed, this time a robbery of Princess Danidoff at her engagement party featuring *le tout Paris*. The Princess is chloroformed and an expensive necklace stolen, with the robber leaving one large and clearly visible fingerprint on her neck. We are led through another meticulous onscreen session of criminal documentation, this time directed to the photography of the human trace left on the victim's neck. When the investigation returns to the police lab the verdict is clear – this is without a doubt the dead man's imprint found in the photograph taken from the crime scene, a scenario made even more troubling by the earlier information that Dollon's body had vanished. The ghostly criminal appears to strike again as Danidoff's fiancé, Thomery, is strangled (with the police chief's scarf no less) and again Dollon's impossible fingerprints are found at the scene. Ultimately, the resale of Thomery's stolen stock shares by Fantômas, now posing as the banker Nanteuil, leads Juve to the criminal and a brutal revelation. Fantômas had skinned Dollon's hands and wears the skin as gloves over his own hands

– hence the 'deceptive' fingerprints at the crime scenes. If this seems an unlikely possibility, the sequence presents us with a close-up of Dollon's skin peeled back from Nanteuil's hand by Juve – a gruesome 'unmasking' of the deception. Juve proclaims the re-establishment of the legal and rational order of things by noting to Nanteuil that his disguise is now exposed and states: '*C'en est fini Fantômas*'. No sooner does Juve makes his pronouncement than two hidden doors behind the criminal open and Fantômas slips through before they quickly close, leaving Juve and Fandor to curse '*L'Insaisissable*'.

Fantômas is never successfully punished in the five films in the series, although he is frequently trapped, arrested and even imprisoned on multiple occasions. In the last film, *Le Faux magistrat*, Fantômas is released not once but twice. In the first instance, Juve – in disguise – aids his escape from a Belgian prison in order to bring the criminal to justice in France. Fantômas does return to France, this time taking on the identity of a judge he has murdered, and as the police and Juve close in once more for an arrest, he signs his own warrant of release from prison (his last act as the *faux* judge).

In none of these films do we see any emotion from Fantômas, with the exception perhaps of a sneer – he does genuinely seem to enjoy his work. However, the deception of the criminal is mainly one of physical disguise and identity theft, and there is almost no need for Fantômas to sell his multiple characters through lengthy discussions or theatrical tactics. His absence of any recognisable personality aids in his transformation solely through visual details.

As the series ends, his one recurrent visual marker, the black bodysuit, is transferred to a new series and now a different set of villains, the criminal gang, *Les Vampires* (1915–16). Interestingly, while multiple members of the gang take on this costume, the attire becomes affixed in cinema history with a female character, Irma Vep, and the silent-era star, Musidora, although the actress only wore the outfit in this one film series and indeed only for about fifteen minutes of screen time. As Monica Dall'Asta points out, Musidora's bodysuit was quite distinct from that of her male predecessor, being made of silk, thus revealing more of the body, highlighting the transgressive modern woman and marking the criminal body distinctly as difference.[15] The oblique transfer of the bodysuit to its iconic new site takes place at a prescient locale, the theatre. Here, the intrepid crime journalist Philippe Guérande is watching his fiancée, Marfa, clothed in the *maillot de soie*, perform in a ballet ripped from the lurid headlines entitled *Les Vampires*. The sensational topic for the ballet is overlaid with an equally scandalous dance as Marfa suggestively and in a threatening manner circles the body of a sleeping woman. As Marfa closes in on her victim, she suddenly collapses and dies on stage (due to her poisoning by a Dr Nox, the leader of the Vampire gang). With that, Marfa's presence is effectively wiped from the narrative, but the indelible image of the black bodysuit is now marked and aligned with the female body and with performance.

Tellingly, our only return to Marfa's character occurs in a later episode as Irma sees a photograph of Philippe's fiancée and her response suggests a moment of shocked (self-)recognition; at that moment the transfer of the bodysuit as Irma's visual motif is solidified.

When we are formally introduced to Irma Vep, our lead female villain, in the third episode of the series, *Le Cryptogramme rouge*, she is, like Marfa, performing onstage, but in this case at a working-class cabaret. Irma Vep (her name an anagram for 'vampire') is a crucial component of the series, not simply due to her alluring attire but also as she becomes the most consistent face – and body – of the Vampire gang as the designated (male) leaders come and go repeatedly throughout the ten films. She has a succession of boyfriends, mostly the gang's leaders, and no real or discernible attachment to any of them. In the one case where there does seem to be passion, Irma's romantic relationship with the gang's rival, Juan-José Moréno, is explained by his talent for hypnotism, but even here Moréno quite quickly comes under *Irma's* spell.

If Irma has picked up the visual mantle of criminality from Fantômas, she alters the profile somewhat and not only on the basis of gender. Like Fantômas, Irma Vep takes on a number of identities, but here, unlike with her predecessor, disguise is not crucial to her persona. Even when Irma cross-dresses, the salient point is that she is almost always easily recognisable by those in pursuit. Most of her 'disguises' are more appropriately labelled as 'costume changes' for a variety of roles, and unlike Fantômas's detachment, we often get to see an array of clearly performed emotions in the series. Frequently, Vep's duplicitous roles are portrayed as the deferent household servant or servile clerical worker (such as Philippe's maid in *Le Cryptogramme rouge*, the bank secretary in *Le Spectre*, the switchboard operator in *Satanas*), which serve as a front and counterpoint to her ruthless crimes (from robbery to murder). Her actions are quite brutal, as evidenced in *Le Spectre*, where she demonstrates 'the proper use of a hatpin' by killing the bank courier, M. Metadier. None of her responses match Fantômas's occasional glee, but her only emotions come through her performed roles with little to no insight into the character's inner thoughts, and general workmanlike detachment accompanies her activities.

By the end of the series, it is clear that Irma Vep is more than our visual cue for criminality; she is the ethical focal point of the series. While Philippe is the male lead in pursuit of the gang and the putative hero, alongside his comic sidekick Mazamette, he, like Juve, repeatedly fails in his effort to corral the gang and as a journalist is only tangentially related to the law through his parallel investigations and periodic alliances. His representation of the social order fares no better with regard to his representation of heterosexual bourgeois order. His romances are bland and mainly off screen, moving quickly into boring domestic life with his marriage to Jane. Jane appears with no narrative set-up or backstory in the next to last film in the series, *L'Homme des poisons*. We have no sense of Jane and Philippe's life together, and her nondescript character seems only to serve one truly useful function, which is to kill Irma at the end of the series; this act was more of a reaction to opportunity than down to any particular skill or strength of her character. Jane's shooting of Irma serves as an alert that the true force of evil has been eliminated from the film and the moral order restored, signified not just by her return to her home with Philippe, but by Mazamette's whirlwind romance and marriage of Jane's maid, Augustine. Thus not only has Irma Vep been killed, but her unorthodox and serial romances in the series have been replaced by the closing shot of not one but two couples embracing (the Guérandes and the Mazamettes).

As Maggie Cheung, in character as herself, comments in *Irma Vep*, Olivier Assayas's 1996 homage to the icon and poetic cinema: 'She has no morals . . . is that a problem?' Cheung's dialogue points to the centrality of Irma Vep to Feuillade's representation of evil in his series, and also the marginal, outsider or disruptive status of Vep with regard to the ruling order. Cheung has been tapped in the film as the logical successor to Musidora and the best performer to incarnate Irma Vep since she is a non-Western star from a Hong Kong cinema driven more by action and aesthetics than linear, rational order as designed and relayed in Hollywood cinema.

Irma Vep and Musidora – the two are inseparable – evoke strikingly the ethos of Feuillade's films and in his next serial, *Judex* (1917), the filmmaker converts Irma into the character Diana Monti, an explicit central figure of illegal and immoral behaviour and driving force in the narrative. While Judex, the lead male character of vigilante justice, is also a key factor, after his opening gambit of 'poisoning' and then kidnapping the disreputable banker Favraux (the concoction he drinks simulates death), his actions are mainly reactive to Diana's ongoing crime wave.

Diana as a character at times seems more attuned to Fantômas's persona, not with regard to disguise and identity, but rather in terms of her cold-blooded and calculated approach to mayhem and romantic alliances. Unlike Irma she does not drift from one sexual intrigue to another, but rather she carefully selects as lovers men who might be valuable to her objectives. Heterosexual desire seems far removed from her calculus, and her flirtations from Favraux to Cocantin (the comical private detective) and the hapless Moralés are all instrumental considerations. Like Fantômas, money is an ostensive motivation, but the schemes she organises around financial gain are noteworthy for the relentless cruelty that exceeds necessity. A case in point is the repeated kidnappings and attempted murder of Favraux's daughter, Jacqueline, with whom Judex is in love. As Jacqueline has given away her fortune upon learning of her father's transgressions with his poisoning 'death', it is not completely clear what Diana gains from these acts, beyond her excessive revenge for Favraux's death (whom she was planning to marry, again solely for financial reward).

Similarly to Fantômas, Diana has no love for the ruling classes and her targeting of Favraux and Jacqueline at times suggests class warfare, given she was the household nanny to *le petit Jean*. However, her role as nanny was simply an assumed identity or performance to gain access to the banker; we have no sense of Diana as we did with Irma Vep of a consistent alignment of roles that are working class.

Due to a similar blankness of character history, motivation, identity or emotion, Diana follows closely in the opaque shadows of Fantômas, Vep and the men of noir. The character of Diana refines Vep from the silent-era 'vamp' aligned almost exclusively with sexual disorder to a more profoundly disturbing femme fatale who destabilises all she touches across an array of social, cultural and economic categories, in large measure due to her essential autonomy (unlike Irma who is an active agent, but part of a gang). As the father of the bandit Moralés notes: 'Here's my son that a wicked woman [Diana Monti] has pushed to the abyss'. The narrative engine is primarily Diana in *Judex* and the trio of Irma/Diana/Musidora seems to circulate endlessly in Feuillade's films and then in noir through the femme fatale. Feuillade himself points to the significance of Diana in an extra-textual reference in the scenario for *La Nouvelle mission de Judex* when he claims that his new villain in the series, the Baronne d'Arpemont, is a worthy successor of Monti.[16]

Daughters of Diana Monti – Noir's Femme Fatale

In film noir, the femme fatale rarely fits one personality profile, but like her noir male counterparts her motivations are equally obscure and opaque. Barbara Stanwyck seems to have perfected this role especially, and her performances across a variety of films – noir and otherwise – are characterised by a certain ambiguity of intent with an emphasis on the performative component of her character. That is to say, her character is not performing an act in some theatrical sense, but rather any given character 'identity' and 'behaviour' are appropriated specifically for the circumstance, as ultimately there is no 'true' essence or person behind this 'performance'. In *Baby Face* (1933), *Double Indemnity* (1944) and *The Strange Loves of Martha Ivers* (1946), Stanwyck portrays a succession of such characters, whose primary motivation seems financial, but the sheer repetition of ruthless actions outdistance monetary reward or social success. To put this another way, money is simply an excuse or justification for her crimes, with the true driving mechanism of the crime, like her male counterpart in the genre, being the disengagement or alienation from a system of bourgeois heterosexuality.

Stanwyck's Dietrichson in *Double Indemnity* is perhaps the quintessential exemplar here and a direct descendant of Diana Monti. Dietrichson takes on and casts off men casually and quickly as needed for the circumstances; from

Figure 1.1   Diana Monti and Moralés arrange their kidnapping, *Judex*.

her husband to Neff to Nino Zachetti, she is as ruthlessly instrumentalist as Monti and Fantômas in her relationships. In her final showdown with Neff she admits it was all a ruse, and that there was absolutely nothing to their romance or her own core being 'No, I never loved you, Walter, not you or anybody else. I am rotten to the heart. I used you just as you said'.

If Phyllis represents the femme fatale as cold calculation and instrumentalism, then Vera in *Detour* spectacularly inhabits a similar terrain. Unlike Phyllis's detachment and performative qualities, Vera's utilitarian ethos is vocalised in increasingly strident registers. However, like Phyllis – and her Feuillade predecessors – there is no achievable financial goal but simply an ongoing loop of accumulation and consumption as her plans for Al and the Haskell payout quickly expand from selling the dead man's car to taking over his identity and inheritance. But Vera is the antithesis of the rapacious capitalist as her objective is not an ever-expanding empire, but rather an unlimited ability to spend. The excessive and catastrophic nature of her desire is signalled for us not only by her vocalisation but also by the tubercular cough that periodically intercedes into her relentless commentary to Al.

Vera may well be transparent in her immediate desires and goals, but her character is no less opaque. We know little to nothing about her past, besides her fight with Haskell, and her objectives, hopes, future plans or intended destination are completely unknown. She is attached to Al's trajectory from the moment she enters the car as a hitchhiker. In addition, for all the intensity of her vocal register, the emotional depth of her character is almost non-existent, especially since we get no insight or backstory to explain her manner.

Less high-pitched but equally ruthless is Elsa Bannister (Rita Hayworth) in *The Lady from Shanghai*. Elsa represents a different variant of the femme

THE CINEMA OF UNCERTAINTY AND THE OPACITY OF INFORMATION

Figure 1.2   Phyllis Dietrichson (Barbara Stanwyck) as Diana Monti's direct descendant, *Double Indemnity*.

fatale, whereby now the 'opaque' quality is rather one consistent disguise that masks her true intent with romantic possibility. In this case, we are unable to see through her lie or 'true identity' until the last funhouse sequence. We believe she cares for Michael as she expresses repeated concern for his well-being and looks out for the trick or frame-up from her jealous husband. The scene at the aquarium visualises the density of the disguise for us; when she and Michael meet, they both drift in and out of darkness and half light, but tellingly, as she says, 'yes, my beloved, my beloved fool' and seals Michael's fate with a kiss, the camera keeps her solidly in the frame. Her duplicitous nature is revealed in the funhouse sequence in a dramatic expressionist visualisation of Elsa as a character located in multiple places; there is not 'one' person before us but many, cast in shadows and layered on the screen. Her personality has now dramatically changed and the romantic tone has been exchanged for a voice worthy of Phyllis Dietrichson, but even here she manages an affectless and unconvincing 'I love you' to Michael as he recounts her criminal acts.

Kathie (Jane Greer) in *Out of the Past* may well be Elsa's double, for duplicity disguised through romance. Like Elsa, Kathie moves quickly and astonishingly from a perceived 'victim' of domestic violence to a woman capable of murder with her shooting of Fisher. The shock of that event is equalled in force by a later moment in the film when we see her casually enter into a domestic breakfast scene, where the thuggish Whit has summoned Jeff for some unfinished business. Throughout the film, Kathie shifts from the role of victim to that of culprit with little hesitation, remorse or explanation. Like almost all of our noir leads, Kathie provides little insight into her 'true' motivations, beyond self-interest.

While most of the femme fatale characters are emotionally detached or place an ambiguous layer of romance over what ultimately turns out to be a cold, calculating personality, Brigid O'Shaughnessy's representation of the character in *The Maltese Falcon* perfects Phyllis Dietrichson's performative strategies. What is unusual about Brigid's actions, or more clearly, 'acts', is that they are repeatedly called out as a performance by the detective Sam Spade: 'Oh that, we didn't exactly believe your story, Miss umm, what is your name? Wonderly or LeBlanc?'; 'You won't need much of anybody's help, you're good. It's chiefly your eyes, I think, and that throb you get in your voice when you say things like, be generous Mr. Spade'. Brigid's convoluted and far-fetched stories (of her sister or relationship with the film's trio of thugs), alongside her physical mannerisms of nervous laughter and shifting eyes, transmit a message that is highly unreliable, and Astor's performance presents a highly nuanced display of these physical tics. Brigid, like other femmes fatales, but also her Feuillade forerunners, seems to take on and dispense with alliances with remarkable speed, the falcon itself being her only 'stable' relationship, which of course we learn is a false one. Moreover, O'Shaughnessy's facility with performance is contagious. Spade himself takes on a number of explicit performances throughout the film, including the angry negotiator (with Gutman) and the 'lover' willing to wait out Brigid's return from Tehachapi.

Chasing the Phantom: The Recursive Story Structure

The opacity of character and the lack of clear motivation and connection to internal states, emotions or subjectivity facilitate the repetition of the noir elements of uncertainty across diverse story lines and styles, hence the wide-ranging nature of the 'genre' and in part why we see noir as such disputed terrain, both in terms of what appropriately fits into the category or indeed whether or not the genre in fact exists. Our ability to 'recognise' the genre is actually a troubling of our facility for recognition, a disorientation that occurs outside of a dream state and often within a clearly defined and unencumbered visual field. The shadows of noir are the least of our problems with regard to knowledge, rather we are thrown into a world without a logic or a point of access (or point of view) to an alternative logic.

For Thomas Schatz, the disorientation in noir is linked to a non-linear story structure, often utilising a flashback or dual-time structure, whereby the fatality of events can be emphasised and an enigma explored.[17] While flashbacks are a typical device employed in noir, non-linearity is perhaps most intriguingly played out in noir through the repetition of unlikely events that often move tangentially from the originally stated story line. In *Detour*, Al Roberts starts off on a cross-country hitchhiking trip to LA to reunite with his girlfriend, Sue, but is sidetracked by the accidental death of the car's driver,

Charles Haskell. Roberts gets closer and closer to LA (and does finally arrive) but further and further from connecting with Sue as he picks up a hitchhiker, Vera, who had earlier ridden with Haskell. It is Vera's 'accidental' death that doubles Al's fear and guilt (believing he will be labelled the murderer in both cases), and restarts his hitchhiking, this time to points unknown. *The Postman Always Rings Twice* has a similar structure; an adulterous couple, Cora and Frank, decide to murder the woman's aging and miserly husband and, having failed once, manage to kill him in a staged car accident. The couple defeat the murder rap and a fractious post-trial period, but at the moment of their romantic reconciliation, Cora and Frank are in another car accident, this time unintended, whereby Cora is killed and Frank given a death sentence for her murder.

In *The Maltese Falcon* the repetition takes the form of a series of hostile and at times violent encounters between Sam Spade, Brigid O'Shaughnessy, Joel Cairo, Wilmer Cook and Caspar Gutman as the group in various and shifting alliances pursue the treasured black bird. Complicating their chase of the bird is the police and Sam's pursuit of those responsible for the murders of Miles Archer (Sam's detective agency partner) and Brigid's unseen accomplice, Floyd Thursby. Further entangling the story is the relationship between Spade and O'Shaughnessy that begins with a series of lies by Brigid, which are dutifully noted by Spade before he agrees to help her. Their 'romance' is a series of lies and performances from both sides, until the climactic finish when Spade forces her confession, or rather narrative clarification, before 'sending her over'.

These repetitive forms, multilevel chases and shifting alliances are all standard fare in the Feuillade crime films. In *Fantômas contre Fantômas*, a high-society masquerade ball features not one but three black-clad phantoms on site, Fandor (Juve's journalistic ally), a policeman and the criminal, Fantômas. Comically, two of the trio bump into each other while dancing and take off in pursuit with the third following close behind, with the audience having no clue as to who is who in the chase. Finally, one of the men is killed and another wounded, leaving a severe mark on his arm. We learn with the unmasking of the other two, Fandor and the policeman (who was the murder victim), that logically the wounded man must be Fantômas. The police, whose suspicions of Juve as the real Fantômas have led to his incarceration, decide to visit the inspector in his prison cell, where they discover a scar identical to the wounded man's injury. Juve is ultimately freed but the duplicity and false identities continue, with Fantômas amusingly taking on the role of a detective, Tom Bob, and Juve taking on the role of the criminal mastermind as he tries to entrap the villain's gang, at one point declaring to them: '*Je suis Fantômas*'. Fantômas, for his part, has no real alliances and, as noted earlier, feels no qualms about double-crossing his fellow gang members.

A similar structure is found in *Les Vampires*, where rival gangs stealing and chasing each other mirror Philippe and the police's pursuit of the gang. The vampire gang uses their real estate agency to set up a robbery of an 'innocent' client, but their initial break-in to his rented space reveals he is a fellow thief, Moréno. Moréno returns the favour by robbing the gang twice as well as kidnapping Irma Vep, with whom he then falls in love; they start a new alliance, which is ultimately folded back into the vampire gang.

Kidnappings and attendant rescues are crucial repetitive structures in the later Feuillade crime serials, *Judex*, *La Nouvelle mission de Judex* and *Tih Minh* (1919), and these often take place with little or obscure narrative motivation in place. With a few exceptions, notably when Judex abducts the banker Favraux, most of the kidnappings have less to do with direct financial gain than a disruption of heterosexual romance with the rescue of the female beloved – sometimes unconscious, sometimes amnesiac – played over again and again in the serials.

These repetitive patterns in Feuillade and noir are crucial markers of the cinema of uncertainty and serve as a key connection between the French filmmaker's silent-era serials and a block of Hollywood 'crime' films. In both instances, the films begin with a putative classical initiation of events, a crime to solve, a kidnapping, a murder, but unlike most detective stories, there is no necessary unravelling of 'facts' towards a logical resolution. Rather, what we have is a repetitive spiral of often unlikely, irrational events as in *The Postman Always Rings Twice* or *Detour* that ends in death or the unknowable void (such as the ghostly police car that 'somewhere' 'some day' picks up Al). Walter Neff documents this pattern well in his last conversation with Phyllis right before they shoot each other: 'You got me to take care of your husband for you, then you get Zachetti to take care of Lola, maybe take care of me too, then somebody else would come along to take care of Zachetti for you'.

The purpose of this repetition is twofold, which in the first instance and at its most obvious is to propose a random and chaotic rather than a linear, rational and teleological world-view (for example, 'good always triumphs', or even 'crime always pays'). The second purpose is what I have labelled the cinema of uncertainty's 'recursive function', that is, the repetition leads to simpler versions of itself, or rather to an abstraction of a form. In the case of Feuillade, the recurrent kidnappings, rescues and multi-layered pursuits point us towards the chase function in the text. This chase function points to the unreliability and instability of the legal/illegal divide.[18] In noir, the seeming 'death spiral' noted above is not about the inevitable fate for wrongdoing (or the censoring hand of Hollywood's 'Hays Code'), but the literal 'fade to black' of everything we might know – from a lover to a spouse, to the law, or even to a logical event. That is, the rational world that we have been promised from our visual culture to the social and economic order cannot be found; neither capitalism, bourgeois sentiment, heterosexuality nor monogamy provides any consistency of motivation or logical order. In this way, noir pushes the Feuillade crime films to their logical conclusion, whereby 'the more you see, the less you know'.[19] Hence, our 'recognition' of the dramatic dark shadows across the noir landscape is enabled by the mnemonic trace of the black bodysuit in Feuillade's crime films and the cinema of uncertainty.

Filmography

Baby Face (Alfred E. Green, 1933)
Broken Blossoms (D. W. Griffith, 1919)
Detour (Edgar G. Ulmer, 1945)
Double Indemnity (Billy Wilder, 1944)
Fantômas (Louis Feuillade, 1913–14)
Irma Vep (Olivier Assayas, 1996)
Judex (Louis Feuillade, 1917)
La Bête humaine (*The Human Beast*, Jean Renoir, 1938)
La Nouvelle mission de Judex (*The New Mission of Judex*, Louis Feuillade, 1918)
Le Jour se lève (*Daybreak*, Marcel Carné, 1939)
Les Vampires (Louis Feuillade, 1915–16)
Murder, My Sweet (Edward Dmytryk, 1944)
Out of the Past (Jacques Tourneur, 1947)
The Lady from Shanghai (Orson Welles, 1947)
The Maltese Falcon (John Huston, 1941)
The Man Who Wasn't There (Joel and Ethan Coen, 2001)
The Naked City (Jules Dassin, 1948)
The Postman Always Rings Twice (Tay Garnett, 1946)
The Strange Loves of Martha Ivers (Lewis Milestone, 1946)
Tih Minh (Louis Feuillade, 1919)

Bibliography

Andrew, Dudley (1995), *Mists of Regret*, Princeton, NJ: Princeton University Press.
Bordwell, David (2005), *Figures Traced in Light: On Cinematic Staging*, Berkeley, CA: University of California Press.
Brook, Vincent (2009), *Driven to Darkness: Jewish Émigré Directors and the Rise of Film Noir*. New Brunswick, NJ: Rutgers University Press.
Callahan, Vicki (2005), *Zones of Anxiety: Movement, Musidora, and the Crime Serials of Louis Feuillade*. Detroit, MI: Wayne State University Press.
——. (2000), 'The evidence and uncertainty of silent film in *Histoire(s) du cinéma*', in Michael Temple and James S. Williams (eds), *The Cinema Alone: Essays on the Work of Jean-Luc Godard 1985–2000*, Amsterdam: Amsterdam University Press, pp. 141–57.
Copjec, Joan (1993), 'The phenomenal nonphenomenal: Private space in *film noir*', in Joan Copjec (ed.), *Shades of Noir*, London: Verso, pp. 167–97.
Dall'Asta, Monica (2013), 'Pearl the swift one', in Marina Dahlquist (ed.), *Exporting Perilous Pauline: Pearl White and the Serial Film Craze*, Urbana, IL: Illinois University Press, pp. 71–98.
Dimendberg, Edward (2004), *Film Noir and the Spaces of Modernity*, Cambridge, MA: Harvard University Press.

Feuillade, Louis (1917), *La Nouvelle mission de Judex*. Original Scenario, Paris: Bibliothèque de l'Arsenal.

Naremore, James (2008), *More than Night: Film Noir in its Contexts*, Berkeley, CA: University of California Press.

Place, Janey and Lowell Peterson (1996), 'Some visual motifs of *film noir*', in Alain Silver and James Ursini (eds), *The Film Noir Reader*, New York: Limelight Editions, pp. 65–76.

Schatz, Thomas (1981), *Hollywood Genres: Formulas, Filmmaking and the Studio System*, New York: McGraw Hill.

Schrader, Paul (1996), 'Notes on film noir', in Silver and Ursini (eds), *Film Noir Reader*, pp. 53–63.

Sekula, Allan (1981), 'The traffic in photographs', *Art Journal* 41(1) (Photography and the Scholar/Critic, spring 1981), 15–25.

Vernet, Mark (1993), 'Film noir on the edge of doom', in Joan Copjec (ed.), *Shades of Noir*, London: Verso, pp. 1–31.

Vincendeau, Ginette (1992), 'Noir is also a French word', in Ian Cameron (ed.), *The Book of Film Noir*, New York: Continuum, pp. 49–58.

Notes

1. For more on the 'cinema of uncertainty', see Vicki Callahan, 'The evidence and uncertainty of silent film in *Histoire(s) du cinéma*', in Michael Temple and James S. Williams (eds), *The Cinema Alone: Essays on the Work of Jean-Luc Godard 1985–2000* (Amsterdam: Amsterdam University Press, 2000), pp. 141–57 as well as Vicki Callahan, *Zones of Anxiety: Movement, Musidora, and the Crime Serials of Louis Feuillade* (Detroit, MI: Wayne State University Press, 2005).
2. Allan Sekula, 'The traffic in photographs', *Art Journal* 41(1) (Photography and the Scholar/Critic, spring 1981), 15.
3. For discussion of the German Expressionist influence on noir and 'visual motifs' that closely align with this aesthetic, see Paul Schrader, 'Notes on film noir' and Janey Place and Lowell Peterson, 'Some visual motifs of *film noir*', in Alain Silver and James Ursini (eds), *The Film Noir Reader* (New York: Limelight Editions, 1996); Vincent Brook, *Driven to Darkness: Jewish Émigré Directors and the Rise of Film Noir* (New Brunswick, NJ: Rutgers University Press, 2009). While Brook notes the international and specifically French cinema connection to noir, he traces these back to German directors bringing the Expressionist aesthetic with them to France and then to Hollywood. Also Place and Peterson do not label the style as Expressionist as such but point to visual motifs of low-key lighting and oblique angles that are typically associated with the early German aesthetic.
4. Ginette Vincendeau, 'Noir is also a French word', in Ian Cameron (ed.), *The Book of Film Noir* (New York: Continuum, 1992).
5. Ibid., pp. 49–57.
6. Marc Vernet, 'Film noir on the edge of doom', in Joan Copjec (ed.), *Shades of Noir* (London: Verso, 1993), pp. 8–12.
7. James Naremore, *More than Night: Film Noir in its Contexts* (Berkeley, CA: University of California Press, 2008), pp. 167–8.
8. David Bordwell, *Figures Traced in Light: On Cinematic Staging* (Berkeley, CA: University of California Press, 2005), pp. 43–81.
9. For more on the different ways the 'cinema of uncertainty' deploys strategies of 'shock' in Feuillade, see Callahan, *Zones of Anxiety*, pp. 8, 26–7, 77. For more on the topic in more extended context see also Callahan, 'Evidence and uncertainty'.

10. Edward Dimendberg, *Film Noir and the Spaces of Modernity* (Cambridge, MA: Harvard University Press, 2004).
11. Naremore, *More than Night*, pp. 220–5.
12. A quite different approach and conclusion, but a related argument concerning Keyes' representation of rationalist logic and the threat that this offers to Neff, can be found in Joan Copjec's excellent essay, 'The phenomenal nonphenomenal: Private space in *film noir*', in Copjec (ed.), *Shades of Noir*, pp. 167–97.
13. Dudley Andrew, *Mists of Regret* (Princeton, NJ: Princeton University Press, 1995), p. 36.
14. Jean Grémillon, as quoted in ibid., p. 38.
15. Monica Dall'Asta, 'Pearl the swift one', in Marina Dahlquist (ed.), *Exporting Perilous Pauline: Pearl White and the Serial Film Craze* (Urbana, IL: Illinois University Press, 2013), pp. 75–9.
16. Louis Feuillade, see the original scenario for *La Nouvelle mission de Judex* (prologue) at the Bibliothèque de l'Arsenal.
17. Thomas Schatz, *Hollywood Genres: Formulas, Filmmaking and the Studio System* (New York: McGraw Hill, 1981), pp. 116–30.
18. Callahan, *Zones of Anxiety*, pp. 10–11.
19. Joel and Ethan Coen's *The Man Who Wasn't There* (2001) serves as the site of this quotation as well as an updating on noir as the 'cinema of uncertainty'. The film features a character, Freddy Riedenschneider, who delivers a mini-lecture on Heisenberg's Uncertainty Principle as he plots out a trial defence as illogical as Walter Neff's murder scheme in *Double Indemnity*.

2. WARNING SHADOWS: GERMAN EXPRESSIONISM AND AMERICAN FILM NOIR

Janet Bergstrom

Prologue

German Expressionism is called one of the most important influences on American film noir so often as to seem self-evident. What is usually meant, though, is not the Expressionist movement in the arts. When it comes to film noir, (German) Expressionism stands for *The Cabinet of Dr. Caligari* (1919/20) and the dark distinctiveness of the best-known films of the Weimar Republic that followed, from 1919 to early 1933, the end of World War I to the Nazi regime. Many films produced in Germany during that time are far from noir, but memory and viewing availability have been selective. Certain Weimar titles and directors come back again and again in the vast literature on film noir.[1]

Noir's inheritance from Weimar cinema has been seen in two different ways: (1) resemblances in style, structure and themes, especially a visual language that menaces the characters while seducing the audience, conveying anguish or worse for characters trapped by uncertainties and betrayals. Framing stories sometimes lead to the past (via flashback) where most of the story takes place, a structure that, in this kind of film, underscores fatalism: it is too late – it has already happened; and (2) skills and cinematic experiences brought to Hollywood by the flood of émigrés from the German film industry (regardless of national origin) fleeing the Hitler regime during the 1930s – directors, cinematographers, editors, writers, composers, producers, actors and almost every other trade – that could be put to new use when the time came.

Paul Schrader's 1972 'Notes on film noir' is still one of the most influential essays on the subject. Schrader devotes an entire section to 'The German Influence':

> Hollywood played host to an influx of German expatriates in the Twenties and Thirties, and these filmmakers and technicians had, for the most part, integrated themselves into the American film establishment ... But when, in the late Forties, Hollywood decided to paint it black, there were no greater masters of chiaroscuro than the Germans. The influence of expressionist lighting has always been just beneath the surface of Hollywood films, and it is not surprising, in *film noir*, to find it bursting out full bloom. Neither is it surprising to find a larger number of Germans and East Europeans working in *film noir*: Fritz Lang, Robert Siodmak, Billy Wilder, Franz Waxman, Otto Preminger, John Brahm, Anatole Litvak, Karl Freund, Max Ophuls, John Alton, Douglas Sirk, Fred Zinnemann, William Dieterle, Max Steiner, Edger G. Ulmer, Curtis Bernhardt, Rudolph Maté.[2]

Robert G. Porfirio summarises the double influence similarly:

> By now both [film noir's] foreign and domestic roots (German expressionism, French poetic realism, the gangster film and the hard-boiled novel) have been clearly established. The mordant sensibilities of the 'Germanic' émigrés and their penchant for a visual style which emphasized mannered lighting and startling camera angles provided a rich resource for a film industry newly attuned to the commercial possibilities of that hard-boiled fiction so popular in the 1930s ... Following the success of *Double Indemnity* and *Murder, My Sweet*, both made in 1944, this 'Germanic' tradition was quickly assimilated by others and the era of *film noir* was in full bloom.[3]

Schrader and Porfirio take into account the time-lag between film noir and the earlier arrival of the German-speaking émigrés and the 1930s publication of noir source fiction that certain academic arguments that would use to deny both influences, if not to deny film noir entirely, citing other forerunners and influences (noir was nothing new).[4] Both writers point to the readiness of elements that could come together at the right time and place to create a popular trend. Schrader does not try to claim, needlessly, that all noir films all had ex-Weimar cinema personnel nor does he claim that ex-Weimar cinema personnel necessarily had made noir-like films before they did so in Hollywood. They had come of age in that environment, even if their careers were only beginning in some cases.

Porfirio includes French poetic realism, a tendency at least as slippery to differentiate from neighbours and forerunners as film noir. Like noir, poetic realism is a tastemaker's post-facto categorisation, in which mood and atmosphere predominate over plots that can somehow, for connoisseurs most of all, absorb narrative disintegration, including dissonant flashbacks.[5] The German influence on French film goes back earlier, to many exchanges between French and German film and personnel during the late silent and early sound eras, a rich area still under-researched in depth and scope despite some encouraging work.[6]

Expressionism

Film noir is notoriously difficult to define, but so too is Expressionism. Art historian John Willett's description of the elusiveness of Expressionism could be transposed, without many changes, to film noir:

> Expressionism was never, like Futurism or Surrealism, a conscious grouping which can be related to a common program (however loosely worded) or to certain collective demonstrations and publications. It is one of those rarer concepts which get used more or less retrospectively to describe something already felt to be happening, or else a permanent basic element in all art which the times seemed to have brought to the surface ... Some of the very people whom any outsider would at once associate with it became the keenest to disown it.[7]

Keeping in mind that there are wide differences of opinion on the subject, Expressionism in Germany is generally considered to have started around 1905 with the artists of *Die Brücke* (The Bridge) in Dresden, founded by architecture students Ernst Ludwig Kirchner, Fritz Bleyl, Erich Heckel and Karl Schmidt-Rottluff, joined by others including Emil Nolde and Max Pechstein. They moved to Berlin in 1911, where they lived, worked and held exhibitions together until 1913 when the group disbanded. Their 1906 manifesto announced their 'passion for art and a burning desire to free themselves from the constraints of social convention; they sought to establish a "bridge" to the future'.[8] A second group, *Der Blaue Reiter* (The Blue Rider) was founded in Munich by Wassily Kandinsky and Franz Marc, who were moving toward an aesthetic of non-objectivity. The *Blaue Reiter Almanac* was published in 1912, devoted to modern art, music and theatre. Divergences among the artists and the ways in which their work broke with, or negated, accepted European art traditions were among the reasons that the Expressionists never cohered as a movement with a future direction, although important journals acted as catalysts for a sense of commonality, for instance Herwarth Walden's *Der*

Sturm (The Storm). His Berlin Galerie Der Sturm was credited with bringing the European avant-garde to Germany, with shows of Futurism, Cubism and the Russian avant-garde. Expressionism, from this perspective, seems to have been the accumulation of reactions on the part of different kinds of artists – painters, artists working with woodcuts, sculptors, architects, poets, writers, musicians – against traditional European arts who were finding inspiration in other European avant-gardes or African and Oceanic art but at the same time were moving away from each other. Expressionism seemed to die with the onset of World War I, when many artists enlisted or were mobilised. *Der Sturm*, however, continued to be published as a weekly from 1912 to 1929, and then less regularly up to the Nazi regime.

A 'second generation' of Expressionists – which was not recognised as such until perhaps as late as the 1980s – became active in the aftermath of the war which these artists had experienced first hand. This tendency was thought to end with the stabilisation of runaway inflation in the mid-1920s that ushered in the Neue Sachlichkeit (New Objectivity) movement across the arts in Germany. To understand the influence of Expressionism on Weimar cinema and from there to American film noir, the work of the 'second generation' of Expressionists – the same generation as the Weimar filmmakers who began making films in or around 1919 – was probably critical, although its graphically explicit depictions of extreme violence would have to be sublimated and transformed for the screen.

An important exhibition, 'German Expressionism 1915–1925: The Second Generation', that originated at the Los Angeles County Museum of Art in 1988, displayed huge, lurid, aggressive paintings by Max Beckmann, George Grosz, Otto Dix, Max Pechstein and Conrad Felixmüller, among others, depicting ghastly suicides, drug addiction and all manner of deformed bodies with their parts skewed at broken, inorganic angles.[9] Scenes of anti-erotic sexual butchery are horrifyingly common, such as could never have been staged in a theatre or appeared in film.

Maria Tatar sees the wartime experiences of artists Otto Dix and George Grosz as one of several probable causes for these obsessions in her study *Lustmord: Sexual Murder in Weimar Germany*:

> For the painter Otto Dix, who experienced combat at first hand, four years at the front led to fundamental shifts in personal convictions and aesthetic positions ... Dix's postwar artistic production – whether it takes the form of bloody battle scenes, mutilated female corpses, grotesque urban streetscapes, or serene neoclassical portraiture – seems singlemindedly devoted to working through primal fears aroused in combat situations, both military and sexual.[10]

Tatar points to 'the subterranean working through of gender conflicts in this war experience' as she shows the 'drive to disfigure the female body' in Dix's work 'that becomes evident in the many post-World War I works bearing the title *Lustmord*'.[11] Dix's etching, *Sexual Murder* (1922), shows the body of a dehumanised woman on a narrow bed, the centrepiece a bloody, dark hole in the area of her open-legged crotch.[12] *Sex Murderer: Self-Portrait* (1920) shows the artist 'slicing body parts in a moment of savage homicidal frenzy. Notwithstanding the cartoonlike, surreal style, the painting conveys both the rage of the assaulter and the terror of the victim'.[13] Tatar sees a similar underlying motivation in George Grosz's wartime and postwar paintings and drawings that repeatedly depict 'the repulsive side of corporality – folds of fat, legs scarred by varicose veins, bloated bellies, and sagging pouches of flesh'.[14] With occasional exceptions,

> Grosz portrays naked female bodies which, despite the sexual context in which they appear, are designed to arouse little more than horror and revulsion in the mind of the viewer. Bloated corpses, hacked body parts, and cut throats are put on display with whimsical artistic touches that blunt the notion of seeing the drawings as weapons in Grosz's arsenal of social criticism.[15]

Parts of a female corpse stick out of a crate that a 'grinning cardplayer' is using for a chair in *When It Was All Over, They Played Cards* (1917). In *Murder on Acker Street* (1916), a man washes his hands next to the decapitated body of a woman on a bed.[16]

Disfigured men, as if refuse from the nightmare of combat, also figure in these postwar urban landscapes, where the metropolis is violently coloured, threatening and claustrophobic. Oscar Kokoschka's prewar Expressionist play, *Murder, Hope of Women*, was revived in many versions. If seductiveness is represented, it is the lure of death and its substitutes, morbidly, relentlessly deglamorised.

(German) Expressionist Film

These second-generation works were not the models for Expressionist cinema, at least not directly. Following the war, prewar Expressionist art had become collectible. Fritz Lang's *Dr. Mabuse, the Gambler* (1921/2) shows a party in the home of a wealthy art collector filled with paintings and art objects that are Expressionist or the kind of art that inspired the prewar movement. Mabuse, posing as a psychoanalyst, is asked what he thinks of Expressionism. He replies that it is a game, like everything else. Indeed, Expressionism had become a parlour game.

GERMAN EXPRESSIONISM AND AMERICAN FILM NOIR

Figure 2.1 *Dr. Mabuse, the Gambler*: the party at Count Told's home.

Expressionism entered German cinema after the war with *The Cabinet of Dr. Caligari*, the most famous, uncontested example of Expressionist cinema. It remained the standard bearer for a new type of film, even if the prototype did not generate many others that, strictly speaking, would count as 'Expressionist'. *Caligari* came to stand for a radical break with the previous generation of German (and other) filmmaking. Its anti-realistic, claustrophobic sets and its harsh, high-contrast darkness coupled with feverish anxiety entered the vocabulary of filmmakers and film viewers. Any image from *Caligari* evokes its provocative difference from the status quo. Who can forget Conrad Veidt as Cesare, the most eye-catching somnambulist in film history, like a ballet dancer as he steps along a zigzagging ridge of artificial rooftops holding a woman's limp body? During his first appearance as a fairground attraction, Cesare's widened eyes, exaggerated by makeup and close shots, seem to penetrate his questioner's inner life, his answer voicing unsuspected fears. 'How long do I have to live?' 'Until morning'. The questioner recoils, unable to control hysterical facial grimaces. He does die before dawn, played out as a combination of dissimulation and destiny. As later in Weimar cinema and also in American film noir, fatalism is psychologised and subjectivised, inspiring terror that exceeds any specific fear.

Caligari's imagery and its hallucinatory story convey an idea of the anxiety ambiance of German Expressionist cinema very quickly. Technically, it functioned as a point of departure for the wave of Weimar films that conveyed similar preoccupations in much more cinematically innovative ways that would influence film noir directly. The paradox of *Caligari*, as inspiration for Weimar cinema and films made far away, was that cinematography and lighting play

Figure 2.2   Cover of the 1965 reprint of Kurtz's 1926 *Expressionismus und Film*.

a very limited role: far from chiaroscuro or the art of 'painting with light', in *Caligari* exaggerated shadows and highlights were flagrantly painted on the sets and the actors alike. Karl Freund, one of the most important cameramen in Weimar cinema, responsible for *The Golem* (1920), *Metropolis* (1925/6), *The Last Laugh* (1924) and *Variety* (1925), among other achievements, was asked later if he had been involved with *Caligari*. He replied, 'I had nothing to do with it, and I'm glad I didn't because it was not a cameraman's work. Everything was painted by the architects. And so a cameraman had to flat-light it, and that was it'.[17]

By the time *The Cabinet of Dr. Caligari* was released, pre-war Expressionism had become domesticated. It was a risky bet that succeeded, a breakthrough for German cinema at home and internationally with incredible staying power. As Werner Sudendorf pointed out, '*Caligari*'s carefully balanced position between vanguard and convention made it a great success with the audience'.[18]

In 1926 Rudolf Kurtz published *Expressionismus und Film*, the first monograph devoted to the subject, in which he discusses only six films in this light: *The Cabinet of Dr. Caligari* (Robert Wiene, 1919/20), *From Morning to Midnight* (Karlheinz Martin, 1920), *Genuine* (Robert Wiene, 1920), *Haus zum Mond* (*House on the Moon*, Karlheinz Martin, 1920), *Raskolnikov* (Robert Wiene, 1922/3) and *Waxworks* (Paul Leni, 1923/4).

Specialists since then have agreed that essentially the same few films from the early Weimar period qualify as truly Expressionist. Jürgen Kasten's influential study, *Der expressionistische Film* (1990), adds *Torgus* (Hanns Kobe, 1920/1).[19] Barry Salt's much-cited, fanciful, error-prone essay 'From Caligari to who?' ridicules extending the designation beyond the titles mentioned, although he considers that *Metropolis* (Fritz Lang, 1925/6) might belong to the group.[20]

Lotte H. Eisner's *The Haunted Screen* was recognised as the most important study of Weimar cinema from an aesthetic perspective on its publication in 1952 in French, and it remains so to this day. In the early chapter devoted to Expressionist film, Eisner discusses *The Cabinet of Dr. Caligari*, *Genuine*, *From Morning to Midnight*, *Torgus* and *Raskolnikov*.[21] Eisner has been reproached in some quarters for characterising the entire Weimar period as Expressionist and leading others to do so, but that would be a misunderstanding. She attempted to clarify her views in later essays on Expressionism and film by emphasising that Expressionist moments or scenes appear in many films that would not be characterised as such in their entirety. She could not control the fact that, for many, 'countless films from the 1920s contain some Expressionist shots that have caused them to be called Expressionist'.[22] In a similar way, writers and programmers of film noir are attuned to any scene or shot they might consider to be noir, perhaps noir enough to qualify another film for the ever-growing canon.[23]

In another parallel with writing on film noir and partly as a result of her training as an art historian, Eisner is interested in showing how composite and sometimes conflicting styles co-exist in the same film. The full title of the English-language version of Eisner's book is *The Haunted Screen: Expressionism in the German Cinema and the Influence of Max Reinhardt*.[24] That title may be misleading – the subtitle is either absent or is worded differently in French and German versions – because Eisner states at the beginning of her study that 'Expressionism' and 'Max Reinhardt' represent contradictory tendencies that were, nonetheless, brought together in Weimar cinema. Throughout her book she draws attention to variances on this work of recombination.

In a 1978 essay in the book published with the huge 'Paris-Berlin' exhibition in the Centre Georges Pompidou, which was accompanied by an important film retrospective, Eisner emphasises the importance of the pre-production art created for these films, painted or drawn images of shots and sets which were sometimes much more explicitly Expressionist than the films. (One might observe the same for posters advertising films of this period created by artists such as Josef Fenneker.[25])

> These effects of lights and shadows are inseparable from the set designs. It is through them that the best resonances of Expressionism are attained. It is also by them that an equivocation presents itself: where does the magic of lighting in the style of Max Reinhardt end, with its luminous effervescence and modeling with shadows, and where does the shock of brilliant light and deep shadows and the flamboyance of cascades of expressionist light begin? It is this ambiguity that has caused French critics to proclaim that all German films of the 1920s are expressionist.[26]

In 1981, Eisner asks at the beginning of her essay 'Ambivalences du film expressionniste' 'Do we need to repeat one more time that only a few films are *fully* Expressionist?'[27]

In 1967 at a round table on Expressionism, which included Eisner, at the Venice Film Festival, Fritz Lang declared that his work had nothing to do with Expressionism. 'He needed to be reminded,' Eisner recounted,

> of certain Expressionist elements, specifically in the two Dr. Mabuse films (1921/2) and that, like most of the artists of the period, he had passed through an 'Expressionist experience', perhaps without being aware of it – but that had left clear traces in his work. There are countless visions that derive from a rather eclectic Expressionism,

for instance, when Mabuse is brooding underneath the painting of Lucifer in the first Mabuse film or, much later, in *The Testament of Dr. Mabuse* (1932) when Mabuse's ghost appears in the office of the doctor of the mental clinic and merges with his body through superimposition, and later, in the car chase near the end, when the translucent ghost of Mabuse commands the doctor as he drives.[28]

The violence of the second-generation Expressionists is not addressed by Eisner, but the conditions that helped inspire that art also influenced Weimar cinema, although in a largely sublimated, disguised form of representation, even in the case of the (offscreen) axe murder in *Hintertreppe* (*Backstairs*, Leopold Jessner and Paul Leni, 1921) or the serial killer in Lang's *M* (1931). G. W. Pabst's *Pandora's Box* (1928/9), a key memory-film for American film noir, romanticises and eroticises ambiguities surrounding the femme fatale and the possibilities or limitations of her independent agency. Lulu (Louise Brooks) is about to marry Dr Schön (Fritz Kortner). The marriage would mean her class rise from a showgirl and kept woman to a wife with social status and money. Instead, Dr Schön, in a jealous rage, orders her to shoot herself with a gun that he pushes into her hand. In the struggle between them, he himself is shot and dies. Lulu is sentenced to death but she escapes from the courtroom and returns to Dr Schön's luxurious apartment, smiling as she opens the closets to look at her beautiful clothes. While she runs bathwater in a deep, temperature-controlled tub, she happily leafs through a women's fashion and leisure magazine, *Die Dame*, as Patrice Petro pointed out in her study of female readers of the Weimar illustrated press in *Joyless Streets: Women and Melodramatic Representation in Weimar Germany*.[29] Eventually she will come to a bleak ending, victim of a sexual murder that is presented to us as soft, seductive, chiaroscuro cinema. Lulu, now a fugitive in London, is forced by poverty into menial prostitution. She directs her warm smile towards a stranger who follows her to her room, dropping a knife held behind his back in response to her tenderness. Inside, she sits on his lap and he holds her against him in a moment of quiet comfort. She cannot see his eyes widen when a knife on the table reflects the candlelight, triggering his compulsion to kill. We see his back, not Lulu, as she drops away from him, except for her hand as it loosens, the ugliness of murder suppressed.

Expressionism and American Film Noir

The Expressionist heritage extended far beyond German Expressionism. American film noir played out in another country, another time. Edward Dimendberg emphasises the historical specificity of each of the two film movements, and that they should not be collapsed into each other, in the context of a 1946 essay by Siegfried Kracauer on 'Hollywood's Terror Films'.[30]

> If the cultural resonance of film noir in the United States remains irreducible to the valorization of German silent cinema, Hollywood B movies, and pulp crime fiction by French film critics, the significance of urban space in the 1940s and 1950s is similarly irreducible to that of the Weimar cinema. The dark alleys and deserted streets of 1920s Weimar cinema engage as a set of social and historical referents vastly different from those which establish the conditions of the spatiality of film noir and its allegorical treatment of the experience of exile.[31]

The specificity Dimendberg argues for in this essay and throughout his book *Film Noir and the Spaces of Modernity* counters Thomas Elsaesser's notion of the 'historical imaginary' of film noir which, in Dimendberg's words, has the function of simultaneously 'covering up' and 'preserving' the inconsistencies, multiple realities, and incompatible entities named by German Expressionist style, political exile and the Hollywood film industry, construing an effect of self-evidence by giving them a single name and a cause-and-effect 'history'.[32]

Given the differences in time, place and lived experience, one might compare the impossibility of the direct cinematic representation of post-World War I Expressionist violence in Weimar cinema with the impossibility of a direct transfer of post-World War II violence in American film noir. Edward Dimendberg's insightful analysis in his chapter 'Naked cities' in *Film Noir and the Spaces of Modernity* takes into account the book of crime scene photographs titled *Naked City*, published by Weegee in 1945, and Jules Dassin's 1948 film *Naked City*, which was influenced by them, but in a necessarily subdued form for an American (or any) film audience.[33]

The postwar possibilities for realism in American film noir were matched by the excitement of welding an Expressionist look with blacker darkness, harder-edged shadows, higher-contrast lighting and sometimes psychologically motivated skewed angles to actual, non-studio locations, as can be seen in heightened-realism films photographed by John Alton, such as *Raw Deal* (Anthony Mann, 1948), *He Walked by Night* (Alfred Werker and Anthony Mann, 1948), *Border Incident* (Anthony Mann, 1949) or *The Big Combo* (Joseph H. Lewis, 1955). Paul Schrader put this well: 'The best *noir* technicians simply made all the world a sound stage, directing unnatural and expressionistic lighting onto realistic settings. In films like *Union Station, They Live by Night, The Killers* there is an uneasy, exhilarating combination of realism and expressionism'.[34]

Extremely dark scenes were used for expressive psychological purposes, ratcheting up the uncertainties inherent in the double-cross. Towards the end of *Double Indemnity*, the shoot-out in near darkness between Walter Neff (Fred MacMurray) and Phyllis Dietrichson (Barbara Stanwyck), the woman Neff can't stop himself from loving except in this way, feels like a double suicide. After the gunfight between the police and the criminals in the huge dark house as *The Killers* (1946) is winding down, the camera moves to tighter and tighter close-ups of Kitty (Ava Gardner) and her dying husband, Colfax (Alfred Werker), as she frantically tries to get him to clear her from their network of double-crosses and murders. Even when Kitty is told he's dead, she doesn't stop: 'Come back, Jim, tell them. Come back, save me . . . Jim . . . Kitty is innocent. I swear, Kitty is innocent. Kitty is innocent, I swear, Kitty is innocent, Kitty is innocent'.

Not every noir dramatic close-out takes place in the midst of expressionistic shadows (not necessarily the last scene, which may be an epilogue). Both

Raw Deal and *The Big Combo* use white mist instead of darkness for the same purpose, literalising the metaphor of being unable to see any future. The ending of *Gun Crazy* (Joseph H. Lewis, 1950) takes place in the hills of the countryside near Bart's home town, where the lovers on the run wake up inside a white blanket of morning fog, unable to see anything but strange shapes of tree branches, almost as inorganic-looking as the trees in *Caligari*. This femme fatale, Annie Laurie Starr (Peggy Cummins), really is in love with Bart (John Dall), but she is still addicted to guns and will kill those who threaten her. The final shots isolate her, showing her growing panic as the voices of Bart's two best friends from childhood call out that they are surrounded, to drop their guns: 'I'll kill you, I'll kill you,' she screams. Looking tortured, Bart shoots her to stop her from killing them. It means his virtual suicide, so closely has he identified himself with her. Then he is shot, falling next to her in death.

The street means something specific in the early years of Weimar culture: the icon of homelessness, inspiring dreadful fears not only for the poor, with less than ever, but now for the newly dispossessed middle class, ruined by calamitous inflation with nowhere else to go. G. W. Pabst's *Joyless Street* (1925) portrays the fears of deprivation and hopelessness on the street, and what people will do to survive. A film called simply *The Street* (*Die Strasse*, Karl Grune, 1923) had to be retitled *Tragedy of the Street* for export to convey this meaning to a foreign audience.

The street in American film noir can be fateful in a different kind of way, especially glistening, rain-soaked streets in the night, such as we see in the first shot of the wildly careening car in Billy Wilder's *Double Indemnity* (1944), or *Gun Crazy*, when the boy trips in the wet darkness, dropping the gun he just stole from a display window that slides across the pavement to stop at the feet of a policeman. Robert Siodmak's *The Killers* opens with a car driving into a town at night. Two men walk into a diner looking for the Swede (Burt Lancaster): they are going to kill him. The highway in the rainy night or the sunny day is equally fateful and ensnaring, despite the open spaces, for Al Roberts (Tom Neal) in Edgar G. Ulmer's *Detour* (1945). World War II combat veteran Sam Fuller's back alley in *Underworld U.S.A.* (1961) is where the young Tolly Devlin (Cliff Robertson) sees his father beaten and murdered in the dark of night, expressionistic shadows of the murderers looming larger than life, the memory that will dominate and limit him.

The passive male is seen again and again in Weimar cinema, much remarked on by later commentators, including Siegfried Kracauer.[35] Myriad variations on the reactive male protagonist exist in American film noir, especially in tandem with a woman – a femme fatale – who influences his course of actions for the worst. Even when he is an experienced, woman-smart detective like Jeff (Robert Mitchum) in Jacques Tourneur's *Out of the Past* (1947), sexual obsession overcomes his better judgment, in this case for Kathy (Jane Greer), whose love he wants to believe in, a separate world for the two of them. He tries to outsmart the frame-ups he begins to realise he is part of, competing with her and her changing allies. He leaves her, returns, leaves again, returns again, until he breaks the cycle by setting up a death trap that will kill both of them. When Kathy sees the police roadblock Jeff has called in, she shoots him, calling him a double-crosser, then is gunned down as she shoots at the police. The French call this *l'amour fou*, beloved of the Surrealists because of the irrational, unpredictable, magnetic pull of the love object.

Visual style in film noir has been a focus of discussion for good reason.[36] I would like to draw attention to the use of reaction shots in film noir, beyond their ordinary use, in carrying the heart of the film, with the eyes and facial expression as window to the character's uncertainty or split belief, not wanting to let go of a hope that – in the end – will not be reciprocated. Reaction shots deepen the impact of noir anxiety cinema, essential for moving the story and emotional uncertainty forward. Sometimes reaction shots are understated, as if the emotion is not deeply felt, but that may or may not be a defensive mask. Throughout the cabin scene in *Out of the Past* reaction shots are provoked by a canny use of offscreen space and sound, in three distinct phases. Jeff and Kathy, on the run and separated for a long time, meet at night at a cabin in the woods, coming together with fresh romance, like the beginning of their passion. They are both startled by the sound of a car door closing outside. Jeff's old partner Fisher has followed Kathy and wants money to remain quiet about their whereabouts. Jeff and Fisher fight, with cutaway shots to Kathy's excited expression. Jeff knocks Fisher to the ground and the sound of a gunshot is heard. Jeff whirls around, looking offscreen towards Kathy, incredulous. She is holding a gun for the first time. Jeff: 'You didn't have to kill him'. Kathy: 'He'd have been against us'. Jeff turns to attend to the body, turning back at the sound of a car motor starting. The door is open, Kathy is gone. Another reaction shot: he looks stunned. Then he sees her bankbook, showing that she lied about stealing money. The trust and the confidence of their bond have vanished, but his expression is almost impassive. He sees her again and again; each time she adds new twists to double-crossing him, appealing to him ever more seductively, the image of nonchalant, expensive glamour. He talks to her as if he hates her, but everyone wonders, to the very end of the film.

Otto Preminger's *Angel Face* (1952) is remarkably similar, with Robert Mitchum again apparently the manly self-reliant decision-maker playing the ambulance driver Frank Jessup. He is persuaded to abandon his normal life to live in the mansion and under the spell of Diane Tremayne (Jean Simmons), whom he comes to detest, his reaction shots registering his disbelief in her, bit by bit, yet not revealing a pain that goes deep. He leaves her, he returns, he leaves again, he is persuaded to return again, until he is implicated with her in a double murder that she planned. The cycle of seduction and rejection is broken similarly to *Out of the Past*, as if the only way out is death.

Edward G. Robinson, playing Professor Wanley in Fritz Lang's *Woman in the Window* (1944), reacts with evident disbelief written on his face when the much younger, glamorous Alice (Joan Bennett) wants to join him for dinner, and again when she invites him to her apartment, and then disorientated disbelief when a man – her patron – bursts into the apartment jealously, attacks him and starts choking him. Wanley's face registers disbelief again after he stabs the man in the back with scissors handed to him by Kitty and the corpse is now on the floor in front of them. His reactions to events caused more or less directly by Kitty structure the film, cued by his reaction shots that are clearly readable, distanced from the core of his being. This was not *l'amour fou*, only generalised seduction and accident.

On the other hand, *Detour*'s many reaction shots of protagonist Al Roberts, anguished and hopeless in a diner where he tells his story through voiceover in multiple flashbacks, go straight to the heart and nerves. His expression is frankly horrified when he realises that Haskell, owner of the car he was driving, is suddenly dead next to him. He shows more anxiety after he hides the body and assumes Haskell's identity. After he picks up the hardened hitchhiker, Vera (Ann Savage), and she asks, 'Where did you leave his body?' – she had previously got a ride with Haskell – Al's face shows his doomed submission to her commands. He unintentionally strangles Vera with a telephone cord running underneath her locked door to stop her from calling the police. The return from the flashback to Al's face at the diner shows his despair. There is no way out, and for no reason. Al's actions have been reactions and unlucky choices.

Wilder's *Sunset Boulevard* (1950) is narrated by the unemployed screenwriter turned gigolo Joe Gillis (William Holden), who is not only passive, he is dead, floating in a swimming pool as the police arrive. Written on his face and heard in his voiceover (the same technique as in *Detour*) is acquiescence, not sexual attraction, as a reason for his failure to leave his patron, the much older Norma Desmond (Gloria Swanson), who turns out to be his femme fatale quite literally.

In Robert Siodmak's *The Killers* and *Criss Cross* (1949), Burt Lancaster – first as the Swede, against Ava Gardner as Kitty, then as Steve, against Yvonne De Carlo as Anna – plays a manly protagonist who is without any trace of meanness or violence, almost an innocent, drawn into an amoral criminal world of cruel betrayal because he wants to believe the woman he loves, who is the centre of his life. He wants to believe that she feels the same way, all appearances to the contrary. But he is buffeted time after time by her unexpected actions that leave him out and at a loss despite what seems like a shared passion. *Criss Cross* begins with an overhead view of the city at night,

Figure 2.3 *Criss Cross*: close-up of Anna (Yvonne De Carlo), frontal, changed angle and black background for emphasis: 'Steve, all those things that happened to us, everything that went before, we'll forget it, you'll see, I'll make you forget it'.

descending to a crowded parking lot behind a nightclub, where a man and a woman are revealed kissing by the headlights of a passing car. The story is perhaps halfway through, on the night before Steve will help Anna's friends rob an armoured car. Steve wants to be sure Anna understands how and when they will meet again. A brief series of shots repositions the camera to show Anna's face in the centre of the frame, surrounded by darkness, trying to convince him to forget the past and believe in a different kind of future, and then Steve's face, slightly at an angle, listening to her, believing her, in love with her.

He explains the plan again as if he is the one in charge. She is saying what he wants to hear. He wants to forget about things that we will see in a series of painful flashbacks, showing Anna repeatedly deceiving him with Slim Dundee (Dan Duryea at his most understatedly powerful and menacing). After one sudden absence, she returns as Slim's wife, yet as if she can still be Steve's girl. In this film, as in *The Killers*, the double-cross cuts the heart out of the male protagonist, leaving him with nothing. We see it in his eyes.

Paranoia and fear are not the same thing. They are both operative when Steve is confined to his hospital bed after the robbery that has gone wrong in a scene where white clouds of tear gas make it impossible to see. Steve's beloved older partner, Pop, dies in the hold-up; ironically, Steve is hailed as a hero who saved part of the money and was badly hurt. His fractured arm hangs in the air, positioned by counterweights. Steve worries about a lone man sitting in the hallway. He keeps looking at him, reflected in a mirror in his room (a favourite Weimar device to show the double), but the nurse tells him he is there for his wife. Accepting this, Steve asks the man if he would stay in his room during the night because he doesn't want to be alone. The man agrees. After Steve falls

Figure 2.4   Reverse close-up of Steve (Burt Lancaster), with anxious hope: 'After it's done, after we're safe …'

Figure 2.5   Return to Anna's close-up: '… it'll be just you and me, you and me, the way it should have been from the start'.

asleep, the man goes to the window, then out the door to bring back a wheelchair. Steve has invited into his room the very man sent to get him out of the hospital for Slim Dundee to find out where Anna is with the hold-up money. The man cuts the cords holding Steve's arm in position, letting it fall. Steve's face registers agony, then the screen blurs as he blacks out from the pain.

That pain is physical. The worst is yet to come, when Steve manages to reach Anna in their getaway bungalow. As soon as she realises that the driver was Slim's man, she starts packing to save herself. Steve can't go; he needs a hospital. Sweating and immobile, he doesn't believe she would leave him: 'All those things you said to me … You weren't lying, you meant it, I know you meant it'. She runs out, then runs back in because Slim is outside the door, about to

Figure 2.6   Orson Welles' *Lady from Shanghai* (1948).

kill both of them. Like the Swede in *The Killers*, Steve was as good as dead anyway. His face showed it.

Regardless of attempts to stop the loose identification of Expressionism with film noir, *Caligari*, *Nosferatu*, *Mabuse* and their Weimar legacy continue to be points of reference for the menacing, ill-fated, hemmed-in and seductive world of film noir, regardless of whether or how many German-speaking émigrés were directly involved in the American productions.[37] No one repurposed this anxiety-cinema tradition better than Orson Welles in *The Lady from Shanghai* (1947). The plot is nearly incomprehensible, despite the voiceover commentaries by protagonist Michael O'Hara (Welles) on its lures, twists and turns, with death warnings in openly symbolic visuals (the aquarium scene) and in direct threats. The climax is an extravagant show of avant-garde visual prowess referencing *The Cabinet of Dr. Caligari* in a combination of realism and its opposite, even more audacious than the dream-like, off-kilter, seductive mise-en-scène leading up to it.

Setting the final confrontation inside a 'real' funhouse motivates multiple trick mirrors, more than could be counted, without being able to differentiate the reflection from the person reflected during the long showdown between two double-dealing death merchants – Arthur Bannister (Everett Sloane) and Elsa Bannister (Rita Hayworth) – now out in the open, so to speak, but impossible to locate in actual space until all the mirrors have been shattered with violent, visual magnificence and they are both dying. Throughout this long scene, it is hard to discern whether Michael O'Hara is in an actual funhouse location or whether this is the mental projection of a paranoid (or terrified) framework of entrapment. Rita Hayworth is as perfect-looking as ever, but with the stony look of a hired gun, certain that she is in control, like some of the femmes fatales before her who were about to die. This scene marks one of the high points in the extreme noir phase, wedding the mood and look of Expressionism, whether through German forerunners or American inheritors, to an eclectic, ever-changing American idiom.

Notes

Translations are my own unless otherwise indicated.
1. This literature includes a substantial contribution published on DVD in the form of commentary tracks, documentaries, interviews and other kinds of documentation.
2. Paul Schrader, 'Notes on film noir', *Film Comment* 8(1) (spring 1972), 10. (A phrase from this statement was omitted in the reprint in Alain Silver and James Ursini (eds), *Film Noir Reader* (New York: Limelight Editions, 1996, p. 55).) James Naremore calls Schrader 'the figure who most shaped American ideas about noir' through this essay that 'became the best-known statement on the topic in the English language', James Naremore, *More than Night* (Berkeley, CA: University of California Press, 1998), p. 33.
3. Robert G. Porfirio, 'No way out: Existential motifs in the *film noir*', in Silver and Ursini (eds), *Film Noir Reader*, p. 77.
4. Thomas Elsaesser, 'A German ancestry to film noir? Film history and its imaginary', *Iris* 21 (spring 1996), and Marc Vernet, 'Film noir on the edge of doom', in Joan Copjec (ed.), *Shades of Noir* (London: Verso, 1993), adopt such perspectives.
5. Dudley Andrew's *Mists of Regret: Culture and Sensibility in Classic French Film* (Princeton, NJ: Princeton University Press, 1995) is the most extended study of poetic realism to date.
6. Alastair Phillips, *City of Darkness, City of Light: Émigré Filmmakers in Paris, 1929–1939* (Amsterdam: Amsterdam University Press, 2004) begins later, but makes an excellent starting point for a study that would begin earlier and that would not be confined to émigrés but would focus on the history of international exchange.
7. John Willett, *Expressionism* (New York: McGraw Hill, 1970), p. 6.
8. Stephanie Barron, 'Introduction', in Stephanie Barron (ed.), *German Expressionism 1915–1925: The Second Generation* (Munich: Prestel Verlag, 1988), p. 12. This section is largely drawn from Barron's summary, pp. 11–13.
9. *German Expressionism 1915–1925: The Second Generation* is generously illustrated in colour.
10. Maria Tatar, *Lustmord: Sexual Murder in Weimar Germany* (Princeton, NJ: Princeton University Press, 1995) p. 68.
11. Ibid., p. 68.
12. Ibid., p. 88.
13. Ibid., p. 16.
14. Ibid., p. 117.
15. Ibid., p. 117.
16. Ibid., pp. 117–18.
17. Karl Freund Interview (in English), 1 June 1964. [Ralph] Freud Collection, Interviews, UCLA Special Collections, Collection 542, Boxes 1 and 2.
18. Werner Sudendorf, 'Expressionism and film: *The Testament of Dr. Caligari*', in Shulamith Behr, David Fanning and Douglas Jarman (eds), *Expressionism Reassessed* (Manchester: Manchester University Press, 1993), p. 95. More context is provided in Mike Budd (ed.), *The Cabinet of Dr. Caligari: Texts, Contexts, Histories* (New Brunswick, NJ: Rutgers University Press, 1990); see particularly Kristin Thompson, 'Dr. Caligari at the Folies-Bergère, or, the successes of an

early avant-garde film'. The most comprehensive current study is Olaf Brill's *Der Caligari-Komplex* (Munich: Belleville, 2012).
19. Jürgen Kasten, *Der expressionistische Film* (Münster: MAkS, 1990); Rudolf Kurtz, *Expressionismus und Film* (Berlin: Verlag der Lichtbildbühne, 1926; reprinted Zurich: Verlag Hans Rohr, 1965).
20. Barry Salt, 'From Caligari to who?', *Sight and Sound* 48(2) (spring 1972). He omits *Haus zum Mond*, which was probably not available to him.
21. Lotte H. Eisner, *The Haunted Screen: Expressionism in the German Cinema and the Influence of Max Reinhardt*, trans. Roger Greaves (London: Thames & Hudson, 1969; paperback edition Berkeley, CA: University of California Press, 1973).
22. Lotte H. Eisner, 'L'influence de l'art expressionniste sur les décors des films allemands des années vingt', in *Paris-Berlin, rapports et contrastes France-Allemagne 1900–1933* (Paris: Centre Georges Pompidou), p. 270.
23. The excitement of discovering new noir titles – a sequence or two may be enough – draws viewers to films called noir by Turner Classic Movies and creates a market for more and more DVDs and special box sets. In April 2013 the Film Noir Foundation and the American Cinematheque co-presented the 15th Annual Festival of Film Noir (twenty-three titles) at the Egyptian Theater in Hollywood, programmed by Eddie Muller, Alan K. Rode and Gwen Deglise.
24. The first French version was an abridged edition titled *L'Écran démoniaque: Influence de Max Reinhardt et de l'expressionnisme* (Paris: Editions André Bonne, 1952), followed by an expanded French version (édition définitive) as *L'Écran démoniaque* (Paris: Terrain Vague, 1965), without the subtitle. The 1969 English translation, again updated, placed the most emphasis on Expressionism: *The Haunted Screen: Expressionism in the German Cinema and the Influence of Max Reinhardt*, while the German translation, again revised and expanded, returned to *Die dämonische Leinwand* [The Haunted Screen] (Frankfurt: Kommunales Kino, 1975).
25. Many coloured examples are included in Lauren J. Miller, *Weimar Rococo: The Cinema Posters of Josef Fenneker as a Reflection of 1920s Berlin Society* (MA thesis in the History of the Decorative Arts and Design, Cooper-Hewitt, National Design Museum, Smithsonian Institution; and Parsons The New School for Design, 2011).
26. Eisner, 'L'influence de l'art expressionniste', p. 270. Despite the fineness of her distinctions, Eisner asked Henri Langlois numerous times to hold an exhibition devoted entirely to Expressionism and film, as described in Laurent Mannoni, 'Lotte H. Eisner, historienne des démons allemands', in Marianne de Fleury and Laurent Mannoni (eds), *Le Cinéma expressionniste allemand, splendeurs d'une collection* (Paris: Éditions de La Martinière-La Cinémathèque française, 2006), p. 67. In 2006 her many years spent securing works for the Cinémathèque française resulted in the exhibition *Le Cinéma expressionniste allemand, splendeurs d'une collection*.
27. Lotte H. Eisner, 'Ambivalences du film expressionniste', in Lionel Richard (ed.), *L'Expressionnisme allemand*, special issue of *Obliques* (Paris: Ed. Borderie, 1981), p. 173.
28. Ibid., p. 173. An interview with Lang along the same lines that was carried out at that event, published as Michel Ciment, Goffredo Fofi, Louis Sequin and Roger Tailleur, 'Fritz Lang in Venice', *Positif* 94 (April 1968), is included in Barry Keith Grant (ed.), *Fritz Lang: Interviews* (Jackson, MS: University Press of Mississippi, 2003).
29. Patrice Petro, *Joyless Streets: Women and Melodramatic Representation in Weimar Germany* (Princeton, NJ: Princeton University Press, 1989), p. 81.

30. Siegfried Kracauer, 'Hollywood's terror films: Do they reflect an American state of mind?', *Commentary* 2(2) (August 1946), 132–6, reprinted in *New German Critique* 89 (2003), 105–11.
31. Edward Dimendberg, 'Down these seen streets a man must go: Siegfried Kracauer, "Hollywood's terror films", and the spatiality of film noir', *New German Critique* 89 (2003), 123.
32. Ibid., 134; Edward Dimendberg, *Film Noir and the Spaces of Modernity* (Cambridge, MA: Harvard University Press, 2004).
33. Dimendberg discusses the significance of Weegee's book *The Naked City* (New York: Essential Books, 1945) in *Film Noir and the Spaces of Modernity*, p. 48 and after.
34. Schrader, 'Notes on film noir', in Silver and Ursini (eds), *Film Noir Reader*, p. 56 and in *Film Comment*, 10.
35. Siegfried Kracauer, *From Caligari to Hitler* (Princeton, NJ: Princeton University Press, 1947).
36. Janey Place's and Lowell Peterson's essay 'Some visual motifs of *film noir*' remains a classic, well-illustrated point of reference, in Silver and Ursini (eds), *Film Noir Reader*, pp. 65–75. Todd McCarthy's *Visions of Light: The Art of Cinematography* has a useful section on film noir (Image Entertainment and Twentieth Century-Fox DVD, 1992; 2000).
37. I am pairing film titles with directors, mainly, as shorthand; in fact, our knowledge of the production genesis and circumstances of most of these films is inadequate and many things will forever remain unknown.

3. HARD-BOILED TRADITION AND EARLY FILM NOIR

Homer B. Pettey

> Partly it may be due to the sense that money as an accounting mechanism submits pleasures to an unforgiving scrutiny, like that of traditional morality. Most of all it has to do with money's anonymity, the sense that the trust it buys is somehow fraudulently acquired, being based on impersonal rules rather than personal understanding. Sexuality is the area of human life most permeated by the ideal of willing and autonomous exchange between partners motivated by convergent desire, and yet it is also the one most poisoned by . . . more indirect and mercenary motive. The indirect masquerading as the direct is likewise at money's very heart.
> Paul Seabright, *The Company of Strangers*[1]

Hard-boiled detective fiction and film noir are almost exclusively aligned with the desires for money and sex, two mirrored conditions of a fragile human economy. *The Maltese Falcon* (1941), *Double Indemnity* (1944), and *Murder, My Sweet* (1944) certainly rely upon economic issues in their adaptations from the Hammett, Cain and Chandler novels. All three novels and their film adaptations deal with sexual exchanges for material possessions: Brigid's erotic enticements to Spade for the mysterious falcon; Phyllis's promise of amorous reward for the monetary compensation from the indemnity policy; and Mrs Grayle's lubricious invitations to Spade in order to guard her jaded secret and thereby her social position. Of course, this concupiscence as capital outlay is hardly limited to feminine desires in film noir, since Spade, Neff and Marlowe engage in this kind of self-interested manipulation for profit. Emerging during the era of the international Great Depression and the rise of global fascism, film noir often addresses the complex, paradoxical interrelationship of economics and passion. Plots and thematic structures of proto-noirs and noirs of the 1940s and well into the next decade reveal the matrix of dependency between money and sex, among them: *The Big Sleep* (1940), *Danger Signal* (1945), *Fallen Angel* (1945), *Mildred Pierce* (1945), *Out of the Past* (1947), *Railroaded* (1947), *Dark Passage* (1947), *Thieves' Highway* (1949), *Too Late for Tears* (1949), *Dark City* (1950), *The Asphalt Jungle* (1950), *Gun Crazy* (1950) and *The Big Heat* (1953). Excess – financial, sexual, material – serves as a central motif in all of these films as it had in the development of the hard-boiled detective genre. While Hammett, Cain and Chandler established a new style and aesthetic for hard-boiled detective fiction and for film noir, their art also reflected the pervasive economic troubles that plagued Depression-era and early postwar American culture.

For the New Deal, Keynesian models for priming the economic pump answered Democratic political needs to justify various promises of reform and relief. Keynes's *The General Theory of Employment, Interest, and Money* (1936) explained how classical economists – the supply and demand apostles of capitalism – could not account for pre- and especially post-1929 market disasters. In particular, Keynes made clear that classical economic theory misplaced emphasis on equilibrium and parallelism of supply and demand; it misunderstood human desire and the concept of demand or fulfilment, but also collapsed the two. Such a dilemma typifies the culprits' desire for the Maltese falcon, Mrs Grayle for her jade, Moose for his Velma, and Neff and Phyllis for wealth. All are incapable of comprehending that a current desire will not fulfil a future need or satisfy a future demand, since time, place, situation and passion are mutable and dynamic, not static. Such is made evident by the twists, turns and betrayals between Spade and Brigid O'Shaughnessy, Moose and Velma, Neff and Phyllis. Like classical economists, they misjudge and delude themselves:

> Those who think in this way are deluded, nevertheless, by an optical illusion, which makes two essentially different activities appear to be the same. They are fallaciously supposing that there is a nexus which unites decisions to abstain from present consumption with decisions to provide for future consumption; whereas the motives which determine the latter are not linked in any simple way with motives which determine the former.[2]

Desire thereby clouds the realities of demand in the same way that classical economists' blindness could never account for the booms and spectacular busts in the capitalist market system. This misconception of economic realities

Hammett, Chandler and Cain exploited by describing aberrant sexual desires and deadly fetishistic attractions in terms of monetary schemes. Speculation to acquire material gain eventually brings about characters' demise – economic, social, psychological and physical deaths.

Hard-boiled fiction for men, nearly a decade before the Great Depression, confronted these issues. In 1920, *Black Mask* included as its subtitle 'An Illustrated Magazine of Detective, Mystery, Adventure, Romance, and Spiritualism', but by the late 1920s, it dropped spiritualism and romance stories, re-subtitling itself as 'The He-Man Magazine'.[3] Hard-boiled masculinity, however, cannot be shrugged off as mere macho fantasies, because from its inception, *Black Mask* had a political and economic agenda against homegrown American fascism. From the early 1920s, *Black Mask* attacked openly in its pages the greatest threat to American politics and social stability – the Ku Klux Klan. In its columns and short stories, *Black Mask* waged a war against the KKK's ultra-conservative rhetoric and Nativist ideology that targeted racial, ethnic and religious minorities and that raged against their contributing to the corruption and decline of Protestant morality. Sean McCann's admirable study on hard-boiled fiction and the New Deal argues that Chandler and Hammett challenged the monolithic vision of a unified racial community and mocked the KKK for its illogical demagoguery and hypocrisy. In particular, Hammett's fiction, while employing ethnic types, undermines ethno-racial stereotypes with its mocking scepticism and its trenchant analysis of economics and class in America:

> Such is the egalitarianism of Hammett's underworld – a fantasy of purely profit-driven society, in which the only meaningful social forces stem from the pursuit of individual interest. In such a milieu, Hammett implies, ethnic distinctions become ultimately insubstantial . . . What counts for him is not the border between ethnic groups, but those occupational and class positions (yegg, detective, settlement worker) that situate people in relation to the underworld . . . Commerce and self-interest dissolve those ethnic boundaries that the Klan sought to cast as metaphysical principles, and when race is summoned, it tends to be a cover for the profit motive.[4]

In this sense, then, Hammett exposed American culture as ultimately an expression of absolute individual self-interest, both economic and sexual. Perhaps the most striking cinematic example occurs with Joel Cairo (Peter Lorre), the fey, foppish Levantine, having his first encounter with Sam Spade (Humphrey Bogart) in the detective's office. Smart-mouthed secretary Effie Perrin (Lee Patrick) hands Spade Cairo's scented card and, in a mockingly suggestive tone, says simply: 'Gardenia'. After a cautious introduction and taking a seat, Cairo offers his condolences for the loss of Spade's partner due to an 'unfortunate death'. While playing provocatively with his walking stick, Cairo quickly shifts to his economic interest:

> 115. CS: *Cairo from a low angle.*
> CAIRO: More than idle curiosity prompted my question. See, Mr. Spade, I'm trying to recover an ornament that, shall we say, has been mislaid. (*He places the top of his walking stick to his lips as he looks at Spade.*)[5]

How Cairo's fellatio gesture passed by the Breen Office remains a wonder! Cairo's speech plays off Spade's emotional loss in order to entice him to monetary gain: Cairo offers Spade $5,000 for the recovery of the black bird statuette. After Effie calls to inform Spade that she is leaving for the night, Cairo exchanges his phallic walking stick for a diminutive, impotent pistol, of which Spade easily disarms him. Now, Cairo's short-lived, highly speculative scheme misfires as Spade, with a satanic grin, knocks him unconscious. Sexuality and economics are clearly paired in this classic noir moment, as they are in the next scene between Spade and Brigid O'Shaughnessy (Mary Astor) in her apartment. After Spade informs her that Cairo has offered him $5,000 for the black bird, she counters with an offer of sex for his loyalty: 'What else is there I can buy you with?' Brigid is an expert at manipulative strategies for achieving success from failure, as Spade recognises: 'You're good; you're very good'. Zero-sum mathematics of competition, then, replaces ethnic, even gender status in the hard-boiled world.

In Hammett's *The Maltese Falcon*, Spade, a metaphorical name implying sexual and pragmatic utility, exemplifies the modern, urban American myth: the system – economics, jurisprudence, politics – forces individual autonomy to be determined by the result of a zero-sum game in which another is deprived of freedom. In short, both the novel and the 1931 and 1941 films conclude that Brigid O'Shaughnessy must go to prison in order for Sam Spade to remain independent. In some respects, Hammett's hard-boiled fiction critiqued and replaced the antiquated, naive view of the individual in modern society that had been fostered by Herbert Hoover's faith in laissez-faire economics and free enterprise autonomy. As emphasised in his *American Individualism* (1922), Hoover sustained the genteel myth of the individual as 'self-contained and to a considerable extent self-created', but social reality, or rather the prevailing social metaphors, conceptualised the individual as self-seeking fortune and status in the marketplace against others, who were only viewed as competitors.[6] In this sense, zero-sum metaphors for the game, competition or marketplace underwrite the modern American allegory. Hammett's new world reflects this harsh, bleak reality as do the conclusions of hard-boiled films noirs.

The metaphor of hard-boiled, used to define the fictional and film genres, has a fascinating etymology derived from the ruthless spheres of warfare, competition and economics. In World War I, the American Expeditionary Force took to France more than men and supplies; it brought American slang, particularly army argot, such as 'hard-boiled', which was usually applied to a demanding sergeant or to tough soldiers like General Ryan's New York National Guard troops, O'Ryan's Roughnecks.[7] In 1926, *Liberty* magazine included a short economic etymology for 'hard-boiled':

> The term originated in Jack Doyle's billiard academy in the heart of Broadway. The term was invented by Jack Doyle, who described a certain class of pool and billiard players as hard boiled eggs, meaning tight in their play, close in their finances, and in everything else.[8]

Cartoonist and sports writer for the New York *Evening Journal* Tad Dorgan, who coined such expressions as 'cat's meow', 'cat's pajamas', 'twenty-three skidoo' and 'Yes, we have no bananas!', was also reputed to have introduced 'hard-boiled' into modern urban slang.[9] College campuses employed 'tough bunny' or 'tight' as a joke phrase for a 'hard-hearted or hard-boiled person'.[10] Professor George Philip Krapp's *A Comprehensive Guide to Good English* (1927) 'defines *hard-boiled* simply as *sophisticated* or *blasé*'.[11] Krapp's distinction is not so far-fetched as it is muted in terms of hard-boiled, suggesting disregard for others or 'careless of public opinion'.[12] Of course, hard-boiled referred to any rough-and-tumble customer, especially urban gamblers and thugs. In *Middletown*, the Lynds referred to an autoworks company as 'hard-boiled' because it got rid of older employees in favour of younger ones; that is, the company was unsentimental, unemotional and unconcerned about the consequences or appearance of its elimination of less productive workers.[13]

In the novel, the sharp, hard 'V motif' associated with Spade's physiognomy seems like the almost cartoonish hyperboles of the first description of Gutman's obese body: 'fallibly fat with bulbous pink cheeks and lips and chins and neck, with a great soft egg of a belly that was all his torso, and pendant cones for arms and legs'.[14] Spade's hard-boiled exterior contrasts with Gutman's soft-boiled physique. Hammett, however, means for the 'V' to suggest a parabolic shape as well. Missing from all film versions is the famous Flitcraft parable, although its economy of loss and gain do play out in their plots. Brigid's comment that Spade is 'wild and unpredictable' proves to be a prophetic misreading of him, especially after his telling her the Flitcraft parable. Spade is not unpredictable, any more than the 'V' of a supply-demand equilibrium graph or mirrored points of a parabola are unpredictable.

The parable, derived from the same roots as parabola, geographically and thematically outlines mirroring circumstances. One afternoon, Flitcraft, a successful Tacoma real estate businessman with a wife, two children and a comfortable middle-class life, is nearly struck dead by a falling construction beam. Flitcraft is initially shocked by this moment of random 'blind chance', then disturbed by his own discovery that an orderly life was actually 'out of step, and not into step, with life'; thus, Flitcraft reacts accordingly: 'Life could be ended for him at random by a falling beam: he would change his life at random by simply going away'. Eventually, Flitcraft moves to Spokane, where he resumes a life almost exactly similar to the one he had abandoned. To compensate for his potential forfeiture (death), Flitcraft speculated on an asset (new life), but then it became a deficit (eternal recurrence of the same). The parable is worth noting not only for its parabolic plot points of similarity, but also because Spokane's latitude is the same as Tacoma's – 47°. The parable is literally a parabola.

Many scholars reduce this parable to an existential response to randomness. John Irwin, however, compares Flitcraft to Job and to Hawthorne's Wakefield: the confrontation with death becomes a moment not of repetition, but of the singularity of a black hole, which forces one to confront oppositions of 'life-as-being and life-as-having', and for Spade, it interposes an another view of 'life-as-doing': 'He in effect tells Brigid that for him what he is what he does, not what he has'.[15] Yet the Flitcraft parable underlines more than just this 'doing' as an American work-ethic trait. Instead, Spade tries to explain to Brigid, who has neither eyes to see nor ears to hear, that her random intrusion into his world, even though it brings with it death, will not radically alter him. The ending of Roy Del Ruth's 1931 film adaptation offers a more explicit explanation for Spade's actions: a newspaper article about Miss Wonderly's (Bebe Daniels) conviction includes the eyewitness testimony from a Chinese merchant, whom the audience has observed speaking to Sam Spade (Ricardo Cortez) in Chinese without subtitles: the implication is that Spade knew that Wonderly killed Archer all along. In both Hammett's novel and Huston's film, the knowledge is only a suspicion, the truth of which can only emerge through stratagems of credit and debit, expenditure and accretion.

Huston's adaptation follows closely the economic games of Hammett's final three chapters: the competition for life; the game of trust; and the illusion of loss as gain. Chapter 18, 'The Fall-Guy', plays out Spade's zero-sum economic system of competition among Gutman, Cairo, Wilmer and Brigid, amid which the four unwittingly do not glom onto the fact that Spade controls this particular game by not participating in it. Their willingness to enter into a serious win-lose situation has to do with their fixation on the value of the falcon, not human life. When Gutman eventually gives up Wilmer to be sacrificed, Spade laughs at seeing 'his working hypothesis about the commodification of human relations vindicated'.[16] Gutman sacrifices his 'gunsel' in a way that almost parallels Spade's relinquishing Brigid to the cops in the end.

In Chapter 19, 'The Russian's Hand', Gutman plays his own game of human commodification by palming one of the thousand-dollar bills that was to go into the envelope with the $10,000 as payment to Spade for the falcon. Spade forces Brigid to strip naked before he can be sure of Gutman's legerdemain. Spade simply explains to Brigid that 'I had to find out, angel' as he kisses her. This scene is as significant as the fall guy scene in terms of human competition and economics. Gutman's money game retaliates for Spade's economic experiment in self-preservation. Thus far, Spade and Gutman are on equal footing in terms of controlling others' motivations and the competitions. Spade has Effie deliver the parcel containing the falcon to his apartment. As Gutman pares at the outer layer of the falcon, he soon discovers that the 'inside of the shaving, and the narrow plane its removal left, had the soft grey sheen of lead'. The reverse alchemy of transmuting states – gold turned into lead – corresponds to the film's economy.

In Hammett's *The Maltese Falcon*, Joel Cairo attends a performance of Shakespeare's *The Merchant of Venice* with George Arliss as Shylock. Hammett parodically inverts the three caskets scenes. In Shakespeare's comedy, Portia poses the problem of the three caskets to her suitors, but in *The Maltese Falcon*, it is the suitors who pursue their own caskets by desiring Brigid, an antithetical Portia without a quality of mercy. In the play, the future is determined by which casket is chosen, as Marc Shell explains:

> The suitors that are, to Portia, not even men are threatened with being legitimately unmanned. Should a suitor choose the wrong casket, he must promise never to generate within the bonds of wedlock his own flesh and blood (2.1.41–42). He will be as barren as Antonio believes metal to be. His legitimate genealogical bloodline (if not the flesh and blood of his own body) will be cut. He will become, in this legal sense, a castrate.[17]

In the novel, the three suitors of this modern Portia fatale – Thursby, Archer and Spade – play the roles of the Moroccan prince, the Prince of Arragon and Bassanio. Thursby, who has greedily pursued the golden falcon with Brigid, meets his lead-ridden death for that desire. Archer has chosen the monetary desire for Brigid and for her silver – the hundred-dollar bills that she carries – and receives a leaden response – a gunshot, thereby ending his wedlock. Spade, who desires, but never wishes to possess, the deadly Brigid and the death-making falcon, opts to give up the leaden image, the real representation of Brigid, the 'faux femme'. Spade's acceptance of the real Brigid leads to her future within a casket: her death in prison.

The ersatz falcon was a clever substitution by Kemidov in Constantinople in order to fool the greedy treasure-seekers. The falcon now represents possession as actual deprivation. In a sense, the Russian's game is the same game Spade and Gutman played, one relying upon human greed and desire to overmatch any trust in others. In all these games, winners end up losers, as is clear when

Gutman pulls a revolver on Spade and demands the $10,000 back. At the end of the novel and its 1931 adaptation, Gutman's recovery now becomes his most significant privation – his loss of life. After vanishing from Spade's apartment, Wilmer tracks down Gutman and kills him.

In all three instances, zero-sum games rule, especially for Spade. It would be appealing to read this novel, which was serialised during the last quarter of the disastrous year of 1929 in *Black Mask*, as an allegory of the Depression, as Leonard Cassuto has done: 'The novel captures the Progressive sympathy for the individual worker toiling within the gigantic corporate engine, and it renders the growing anxiety over an overheating economy that would soon ruin rich and poor together'.[18] Still, cynicism pervades Hammett's and later film noir's world. The final zero-sum game in Chapter 20, 'If They Hang You', between Spade and Brigid is a culmination of all of the feints, subterfuges, dodges and substitutions of the previous games. Since the fall guy has vanished, one is still needed to replace that loss. Since Spade has been forced to give up $9,000, that 90 per cent reduction has not yet compensated. Since the falcon has turned out to be a fake, the desire that it represented still needs fulfilment. Just like the Flitcraft parable, Spade explains the situation confronting Brigid in this new system of exchanges. In the film, Humphrey Bogart's speech employs a ledger metaphor of credit and debit for assessing their relationship. Spade lists only seven of his eight reasons why he will not play the sap for Brigid. The first three are business-oriented rationales – partnership, good business practices and the occupation of a detective. The final four deal with a lack of faith and trust, which can only lead to Spade's demise. In the end, Brigid's column is blank, as Spade reminds her, 'a lot more money would have been one more item on your side of . . . scales'. When Detective Tom Polhaus (Ward Bond) arrives, Bogart hands over Mary Astor like so much merchandise: 'Here's another one for you'. The final shots of Astor are quintessential noir:

> 512. CS: *Brigid, staring stolidly ahead as the elevator grate closes in front of her. The bars of the grate resemble prison bars.*

This duplicitous caged bird has been exchanged for the phony falcon that Bogart carries in his hands: 'The, uh, stuff, that dreams are made of '.

The two earlier film versions of Hammett's novel conclude with the Brigid figure in police custody and with both detective and femme fatale left emotionally insolvent. In *The Maltese Falcon* (1931), Spade mordantly raises the hopes of a defeated Miss Wonderly in her jail cell, only to dash them with the 'good news' that she has helped him become Chief Investigator for the District Attorney's office; she, with deadly sarcasm, counters to crush Spade emotionally: 'I assure you, it was a labour of love'. He reaches through the cell bars to

Figure 3.1　Brigid (Mary Astor), the caged bird, *The Maltese Falcon*, 1941.

shake her hand, but she does not return the gesture. Spade has returned, like Flitcraft, to his former existence. Of course, Hammett's novel ends with Sam Spade shivering as Iva is about to enter his office, a moment of Flitcraft recognition that he has acquired less than zero.

At the conclusion of the somewhat madcap, almost screwball adaptation, *Satan Met A Lady* (William Dieterle, 1936), Valerie Purvis (Bette Davis) thwarts private investigator Ted Shane (Warren William) by convincing a African-American ladies' room attendant on the train to turn her over to the authorities, thereby gypping Shane out of the $10,000 reward for her capture. In handcuffs, Purvis gleefully announces her defeat of Shane in their zero-sum game: 'But from me, you'll go through something worse than death. Because you'll always remember me – the one woman you couldn't take for both love and money. The one woman who handed you double-cross for double-cross right up to the end'. Few speeches in proto-noirs better encapsulate the economic and gender struggles that will become standards for plots and characterisation in film noir.

Clearly, from Hammett's hard-boiled fiction, economics determine the structure of American society. Of course, Marlowe's world-view confirms Chandler's own disdain for economic control and corruption in the urban political machine. While often cited as the guide to the gritty, existential ethos of the hard-boiled detective, Raymond Chandler's 'The Simple Art of Murder' devotes ample discussion to monetary and financial issues of the mystery business and business in mysteries. Before the famous final section of this foundational essay on the genre, with its code of the hard-boiled detective and life on the mean streets, Chandler makes no fewer than seventeen references to the business of the writing, the money-making, the selling, the promotion and the nature of this genre as product in the marketplace. Clearly, Chandler has in mind the cold realities bearing on detective fiction writers. His essay's first paragraph concludes with the hypocrisy of cultured, supercilious critics and book clubs, whose aim, like that of vicious racketeers, crooked cops and unscrupulous politicians with whom the private eye must contend, always boils down to a game of economics:

> These are the people who make best sellers, which are promotional jobs based on a sort of indirect snob appeal, carefully escorted by the trained seals of the critical fraternity, and lovingly tended and watered by certain much too powerful pressure groups to think they are fostering culture. Just get a little behind in your payments and you will find out how idealistic they are.[19]

Purveyors of culture belong to that very real world of the hard-boiled detective, who is more or less a poor man, but who refuses to take money dishonestly, unlike those who inhabit this shady world

> in which gangsters can rule nations and almost rule cities, in which hotels and apartments house and celebrated restaurants are owned by men who made their money out of brothels ... where the mayor of your town may have condoned murder as an instrument of money-making.

For Chandler, the subject matter of hard-boiled fiction must always address the corruption that arises from the pursuit of capital and sustaining at all costs material and monetary gain, even at a loss of morality and ethics.

Farewell, My Lovely opens with Marlowe commenting on the racial geography of Los Angeles, where Central Avenue was still a 'mixed block', 'not yet all Negro'.[20] Marlowe's initial case involves a barber named Dimitrios Aleidis, Chandler's pun upon the Greek *aleites*, 'culprit, sinner', originally 'the one driven forth beyond the borders', and a commentary on the outsider status not just of an immigrant, but of a modern man in the urban scene. Chandler clearly knew the urban ethnic and racial topography of 1940 quite well, since, as the census of that year documented, despite white covenants, 'the geographic boundaries of the Central Avenue area had expanded in the prewar years, stretching south to Slauson Avenue and west to Main Street by the time of the 1940 census'.[21] As far back as the turn of the century, Central Avenue marked Los Angeles's economic and racial division of West, primarily white and more affluent, and East, lower-middle-class African-Americans who did not go beyond Avalon Avenue, which ran parallel to Central. Shifts in racial divisions did not occur until the 1940s, when 'Afro-Angelenos [would] be able to push beyond this border'.[22] Subdivisions of Los Angeles, beginning as early as the 1920s, sought to attract the white, upper-middle class, as well as the white working class on the fringes, while restricting access to non-whites by overtly advertising 'Permanent Race Restrictions'.[23] Chandler, however, undercuts and inverts these racial-topographic restrictions in his summation at the end of his description of the outlandishly dressed Moose Malloy:

> Slim quiet Negroes passed up and down the street and stared at him with darting side glances. He was worth looking at. He wore a shaggy borsalino hat, a rough gray sports coat with white golf balls on it for buttons, a brown shirt, a yellow tie, pleated gray flannel slacks and alligator shoes with white explosions on the toes. From his outer breast pocket cascaded a show handkerchief of the same brilliant yellow as his tie. There were a couple of colored feathers tucked into the band of his hat, but he didn't really need them. Even on Central Avenue, not the quietest dressed street in the world, he looked about as inconspicuous as a tarantula on a slice of angel food.[24]

This white outsider stands out even more than usual for a white man to the African-American residents of this mixed block. Chandler craftily reverses the usual stereotype of loud dress as a racial category for Negroes in the 1940s with the tarantula simile: Moose is now the black intruder in this neighbourhood, the outsider in this world.

The opening of *Murder, My Sweet* retains much of the novel's economic contrasts, as Marlowe's (Dick Powell) voiceover relates his failures: a barber he was supposed to find, but never did for the client-wife, and his penury: 'My bank account was trying to crawl under a duck'. Dmytryk's urban montage portrays the cityscape of Los Angeles at night, revealing both its prosperous and downtrodden symbols of commerce. A dolly shot moves from Marlowe out the framed window then zooms slowly downward to the street. Signs and blinking neon illuminate a deep black street scene along Hollywood Boulevard – California Hotel, Crystal Plaza, Buy Luntz, AWL Drugs, Keiths, as well as signs advertising cars, coffee and sundries. Dissolve to a street-level shot, ironically on the corner of Park Avenue, of men in suits and working-class outfits strolling past signs for alimentary and entertainment consumption: the White Rose Bar, Eva Hosiery, Food Shop, Soda Luncheonette and RKO Theatre marquee announcing a Gala Stage Show, 'Gangsters Boy' and 'Mad Miss Manton'. Dissolve to a shot of automobiles moving diagonally right to left on a trash-lined street; in the lower-right background a billboard ironically proclaims *Bach Festival*. Dissolve to a high-angle zoom shot of the Earl Roy Hotel offering 'Modern Rooms' from 75¢ $_{UP}$ and a busy street. Superimpose to an oblique, low-angle shot of streetcar wires and a radio transmission tower atop a hotel. Dissolve to a shot of Marlowe in his office framed through his window that reads PHILIP MARLOWE CRIMINAL *&* CIVIL INVESTIGATIONS with the reversed reflection of two Chinese characters, indicating the location in the northern section of downtown.

Moose Malloy's superimposed reflection above Marlowe's in his office window also indicates the power of money and sexual desire. Marlowe agrees to follow Moose out of curiosity, but also for pay, which Marlowe recounts as potentially harmful: 'The two twenties felt nice and snug next to my appendix'. Florian's neon sign blinks intermittently with the 'L' and especially the 'A' fading to produce 'Florin' at times, a fine visual pun on the unnatural *flora* that is the debauched, alcoholic widow Florian and, of course, money, the root of all Eves in the film. In *Murder, My Sweet*, Dmytryk relies upon class rather than race to designate Moose, the ex-con, and Marlowe, the impoverished detective, as outsiders to the hierarchy of economic social status. The African-American bar in the novel has been altered, shifting the economic issue from race to class.[25]

The plot of the film, like that of the novel, rests upon a hold-up, theft, ransom, payment and recovery of a jade necklace that never occur. Marlowe's relationship with all members of the Grayle family involve their offering him money, as when Ann, at the Coconut Beach Club, berates him, with an offer of $1,000, for taking money from Mrs Grayle, her lascivious stepmother: 'Surely, I'm not corrupting you. You've been bought off before'. Cinematographer Henry Wild captured Ann's ambivalence toward Marlowe by subverting typical studio three-point lighting so that her face is only half-illuminated, with the lighted side 'darkened by a carefully motivated crisscross pattern'.[26] Ann obviously equates Mrs Grayle's sexual disloyalty to Marlowe's apparent monetary corruptibility. Later, in front of the Grayle mansion, Marlowe defies cupidity, literally, by striking a match on the buttocks of the Cupid statue in the fountain. Marlowe becomes ever more frustrated with the manner by which the wealthy desire to manipulate him through money: 'I get dragged in, I get money shoved at me. I get pushed out, I get money shoved at me'. Marlowe realises that he is caught in a game of shifting and competing monetary interests, all of which will end badly.

Ann joins Marlowe in his investigation, which leads them to the final lair, the Grayle cliffside beach house. Dmytryk has the camera follow the circular beam of Marlowe's flashlight in a point-of-view shot as they search out the dark alcoves and tiers for the hidden threat. As they embrace, Marlowe confronts Ann about her motivations to buy him off, first with money, then with affection. Ann struggles in his arm, as she rants about men and women in a way that conforms to Marlowe's zero-sum view of the world:

ANN
Sometimes I hate men! All men! Old men, young men, football players, opera tenors, smart millionaires, beautiful men who use rose water, and almost-heels who are . . . private detectives –

Figure 3.2   Marlowe's (Dick Powell) hallucination, *Murder, My Sweet*.

The monster in this sexual and material labyrinth – Mrs Grayle – appears but first only as a mocking laugh. Ann shifts her denunciation to Mrs Grayle:

> The rest of it goes like this: I hate their women, too. Especially the Big League Blondes. The silky, selfish ones. The beautiful, expensive babes, who know what they're got. All bubble bath and dewy morning and moonlight. And inside, watchworks, blue diamonds and blue steel. Cold like that – only – [groping for words] – only not that clean.[27]

Ann's gender distinctions are not far off the mark in relation to Marlowe's perception of the hard-boiled modern world of money. Chandler's novel is narrative read in truth and claws. The California Dream is often the California nightmare: its causes remain simply money and desire. In Marlowe's world, no class and no profession are exempt from their corrupting influence: the wealthy are as immoral and venal as the low-down; physicians tend towards quackery; police lean towards thuggery. The urban scene is filled with charlatans, posers, psychotics, alcoholics, vicious underworld figures and depraved, amoral faux aristocrats.

Too often *Murder, My Sweet*, like many adaptations of Chandler's novels, has been found lacking by critics in the kind of social critique found in *Farewell, My Lovely*, which castigates the LAPD as racist and corrupt, 'in opposition to the Production Code insistence that the public be presented with efficient, irreproachable agents of law enforcement'.[28] Such assessments dismiss too readily Dmytryk's fidelity to the spirit of Chandler's Marlowe and his world-view. Exchange value for Marlowe expresses itself in the unpleasant necessities of debit, expenditure and remittance. In Marlowe's world, there is never an equal transference of funds for services rendered or a simple contractual obligation of gain for both parties.²⁹ Instead, loss pervades all exchanges, systematically and paradoxically making zero-sum systematically become a lose-lose outcome. Just as with the sacrificial suicide of Velma (by firing two self-inflicted bullets into her own chest!) at the end of *Farewell, My Lovely*, Marlowe, in *Murder, My Sweet*, must suffer blindness in order to fulfil his sexual desire for Ann. Before he leaves the precinct house, Marlowe hands over the *fei tsui* jade necklace, even though it is now his. In Dmytryk's treatment of Chandler, he remains faithful to the precarious money-sex capital of human exchange, as well as to Marlowe's cynicism that all victories are Pyrrhic.

Certainly, Marlowe's alienation, isolation and sense of futility convey Chandler's brand of American existentialism, one that will become a mainstay of film noir. Both Chandler's and Dmytryk's economic themes go beyond a Faulknerian or Sartrean existential double negation of the world: 'What Marlowe *is* the world is *not*. Thus Marlowe must always be conscious of something *not there*, both in the world (where he is *not*) and in himself (where the world is *not*)'.³⁰ Such a reading draws attention to the paradoxically pervasive absence, in the ontological sense, of substance, morality and reality in the face of artifice and illusion in the novel and film. Still, Chandler's and Dmytryk's vision of Los Angeles more often accounts for negation in terms of a balance sheet, credit and debit working against one another with the result being not a doubling of nothingness, but a less-than-nothing. Like Chandler's Marlowe, *Murder, My Sweet* relies upon the detective's 'bodily helplessness and even impotence', expressed as a noir visual motif with the recurring black pool and the fading to black representing ever new stages of excessive privation for Marlowe.³¹ This form of continual reduction occurs in the famous hallucinatory montage, with Marlowe trying to escape through ever decreasing doorways, then stepping into nothingness, losing balance, falling and spiralling into the abyss as his body becomes ever smaller until it joins the inky blackness engulfing the frame.

Vernon L. Walker, who worked on *King Kong*, *Citizen Kane* and *Stranger on the Third Floor*, employed special effects wizardry to reinforce Marlowe's drug-induced disorientation, which the Breen Office accepted far more than the film's violence.³² This thematic negation also relates to the shifting aesthetic of dynamic black-and-white texture in film noir, such as the contrasts of white, wispy fog and night during the foiled ransom exchange for the *fei tsui* jade necklace, and the spider web lacing over the camera lens as Marlowe regains consciousness from forced hypodermic injections used to find the whereabouts of the *fei tsui* necklace. The first scene induces the inky black pool to close in; the second ensues as black pool dissipates into light; and both punctuate moments of Marlowe's strategic losses and gains in the film. One comic example of noir aesthetic commentary is Dick Powell's ad lib hopscotch shuffle on the black-and-white tiles of the expansive foyer of the Grayle mansion, which is a sardonic jab at upper-class extravagance. Although not generally associated with the HUAC attacks on Dmytryk and his producer, Adrian Scott, *Murder, My Sweet*'s thematic and stylistic coherence surely suited 'the idealism of the Popular Front progressives' with its critique of 'capitalist power relations'.[33]

Conservative panic during the New Deal era was not relegated to the District of Columbia alone. By the mid-1930s, economic and class issues dominated local, state and national elections. In 1934, Upton Sinclair ran in the gubernatorial race on the EPIC (End Poverty In California) Plan, an outgrowth of his two failed runs at the Governor's mansion under the aegis of the Socialist Party. Much of the condemnation came from media executives: Hearst, of course, and studio heads who worried about Sinclair's plans to convert unused film lots and hand them over to unemployed writers, directors and crew members. Sinclair promised that if he were elected the EPIC group would make, distribute and exhibit their own films, thus removing vertical integration from studio moguls' control. Sinclair even attacked the banal aesthetic of studio films, promising a more realistic style of filmmaking. Even though Sinclair's independent film organisation lacked much systematic planning, he did instil fear throughout an already paranoid industry, made so by the Production Code of 1934, with its 'Stop Sinclair' campaign, headed by MGM's Louis B. Mayer, who was also the chairman of the state's Republican party.[34] So fearful of revenue losses, major studios were contemplating leaving Hollywood: 'United Artists, Universal, Paramount, and Columbia were ready to leave town, with MGM and RKO likely to join them'.[35] Not only were studios dead set against Sinclair, but in particular, insurance companies favoured his opponent, a former Iowa State Auditor, Frank Merriam, notorious because he 'pretended to examine insurance companies, and charging big fees for it': 'the Pacific Mutual Life Insurance Company calling in its employees and coercing them to vote for Merriam'.[36] *Double Indemnity* as novel then film was the perfect property to convey the socio-economic milieu of California.

In the screenplay of *Double Indemnity*, as Neff arrives at the Dietrichson house, Chandler and Wilder describe a neighbourhood that corresponds to the economic themes of the film: 'Palm trees line the street, middle-class houses, mostly in Spanish style. Some kids throwing a baseball back and forth across a couple of front lawns. An ice cream wagon dawdles along the block'.[37]

Class status, the American dream and free-market commerce visually announce the monetary desires underlining the plots within *Double Indemnity*. In the film, Neff's (Fred MacMurray) voiceover adds financial details about the house, and functions as a prophetic statement about the film's fixation with debt, credit and literal mortgage ('death pledge'): 'This one must have cost somebody about thirty thousand bucks – that is, if he ever finished paying for it'. Not to be overlooked is the baseball game being played in the lower fore-

Figure 3.3 Girl with bat in front of Dietrichson house, *Double Indemnity*.

ground by three children: a girl in a dress holds a bat as a boy pitches to her, while another boy awaits the outcome of the hit. Visually corresponding to the film's love-murder triangle, the empowered female initially controls the game over two males, but it is also the game itself that is prophetic. Baseball relies upon a zero-sum exchange by which success of the batter is an immediate loss for the pitcher and vice versa, which makes it a perfect prelude to the games about to commence in *Double Indemnity*.

Cain's novel opens with Huff's morbid, yet detached recollection of the Nirdlinger residence as 'the House of Death', with its 'blood red drapes' described in a neutral manner as though it were part of a domestic inventory, like the rest of the furnishings:

> All I saw was a living room like every other living room in California, maybe a little more expensive, but nothing that any department store wouldn't deliver on one truck, lay out in the morning, and have the credit O.K. ready the same afternoon. The furniture was Spanish, the kind that looks pretty and sits stiff. The rug was one of those 12 X 15's that would have been Mexican except it was made in Oakland, California.[38]

Commercial reproduction and ersatz style characterise the artificial existence of Californian modernity and 'the ubiquitous and homogenizing forces of corporate interests on the occupants'.[39] Similar to his other hard-boiled novels of the 1930s and 1940s, Cain's *Double Indemnity* integrates domestic issues within the broader context of the economic effects of the Great Depression and the New Deal. Cain's novels – *The Postman Always Rings Twice*, *Double Indemnity* and *Mildred Pierce* – fit a general thematic structure attributed to the Los Angeles novel of the 1930s and 1940s, as David M. Fine provides in a synoptic view of collapse, endings and breakdown: 'In the fiction the recurring messages are the breakdown of clear boundaries between reality and illusion, the chasm between expectation and actuality – promise and fulfilment – and the collapse of traditional values and standards in the frantic search for 'the good life'.[40] So much of film noir devotes itself to critiquing just this kind of illusory and ultimately destructive search for the American dream.

In the film, Neff, continually eyeing with fetishistic intent Phyllis's (Barbara Stanwyck) ankle bracelet, couches his sexual interest in commercial terms: 'I never knock the other fellow's merchandise, Mrs Dietrichson, but I can do just as well for you'. Once he finally learns that her name is engraved on the bracelet, Neff turns Phyllis into an automobile and insinuates sexual overtones into their auto- and accident-insurance policy discussion: 'I'd have to drive it around the block a couple of times'. This famous scene of not-too-veiled sexual banter between Phyllis and Neff about speed limits and tickets parallels the baseball game, but with words tossed and chords struck. Neff, of course, realises that Phyllis has far more erotic agency than she admits to:

> Phyllis: I wonder if I know what you mean.
> Neff: I wonder if you wonder.

Like the insurance business, the supermarket worked on a scheme of volume and minimal outlay expenditure, a model based upon a high number of customers and a reliance upon automobiles to sustain demand. For insurance in California, automobiles were a first-line item to other types: home, health and especially life insurance. In the novel of *Double Indemnity*, Walter Huff spends considerable time in his automobile as he moves throughout the urban geography from Hollywoodland, Long Beach, Santa Monica, Burbank and Glendale to downtown Los Angeles.

The film also captures this obsession with free mobility, but simultaneously demonstrates that freedom is an illusion of modernity. In the film's opening scene, Walter Neff races his automobile in the early morning hours through downtown Los Angeles, running a stoplight, a visual signal of both his ill-fated plans and his eventual demise. The first insurance case that bothers Keyes's (Edward G. Robinson) 'little man' concerns a phony auto claim, a get-rich-quick scheme that ends up costing the dejected Gorlopsis $2,600, his old truck and his reputation with the insurance company. After Neff's second visit to Phyllis, when he dissuades her about accident insurance and any potential murder of her husband, Neff diverts himself (done by means of montage dissolves) by driving, going to a drive-in for a beer and bowling a few frames – leisure activities that require an automobile for access. All the while, Neff still feels that 'red-hot poker' burning his hand and realises that his attempts at freedom were illusory: 'the hook was too strong, that this wasn't the end between her and me. It was only the beginning'. Neff's first item on his own alibi agenda was to make sure that his car would be washed by the attendant at his apartment building. Of course, the murder itself takes place within the Dietrichson family car, with Barbara Stanwyck staring straight into the camera as the sounds of struggling and muffled groans occur off screen. In chiaroscuro lighting, the play of emotions – fear, elation, shock, satisfaction – across Stanwyck's face during the murder remains a singular, iconic moment for the femme fatale in film noir. After the murder and the faked observation car accident, their freedom is ominously curtailed by the 'nerve-wracking sluggishness' of the car's ignition, until Neff takes control of the key from Phyllis and is able to turn over the engine. Their road to the good life, to freedom, starts off as it will end up, with a shifting power game for control.

By 1940, the Los Angeles County Regional Planning Commission had proposed networks of parkways and freeway systems that would ensure a better way of living for suburbanites as well as maintaining 'social and economic advantages of the urban center'.[41] Along with the automobile as the symbol of Californian independence, consumers navigated through a cityscape that mirrored that sense of freedom, both on its roadways and within its mercantile architectural designs. The space within the grocery store staged a drama of trade and freedom, an interior model analogous to the transformation of the Californian urban scene, with aisles as thoroughfares for mobility, modernity and rapid commerce. Individual movement and choice were accented by market design: 'Aisles were formed by long and comparatively low, multi-tiered shelves, arranged in parallel groups that fostered easy movement from one end to the other. Most goods were thus displayed openly for customers to inspect and choose'.[42] In this sense, the American penchant for mobility, geographically and economically, acquires an aesthetic in the design, access and staging of this literal market. The movement through the market can be likened to the future promise of mobility, which is not only part of the myth of American equality, but also the very basis of insurance schemes, as David M. Potter's postwar study of the American character rightly pointed out: 'The imperceptible way in which the drive of mobility merges with the anticipation of status is suggested by the appeal used by a life insurance company which sells policies to provide for the future'.[43] That Neff and Phyllis clandestinely meet twice in Jerry's Market confirms Wilder's, and especially Chandler's, cynical commentary on their obsession with mobility, as a means not so much to achieve economic or social standing as to escape from the myth of future advancement. Exploiting and perverting both the promise of and necessity for life insurance reveals their distrust for the American dream of upward mobility.

At Jerry's Market, two clandestine meetings between Neff and Phyllis reveal their shifting power struggle: the first concerns the life insurance policy and the new complications thwarting the plans for the murder, with Neff in control;

the second concerns new problems with the indemnity policy payout and a potential legal battle, with Phyllis entirely in control. The zero-sum shifting of acquisitions and depletions take place in this theatre of American consumer capitalism. Neff likes Jerry's Market, because, very ironically he notes, they can meet 'accidentally on purpose', just like the death of Mr Dietrichson. During the first staged, chance encounter in the market, Neff lays out the details of the murder to Phyllis in front of the baby food section, with mass-produced boxes bearing a infant's face staring at them. A mother and her child interrupt them; the mother requests that Neff hand her a box of baby food and walks off complaining: 'I don't know why they always put what I want on the top shelf'. That line ironically sums up both the desire for the American dream and complications imposed against economic and class mobility to hinder achieving the American dream.

In the second market rendezvous, the camera dollies to follow Neff and Phyllis as they walk down an aisle. Unlike the first grocery store meeting, this scene maintains an emotional then physical barrier between them. Neff wants to call things off, worried about Keyes's suspicions. Neff confesses that he has been seeing Lola, Phyllis's stepdaughter, who has told him about the mysterious death of the first Mrs Dietrichson, for which she blames Phyllis. As they argue, Phyllis shifts from jealousy towards Lola to a renewed commitment to Neff. At the very moment that Phyllis tries to take Neff in her arms, 'forgetting where she is', they are interrupted by a store clerk, who pushes a small hand truck with canned goods, a telling moment of commerce and mobility that ironically counters their own stalled transaction and immobility. Now, they move down different aisles, stopping to bicker over the canned goods and the macaroni. With a cold, menacing stare, Phyllis departs with an ultimatum, by which their once-happy, mutual freedom becomes distrustful bondage: 'We went into it together, and we're coming out at the end together. It's straight down the line for both of us, remember'.

The final confrontation occurs where it all began – the living room of the Dietrichson residence – but with a reversal, night rather than day in a darkened room with the only illumination formed between the horizontal entrapment shadows of blinds and crossed, prison-bar-like shadows from the frames in the french doors. The familiar household now becomes the 'house of death' of the novel. When Neff first arrives at the Dietrichson house, the housekeeper sarcastically informed him that the liquor is locked up, to which he retorts in an unconsciously revealing remark, 'I always carry my own keys'. Hence Neff's voiceover Dictaphone narrative to Keyes, a confession that plays out more like a competition. On this night of the second murder, Neff adapts Keyes's 'trolley car' analogy for murder to explain how he intends to get off, figuratively and legally, by blaming Zachetti, Lola's tempestuous, overly jealous boyfriend, since Keyes already suspects him, and by giving Phyllis over to the cops in the bargain. Of course, Phyllis has already planned out her own double-cross, setting up the scene for murder before Neff arrives – unlocking the front door, turning off the lamps, secreting the gun under the cushion of her chair. She shoots Neff, but halts before firing a second shot. Neff cannot believe that Phyllis resisted that homicidal urge out of love. She confesses to Neff that she only used him, never loved him 'until a minute ago. I didn't think anything like that could ever happen to me'. Neff's response, before killing her, articulates the zero-sum ideology of American culture that Hammett, Chandler, Cain and the history of film noir critique: 'Sorry, baby. I'm not buying'.

Notes

1. Paul Seabright, *The Company of Strangers: A Natural History of Economic Life* (Princeton, NJ: Princeton University Press, 2010), p. 76.
2. John Maynard Keynes, *The General Theory of Employment, Interest, and Money* (New York: Harcourt, Inc., 1964), p. 21.
3. Erin Ann Smith, *Hard-boiled: Working-class Readers and Pulp Magazines* (Philadelphia, PA: Temple University Press, 2000), pp. 27–8.
4. Sean McCann, *Gumshoe America: Hard-boiled Crime Fiction and the Rise and Fall of New Deal Liberalism* (Durham, NC: Duke University Press, 2000), pp. 70–1.
5. *The Maltese Falcon*, John Huston, director, William Luhr, editor (New Brunswick, NJ: Rutgers University Press, 1995), p. 45.
6. Alan Lawson, *A Commonwealth of Hope: The New Deal Response to Crisis* (Baltimore, MD: The Johns Hopkins University Press, 2006), p. 17.
7. Mary Paxton Keeley, 'A. E. F. English', *American Speech* 5(5) (June 1930), 384, 375. The phrase 'hard-boiled brass hat' referred to a severe, uncompromising, high-ranking officer; 'hard-boiled regulars' to seasoned troops; 'Hard Boiled Top' to a first sergeant; 'hard boiled', in nautical slang, to a salty, hard-bitten sailor; 'hard-boiled' to instructors of shave-tails, new recruits needing discipline, Jonathan Lighter, 'The slang of the American expeditionary forces in Europe, 1917–1919: An historical glossary', *American Speech* 47(1/2) (spring–summer 1972), 21, 57, 79, 93, 98–9.
8. As quoted in 'Miscellaneous Notes', 'Origin of Hard Boiled', *American Speech* 2(5) (February 1927), 258. See H. L. Mencken, 'XI: American Slang', *The American Language, An Inquiry into the Development of English in the United States* (New York: Alfred A. Knopf, 1937), p. 561, footnote 2.
9. W. L. Werner, 'Tad Dorgan is dead', *American Speech* 4(6) (August 1929), 430.
10. Virginia Carter, 'University of Missouri slang', *American Speech* 6(3) (February 1931), 206. For 'tight' as meaning rough or hard-boiled, see J. Louis Kuethe, 'Johns Hopkins jargon', *American Speech* 7(5) (June 1932), 337.
11. Cited by Lowry Axley in 'One word more on "you all"', *American Speech* 4(5) (June 1929), 351.
12. Carey Woofter, 'Dialect words and phrases of central West Virginia', *American Speech* 2(8) (May 1927), 356, as in the expression 'You need expect no favors from that hard-boiled man'.
13. Robert S. Lynd and Helen Merrill Lynd, *Middletown: A Study in American Culture* (New York: Harcourt, Brace, and Company, 1929), p. 32, footnote 12.
14. Dashiell Hammett, *The Maltese Falcon* (New York: Vintage Crime/Black Lizard, 1992), p. 104 [1929].

15. John Irwin, *Unless the Threat of Death is Behind Them: Hard-boiled Fiction and Film Noir* (Baltimore, MD: The Johns Hopkins University Press, 2006), p. 27.
16. Josiane Peltier, 'Economic discourse in *The Maltese Falcon*', *Clues: The Journal of Detection* 23(2) (winter 2005), 27.
17. Marc Shell, *Money, Language, and Thought: Literary and Philosophical Economies from the Medieval to the Modern Era* (Berkeley, CA: University of California Press, 1982), p. 56.
18. Leonard Cassuto, '*The Maltese Falcon* and the hard-boiled sentimental', *Clues: The Journal of Detection* 23(2) (winter 2005), 46.
19. Raymond Chandler, 'The Simple Art of Murder: An Essay', *The Simple Art of Murder* (New York: Viking Crime/Black Lizard, 1988), p. 1.
20. Raymond Chandler, *Farewell, My Lovely* (New York: Vintage Crime/Black Lizard, 1992), p. 3 [1940].
21. Josh Sides, *L.A. City Limits: African American Los Angeles from the Great Depression to the Present* (Berkeley, CA: University of California Press, 2003), p. 34.
22. Douglas Flamming, *Bound for Freedom: Black Los Angeles in Jim Crow America* (Berkeley, CA: University of California Press, 2005), p. 98.
23. Robert M. Fogelson, *Bourgeois Nightmares – Suburbia, 1870–1930* (New Haven, CT: Yale University Press, 2005), p. 111.
24. Chandler, *Farewell, My Lovely* p. 4.
25. Erin Smith relies upon Pierre Bourdieu's discussion of taste, particularly self-presentation in dress, to reveal the hierarchical distinctions between Marlowe and Moose, but also to reveal how Chandler demystifies the games of style played out by the ruling class. 'Dressed to kill: Hard-boiled detective fiction, working-class consumers, and pulp magazines', *Colby Quarterly* 36(1) (2000), 11–28.
26. Patrick Keating, *Hollywood Lighting from the Silent Era to Film Noir* (New York: Columbia University Press, 2010), p. 256.
27. John Paxton, *Murder, My Sweet*, Final Script (21 April 1944), Shots 291 and 293.
28. John Paul Athanasourelis, 'Film adaptation and the censors: 1940s Hollywood and Raymond Chandler', *Studies in the Novel* 35(3) (fall 2003), 332.
29. See Johanna M. Smith, 'Raymond Chandler and the business of literature', *Texas Studies in Literature and Language* 31(4) (winter 1989), 595, in which the argument moves away from Marlowe's complex exchange economy to a somewhat questionable reading of homosocial friendship: 'As he attempts to transform an exchange economy of client relations into an expenditure economy of homosocial friendships, he sees loyalty and commitment become professional commodities; for sale, they are subsumed into the economy they are meant to oppose' (593–610).
30. William Brevda, 'The double nihilation of the neon: Raymond Chandler's Los Angeles', *Texas Studies in Literature and Language* 41(1) (spring 1999), 79.
31. Megan E. Abbott, '"Nothing You Can't Fix": Screening Marlowe's Masculinity', *Studies in the Novel* 35(3) (fall 2003), 311.
32. Jennifer E. Langdon, *Caught in the Crossfire: Adrian Scott and the Politics of Americanism in 1940s Hollywood* (New York: Columbia University Press, 2008), pp. 81–2.
33. Jennifer Langdon Teclaw, 'The progressive producer in the Studio System—Adrian Scott at RKO, 1943–1947', in Frank Krutnik, Steve Neale, Brian Neve and Peter Stanfield (eds), *Un-American Hollywood: Politics and Film in the Blacklist Era* (New Brunswick, NJ: Rutgers University Press, 2007), p. 154.
34. Upton Sinclair, *I, Candidate for Governor: And How I Got Licked* (Berkeley, CA: University of California Press, 1994), p. 167.
35. Greg Mitchell, *The Campaign of the Century: Upton Sinclair's Race for Governor*

of California and the Birth of Media Politics (New York: Random House, 1992), p. 171.
36. Sinclair, I, Candidate for Governor, pp. 126, 176.
37. Billy Wilder and Raymond Chandler, Double Indemnity (Berkeley, CA: University of California Press, 2000), p. 11.
38. Cain, Double Indemnity, p. 4.
39. Frederick Whiting, 'Playing against type: Statistical personhood, depth narrative, and business genre in James M. Cain's Double Indemnity', JNT: Journal of Narrative Theory 36(2) (summer 2006), 194. Whiting, however, shifts the focus away from the commercial and economic to the existential agency and psychological typing in contemporary culture.
40. David M. Fine, 'James M. Cain and the Los Angeles novel', American Studies 20(1) (spring 1979), 26.
41. As quoted in Scott L. Bottles, Los Angeles and the Automobile: The Making of the Modern City (Berkeley, CA: University of California Press, 1987), p. 226.
42. Richard Longstreth, The Drive-in, the Supermarket, and the Transformation of Commercial Space in Los Angeles, 1914–1941 (Cambridge, MA: MIT Press, 1999), p. 91.
43. David M. Potter, People of Plenty: Economic Abundance and the American Character (Chicago, IL: University of Chicago Press, 1954), p. 106.

4. COLD WAR NOIR

R. Barton Palmer

Half-hearted Paeans to Supremacy

That continuing series of crises in politics, both domestic and international, beginning in the immediate postwar era that gradually came by the 1950s to be known collectively in the United States as the 'Cold War' bears an interesting, complex relationship to film noir, which took shape and flourished in that same era. It is perfectly possible, even useful, to identify Hollywood releases generally known as noir that form a sub-grouping dealing with so-called Cold War themes. These include subversion by Soviet agents, as well as international intrigue in which free world interests more generally and American security in particular are threatened by various communist conspiracies. This chapter will provide a brief anatomy of that tradition. These films partake deeply of the Cold War atmosphere, with its paradoxical mélange of overweening self-confident nationalism and paralysing paranoia. In them the nation appears under constant threat, but government institutions in the end prove equal to the task of defeating even the most sophisticated forms of subversion and espionage, protecting in particular the scientific secrets upon which American pre-eminence, first established by the success of the Manhattan Project, is suggested to continually depend.

However jingoistic, these Cold War noirs also partake of the ways in which film noir explores profound doubts about contemporary American society, problematising the efficacy or even moral fitness of its hallowed institutions, including marriage and the family. In the manner of all Hollywood films that treated continuing conflict with the Soviet Union and its allies, the Cold War noirs conclude with what appears to be the unambiguous triumph of the government agencies that had grown immense during the conflict with Germany and Japan, especially the FBI. No film that interrogated the essential rightness of the official approach to global affairs, or the ability of the government to protect its citizens from organised threats, could possibly have been made in a Hollywood where suspect communist infiltration (and worse) was already under congressional investigation. The House Un-American Activities Committee (HUAC) held hearings in Hollywood that in 1947 led to the conviction of the so-called Hollywood Ten for refusing to answer questions about their political affiliations. What followed was an informal blacklist in which many others in the film industry found their careers ended because of their supposed communist affiliations or sympathies. After the North Koreans invaded their southern neighbours in June 1950, the Cold War became – if only by proxy – a shooting war that lurched into inconclusion only three years later. Questioning American policy after the nation's soldiers were, once again, fighting and dying on Asian battlefields would have seemed at best defeatist. Even suggesting a political position whose anti-communism was moderate or provisional would have been professional suicide for any filmmaker.

It is only incidentally, then, customarily in subplots and with minor characters, that the Cold War noirs engage anomie, psychopathology, homicidal anger and the threat posed to bourgeois propriety by sexual desire, the themes that are featured in the early noirs, particularly those directed by European émigrés like Boris Ingster (*Stranger on the Third Floor*, 1940), Billy Wilder (*Double Indemnity*, 1944) and Fritz Lang (*Woman in the Window*, 1944 and *Scarlet Street*, 1945). A single foundational principle prevails in all of these films. Nothing is as it seems. Everydayness conceals a dark underside, which will out, sooner or later. In the Cold War noirs, that frightening beneath is ideological as well as criminal, international as well as communal, of sufficient collective danger to warrant the vigilant action of powerful law enforcement institutions, not just the local police or a perspicacious private investigator. And yet the inevitable defeat of these threats to the American way, though celebrated, always seems provisional, especially since the class of cultures that is its motor cannot be resolved by open conflict and shows no other signs of how it might be ended. These political facts, of course, suit perfectly noir's deep questioning of social virtues, as the world it conjures up seems populated almost exclusively by characters acting out their own compulsions and pursuing their self-interest with no regard for moral codes or the damage thereby inflicted on others. In a sense, the Cold War writes large this Hobbesian view of experience, with its depiction of a death struggle acted out surreptitiously between irrevocably opposed systems, and thus its politics can easily be accommodated to the solidifying conventions of a cinematic series that had emerged during World War II.

Yet the Cold War not only furnishes the film noir with a repertoire of different, but also immensely useful narrative patterns and themes. More interestingly perhaps, the noir phenomenon is a reaction to the very same developments both domestic and international that conditioned the emergence of the Cold War, which was as much a collective state of mind, especially in America, as a succession of political actions and policy manifestos. The Cold War was defined by a traditional sphere of interest rivalry between the US and the Soviet Union, the two superpowers left standing after the defeat of Germany and the Japanese Empire. But this rivalry, for a variety of reasons, led Americans to adopt a certain view of the world that had been remade by World War II, constituting what is arguably the most important part of their national postwar *mentalité*. The same sense of life's fragility, of the impotence of traditional values and institutions, of pervasive uncertainty found expression in film noir. During the war, filmgoers began to reject the optimistic populism that became Hollywood's default cultural politics during the late 1930s under the profound influence of the New Deal. This production trend is most obvious perhaps in Frank Capra's several paeans to national institutions and virtue, especially *Mr. Smith Goes to Washington* (1939) and *Mr. Deeds Goes to Town* (1936). Capra's *It's a Wonderful Life* (1946) similarly endorses the transcendent, salvational value of community even while acknowledging deep problems in American society. And yet, unlike Capra's previous releases, this film failed to connect with audiences. Writing in *The New York Times*, Bosley Crowther may have been speaking for many when he opined that the problem with *Wonderful Life* was what might, ten years earlier, have seemed its virtue: 'the sentimentality of it – its illusory concept of life'.[1] Only by divine intervention are suicide and communal disaster averted, and audiences were not buying the fantasy. This rejection of idealism about the efficacy of social bonds indexed the darkening of the national mood, which can also be read out from the popularity of the early noirs mentioned above. These films conjure up a world that can be imagined in Capra's box office flop only as an existential nightmare, as the impossible result of non-being that appears to be true only because of misconceived wish fulfilment.

International events, however, prompted an alternative version of where America found itself in the mid-1940s. Unconditional victory against two seemingly invincible military powers seemed to establish the universal rightness of American democracy and the free enterprise system, which had spectacularly succeeded in producing an overabundance of the tools of war, without which final victory would have been inconceivable. The unforeseen consequence of an incredibly accelerating wartime production was that the several related economic crises known collectively as the 'Great Depression' were quickly resolved, a development that, in its effortlessness, seemed truly miraculous, given the only partial success of a decade's worth of deliberate reforms. With its strong advocacy for a United Nations, founded in 1945 at war's end, the United States claimed the fruits of victory by making an audacious attempt, full of misguided idealism, to end international rivalry and the global warfare that had twice in three decades almost destroyed European civilisation, eventually threatening the stability of Asia as well. The United Nations was dedicated not only to ending the destructive play of power politics, but also to the preservation of human rights, which were quickly defined on the supposedly universal American model. If the world were only remade in the national image, justice and prosperity would prevail, or so most Americans were encouraged to believe.

But the triumphalism of victory culture was soon at least partially undone by international developments, as the wartime pragmatic alliance with the Soviet Union soured. Providing an interesting correlative to the noir vision of a deeply troubled society, global politics became yet another realm of threatening insecurity, destructive rivalries, immoral acquisitiveness and opposition to foundational national values, especially Enlightenment concepts of individual freedom and collective liberty. In the first years after the war, Americans became embittered by the debunking of their undoubtedly unrealistic expectation that Eastern Europe, though under Soviet influence, would somehow be reconfigured as a regional community of self-governing republics. In the telling phrase of Winston Churchill, which was carefully tailored to the American audience he addressed, an 'iron curtain' had descended, dividing the socialist republics of Eastern Europe from their Western counterparts. Americans were horrified by what they widely regarded as a Soviet betrayal. Few in the country noted the dangerous chauvinism of Churchill's metaphor, which demonised the Eastern bloc's not surprising desire (after two encounters with German aggression) to constitute a self-enclosed, self-regarding community responsible for its own security and territorial integrity. American fears that the so-called free world was being taken over by a conspiratorial communist expansionism were hardly allayed by subsequent events, especially what became known, rather strangely, as the 'loss' of China in 1948 following the defeat of nationalist forces in the civil war and the retreat of Chiang Kai-Shek's battered followers to the island of Taiwan.

With the promulgation of the so-called Truman Doctrine in 1947, the inevitable competition between the world's two superpowers quickly became moralised, an arena in which what prevailed for Americans was, in historian Nick Smedley's telling phrase, 'a battle between dark and light, between the fundamental forces of good and evil; it was a crusade'.[2] The president committed the United States to defend all 'free peoples' who were struggling against internal subversion or battling external foes determined on subjugation. Competition with the Soviet Union, in other words, was remade as a Manichean opposition of goodness to evil, according to the ideologically understood conflicts, just recently concluded, with National Socialist Germany and a thoroughly militarised Japanese empire. Once again, the enemy was identified with an aggressively expansionist political ideology that rejected parliamentary-based democracy. Responding to domestic political realities (especially the pronounced rightward swing of American culture after New Deal idealism lost its lustre), Truman, Smedley writes, helped dramatise 'a pragmatic political conflict in terms more in keeping with the national mood. It was a universal struggle'.[3] True to the moralising, crusading spirit of the Truman doctrine, however, the threat of political defeat by the forces of anti-democratic evil is always effectively surveilled and eventually contained by the institutions of law enforcement, especially the FBI, which, if such films were to be believed, was rendered invincible by its devotion to scientific investigation, especially the data collection and processing promoted by founder J. Edgar Hoover and developed to a high art during his lengthy tenure (1924–72).

Between Two Worlds

In the political struggles staged in these films, the US usually defends the North American homeland (sometimes areas of confrontation abroad, notably Germany), resisting home-grown subversion perpetrated by 'sleepers' of various kinds who only seem to be ordinary Americans, as well as by easily identified foreign agents, usually Neanderthalish heavies who speak broken English with incomprehensible Slavic accents. If ethical clarity prevails in the end, providing a striking contrast between these films and the noir tradition more generally, the protagonists in Cold War noir also find themselves straddling the border between competing forms of identity, as they often enter, like George Bailey (Jimmy Stewart), the hapless protagonist of *Wonderful Life*, into perilous *rites de passage* through a nightmarish version of contemporary urban reality, where everydayness barely, and at times ineffectively, conceals a much darker underside.

A central feature of film noir in all its forms is this foregrounding of liminality, which in the Cold War noirs is provided with an ideological inflection. Noir characters inhabit two contrasting forms of being that prompt them to adopt irreconcilable identities; in Cold War noir the protagonist is customarily a double agent, someone who must penetrate the threatening conspiracy by pretending to be part of it. This device is convenient for narrative purposes since it permits the investigators and their quarry to at least in part share the same space. But such doubleness is quintessentially noir in other ways. In this, *Double Indemnity* is perhaps foundational. An adulterous couple plot and then carry out a crime that is meant to be understood as an accident. That crime will pay by releasing insurance benefits to one of the perpetrators, and at a bonus 'double' rate, but only if the coroner rules that the death in question is no murder, but the result of an unfortunate and accidental tumble from the back of a train. And so Walter (Fred MacMurray) and Phyllis (Barbara Stanwyck) must become like the crime they commit, which is carefully designed to seem one thing though it is actually something quite different. During the thorough investigation of the 'accident', they must struggle to maintain their ostensibly respectable identities.

To carry off the required elaborate masquerade, Walter and Phyllis become performers as soon as they begin plotting. In addition to playing at remaining 'himself' even as he rejects that identity, Walter is even called upon to impersonate the dead man at one point. After carrying out the murder, the pair must stay 'in character', which proves difficult after the accident theory is shown by the insurance company investigator to be untenable. A key effect of the narrative is that it highlights the willed, constructed nature of social roles, whose 'naturalness' is thereby called into question. For once Walter and Phyllis determine to become other than what they were, they are forced by the very logic of their plan to inhabit self-consciously, and inauthentically, the roles they had previously performed unthinkingly: the pleasant housewife loyal to her husband and the successful insurance agent dedicated to his company's financial well-being and the steady advancement of his own career.[4]

Double Indemnity dramatises this distancing from and yet reflection upon the nature of ordinary experience. Narrator of the flashback in which he is the principal character, Walter is both the subject and the object of the resulting narrative. The disjunction between the experiencing-I and the narrating-I (always a feature of character narration) in this case emphasises an already existing split that opens up within the character as his plot unfolds. *Double Indemnity* evokes a secular limbo as Walter and Phyllis find themselves between contradictory social spaces. Walter cannot be both a law-abiding citizen and a conscienceless, cold-blooded murderer, and yet he manifestly fills both roles simultaneously, until he assumes a third self – confessed murderer – that reconciles them. Within the paradoxical space marked out by the narrative, the ordinary forms of everyday living are shown by Walter and Phyllis as what they always already are, that is, performances whose authenticity is by definition always already in question.

Unstable from the outset, these performances eventually break down completely, as Walter discovers within himself the capacity, and then the desire, to love a decent woman with whom he can imagine an ordinary life. But he cannot reform. *Double Indemnity* exposes the self-defeating nature of Neff's desire for self-fashioning whose trajectory it traces: so powerful is the demand that we be who we are that the shedding of the self can only be achieved through the artfully inauthentic preservation of the self that has been shed.

Change, real change, is only an illusion. A defining quality of noirness is its exploration of such liminal states of being, of a destabilising yet seemingly inescapable betweenness that also suits perfectly the Red Scare view of contemporary American society, in which the apparent ordinariness of everyday life is found to conceal society-destroying threat at every turn. Cold War noir discovered compelling cinematic possibilities in the dramatisation of this terrifying liminality, of social surfaces that could not be trusted, and the inevitable defeat at the hands of law enforcement of the conspirators who inhabit the underside of American life.

Consider *Walk East on Beacon*, a semi-documentary political thriller, thoroughly noir, directed by Alfred W. Werker and released by producer Louis de Rochemont in 1952. The plot is simple enough, lending itself to the easy moralism of all Cold War productions. An anonymous tip warns the FBI that Robert Martin (Ernest Graves) is a Soviet agent. As it turns out, Russian spies and their American operatives in the Boston area are eager to blackmail a scientist into surrendering important defence secrets, which, so the Russians believe, and it seems to be true, are to provide the basis for new forms of technologically based warfare codenamed 'Falcon', confirming an already-achieved US hegemony. Martin was turned by Soviet recruiters during a European trip in the 1930s, but immediately upon his return came under constant FBI scrutiny, although he has been allowed to remain free in case he will lead the authorities to what they call 'bigger fish'. This does happen, as Martin meets with Laschenkov (Karel Stepanek), an experienced and quite brutal Russian also well known to the FBI. Meeting up with Martin's circle of sleeper agents, including a florist, Vincent Foss (Jack Manning), Laschenkov orders them to begin blackmailing the principal scientist working on Falcon, Dr Albert Kafer (Finlay Currie), whose son, a scientist working in West Berlin, has been kidnapped and will only be released when Kafer turns over his finding to the Russians. Kafer does the right thing, informing the FBI, and he immediately becomes the man between, having to pretend to be cooperating with his blackmailers. The Russian confronts the scientist with the information that his son is being held by Soviet police in East Berlin and will only be released unharmed if the man gives vital information about the project he is working on for the government. At this point, agent James Belden (George Murphy) persuades the scientist to hand over false information to the Russians. Belden sets up an elaborate sting operation that almost costs Kafer his life. The FBI proves able to rescue the scientist's son from his captors. The spy network is then quickly rolled up.

The enemy agents in *Walk East on Beacon* are in the end a fairly pathetic lot, easily disposed of by American authorities whose vigilance is not in doubt for long. The principal challenge for the filmmakers (here and in all similar productions) was to make the communist threat fearful enough to energise the narrative, while, at the same time, establishing that the Russians actually pose little threat to national security. The imbalance between the two opposing forces finds an unintentionally humorous reflex in the film's narrative climax, in which the spies attempt to flee Boston harbour in a yacht but are quickly foiled by Belden aboard a huge Navy cruiser. But in this America, however easily defended, there are numerous signs of breakdown. Martin's wife dissolves into hysterics when she learns that her husband, whom she had never suspected of being a Soviet agent, has been whisked out of the country on a Polish freighter, unintentionally abandoning her and his child. Frightened by Laschenkov, and the unexpected news that Martin has been 'sent back' to Moscow, Foss speaks to his wife (Vilma Kurer) about his regrets at having joined the party as an idealistic young man. She confesses that she provided the FBI with the anonymous tip about Martin. Foss says that he wants out of the spy ring, and the film loses track of him until his suicide is reported in the local paper. If Kafer succeeds, with the help of the FBI, in managing his double life, Foss and Martin do not, and each of them, in accordance with the poetic justice that normally operates in the Hollywood film, suffers an appropriate punishment for their betrayal of nation and family. Both men seem likeable enough, however, pathetic dupes of an ideology that in the end does not serve them well.

Containment, Cinematic and Political

A forceful and articulate analyst with unusually extensive diplomatic experience, George F. Kennan became the chief strategic architect of national policy during what became known as the Cold War, that long period of hostility, rivalry, and proxy conflicts that characterised the relationship of the two nations and their clients from the late 1940s to the fall of the Soviet Union in 1991. In the famous 1946 'Long Telegram' that he sent from Moscow to the State Department. Kennan's main argument was that the Soviet Union, by the logic of Marxist-Leninism, was driven towards an expansionist foreign policy that treated the outside world as 'evil, hostile and menacing, but as bearing within itself germs of creeping disease and destined to be wracked with growing internal convulsions until it is given [the] final Coup de grace by [the] rising power of socialism and yields to [a] new and better world'.[5]

Like many in the Truman administration, George Kennan believed that opposition to Soviet designs on an increased sphere of influence and the spread of communism more generally should be proactive: 'the main element of any United States policy toward the Soviet Union must be a long-term, patient but vigilant containment of Russian expansive tendencies'.[6] Kennan's strategy of containment would become the main principle of the Truman Doctrine, promulgated in March 1947, according to which US policy should be directed towards thwarting Soviet (indeed, any communist) initiatives abroad, while resisting presumed efforts at subversion at home. It was in this atmosphere of heightening military threat that American statesman and dedicated internationalist Bernard Baruch dubbed the East/West rivalry the 'Cold War'. While thus acknowledging the proxy, indirect nature of the conflict, Baruch and others recognised that this ideological struggle could break out into actual fighting on any number of barely foreseeable fronts. It was thus not much of a surprise that the North Korean invasion of South Korea in 1950 signalled the advent of a proxy war that dominated world politics for three years, especially after Communist China 'unofficially' entered the conflict.

Could the Korean War have been avoided had a Cold War mentality not taken hold in Washington? As the 1940s drew to a close, Kennan, supported by influential pundits like journalist Walter Lippmann, himself began to argue for the opening of discussions with the Soviets in order to solve or at least mitigate outstanding disagreements and differences of vision about the nature of the postwar world. Ironically, he was quickly marginalised within the State Department by advocates of black-and-white ideological thinking, particularly Secretary of State Dean Acheson. These influential supporters of the Truman Doctrine, so Kennan opined years later, distorted his advocacy of containment, which was initially meant to be largely economic and political. Instead, Acheson and company 'pursued it exclusively as a military concept; and I think that that, as much as any other cause, led to [the] 40 years of unnecessary, fearfully expensive and disoriented process of the Cold War'.[7]

In the first decade or so of the postwar era, however, Hollywood offered no trenchant criticism of the containment strategy and the inevitable, distasteful political compromises such a policy entailed simply on the basis of the strategic principle that the enemy of my enemy is my friend. At least in terms of its releases, the film industry also strongly supported for almost a decade the domestic struggle against enemy espionage and infiltration. The threat from domestic communists and Soviet agents, which was real enough but on a rather small scale, began to be imagined by many as more pervasive, as a clear and present danger demanding action. These films, however, present the domestic threat posed by communism in radically different ways. Americans, Kennan had argued, should not feel powerless, even if they had good reason to fear an ever-watchful enemy. Americans were living in a free and prosperous society whose system of government (unlike that of the Soviet Union) had stood the test of time. The Soviet Union, Kennan presciently believed, might just collapse from the dead weight of its own economic unworkability, especially when the linked benefits of capitalism and participatory democracy became known to those who found themselves trapped behind the Iron Curtain.

Interestingly, one of the earliest films of the Cold War cycle, William Wellman's noirish *The Iron Curtain*, released by Fox in 1948, examines just that feature of the postwar Russian *mentalité*, and is thoroughly noir in its focus on a protagonist who finds himself trapped between competing loyalties. The film dramatises the inherently self-destructive energies and incapacities of the Soviet system, avoiding the black-and-white thinking abhorred by Kennan, which became, unfortunately, the apparent guiding principle of most later Hollywood productions. *The Iron Curtain* is based on the actual experiences of Igor Gouzenko, a Soviet code clerk who is dispatched during the closing days of World War II to his nation's embassy in Ottawa. Establishing a life in Canada with his wife Anna (Gene Tierney) and newborn son, Gouzenko (Dana Andrews) rapidly loses his commitment to the espionage duties he has been assigned once the ostensible enemy turns out not to fit what he had been taught about capitalist exploiters. A trusted colleague, who is a decorated veteran, betrays to Igor his own profound doubts about the morality of the system he has been sworn to support, openly confronts the station chief with the party's hypocrisy and resigns himself to immediate liquidation upon his return home.

Living in democratic Canada and watching their neighbours go about their business with no interference from the government, the Gouzenkos, moreover, begin to resent the constant surveillance they find themselves under from their ostensible colleagues. In a short time, the couple become thoroughly Westernised. With his term of duty about to expire, Igor decides to seek political asylum as a defector. He steals from the embassy files containing the documents that detail the extensive Soviet spy network in the country, which, as the film dramatises, has found success obtaining information about the Canadian contribution to atomic weapons research. In contrast to those in his own embassy, who are dominated by distrust and paranoia, the Ottawa officials to whom he shows the documents do not at first take Gouzenko seriously. The truth, so the film's narrator proclaims, is simply 'too big, too incredible'. Gouzenko, however, puts his faith in an institution whose function in a free society he has only recently come to realise: the press. Only when he goes to a leading newspaper does he find one reporter willing to believe what he says and help Gouzenko get his information to the proper authorities. Resettled in a remote part of Canada, Gouzenko must live out the rest of his life in fear that Soviet agents will find and kill him; protecting police can never leave his side, an ironic comment on the fact that the refugees now live in a free country.

The Iron Curtain reveals the substantial threat of Soviet spy networks, whose most dangerous members are committed native Communists. John Grubb (Berry Kroeger), head of the Canadian communist party, is a smarmy yet effective seducer of the intellectually gullible who manages to 'turn' both a high-ranking airforce officer and also a scientist (a character clearly based on the notorious Alan Nunn May, who served ten years for espionage) with access to atomic secrets. In his mistaken liberalism, the man supports the 'peoples' war' against fascism and is convinced by Grubb that only if Russia also possesses the bomb will there be an end to global conflict. It turns out that these efforts to subvert the West are undone not by the Canadian authorities, but by a man of conscience within the spy ring itself who is not persuaded to betray his country by anything more dramatic than the evidence of his own experience.

Other films of the late 40s and early 50s offer noirish glimpses into what was thought to be going on in the lives of ordinary people living behind the Iron Curtain, who are trapped between their presumed desire for democratic freedoms and an oppressive system. Like *The Iron Curtain*, Felix Feist's *Guilty of Treason* (released by Eagle-Lion in 1950) also offers a thinly fictionalised version of Soviet and Eastern European experience, using the arrest and trial of Hungary's Catholic primate, Cardinal Mindszenty, as a framework for exploring the growing disillusionment of Soviet subjects with the system. Mindszenty (Charles Bickford) heroically resists an inexpertly organised attempt to paint him as a traitor because of his public criticism of the continuing Soviet occupation; the film grimly details the various forms of torture, both psychological and physical, to which the cardinal is subjected and over which in the end he is perceived as triumphing despite an obviously drug-induced 'repudiation' of 'past errors'. *Guilty of Treason*, however, is most effective in dramatising the growing rift over the Mindszenty affair that soured relations between Russia and its erstwhile client state. The cardinal's arrest fatally strains the romantic relationship between Hungarian artist Stephanie Varna (Bonita Granville) and Russian Colonel Alex Melnikov (Richard Derr), who works for the occupation force. Varna, who fought with the French resistance during the war against Hitler, finds herself persuaded of the cardinal's innocence and puts herself in danger by speaking out against it. Her lover tries to spirit her out of the country, but she refuses to abandon Hungary. Agonising over his affection for the beautiful woman (which, if revealed to his superiors, could end up destroying him), Melnikov decides to remain faithful to his political beliefs and eventually gives Varna up to the secret police, who then torture her to death in a failed attempt to extract a confession.

Broken-hearted, Melnikov returns to their love nest where he is discovered by the secret police and killed. American journalist Tom Kelly (Paul Kelly), who has been sent to Budapest to get the 'real story' of the Mindszenty affair, functions as the film's moral centre. He tells Melnikov he is supporting a system that is just as evil as the Nazism he struggled so valiantly in a defensive war to resist, in effect simply exchanging one tyrant (Stalin) for another (Hitler). Badly beaten by a gang of former Hungarian Nazis turned Communist thugs, Kelly leaves Budapest after Mindszenty is predictably found guilty at the end of his show trial. If he returns to the safety of Paris, however, it is to deliver a stirring address to the Overseas Press Club. Kelly reminds his fellow members of the 'free world' that the countries behind the Iron Curtain are not surrendering meekly to Soviet overlordship and that 'liberty is everybody's business'. Kelly is certain that the Russian domination of Eastern European countries will continue to be resisted; the film presciently anticipates the dissatisfaction that would break out into widespread social unrest and work stoppages through East Germany in 1953 and then, soon afterwards in 1956, into open revolt in Hungary. In such circumstances, the American role, Kelly proclaims, is to support the restoration of political freedom, especially by making sure the truth about the emerging Soviet system continues to be made known throughout the free world.

Diplomatic Courier, directed by Henry Hathaway and released by Fox in 1952, offers a dark, suspenseful tale of postwar espionage in the divided city of Trieste. The film ends with the improbable, if ideologically satisfying, conversion of the beautiful Russian agent (Hildegarde Neff) to democratic principles as well as a romantic commitment to her handsome American counterpart (Tyrone Power). Victor Saville's *Conspirator*, released by MGM in 1950, updates the threatening husband gothic romance popularised by Hitchcock's *Rebecca* (1940) and George Cukor's *Gaslight* (1944) by providing it with political relevance. Starry-eyed newlywed Melinda Curragh (Elizabeth Taylor) slowly comes to realise that handsome but maddeningly remote husband Michael (Robert Taylor), a British major entrusted with sensitive intelligence work, is actually funnelling state secrets to Russian agents. The film's political content is strikingly thin, certainly politically incorrect by current standards. Somewhat shockingly, it is revealed that Curragh's motive for treason seems to have little to do with the Cold War, but instead is the standard one provided for British traitors in World War II dramas. Curragh, we learn, is Irish, which seems to be all the explanation needed for his conversion to communism and subsequent betrayal of the government he had fought and bled for during the German war.

Hollywood's films dealing with the various European developments and foreign intrigues of Cold War politics nicely demonstrate how no thoroughgoing 'fatalism' as such, despite Kennan's worries, can in fact be glimpsed in Hollywood's initial response to the Cold War. And this was true even though the deficiencies of American society, particularly its pervasive racism, were then being interestingly anatomised, albeit from a positive, progressive perspective, in a series that became increasingly prominent in the early postwar years: the social problem film. And so, despite the persistence of the cliché, the films of this early era only sporadically exemplify anything like a collective hysteria over some supposed 'Red Scare'.

Perhaps a more plausible danger was subversion of the American system from within, the diversion of domestic discontents of various kinds into an ever growing support for communism as a political philosophy. R. G. Springsteen's

Red Menace, released by Republic in 1949, traces how an ex-serviceman, Bill Jones (Robert Rockwell), comes to flirt with communism after he becomes disenchanted with government attempts to recover money embezzled by a crooked home builder who is exploiting the recently instituted housing provisions of the G.I. Bill of Rights. Bill's fiancée deserts him after they are bilked of their down payment, putting an end to his dreams of postwar middle-class respectability. At the Veteran's Service Center, Bill is approached by Jack Tyler (William J. Lally), a member of the local communist party who hangs out there in order to prey on the disgruntled. Apparently in an attempt to complete this seduction, Tyler introduces Bill to a beautiful woman, Mollie O'Flaherty (Barbra Fuller), who quickly beds him down. Bill, escorted by Mollie, soon meets up at party headquarters with a stereotypical gallery of other disgruntled citizens: a Jewish poet/intellectual, Henry Solomon (Shepard Menken), a Negro writer, Sam Wright (Duke Williams) and a Russian party leader now resident in the US, Nina Petrovka (Hanne Axman).

In just a few weeks, Bill witnesses the thorough disillusionment of this group with Soviet-style ideological rigidity and inclination toward violence. Solomon publishes a poem that calls attention to Marx's expression of long-held ideas within Western culture about emancipation from tyranny. But party officials will not allow that Marx belongs to any tradition at all save that of the system he invented, and Solomon is asked to recant. He refuses and, after denouncing local leaders as perverting the real nature of Marx's thought, is condemned as a Trotskyite. Shunned by the group, Solomon soon commits suicide, leaping to his death through the party office window to the street below. Nina and Sam Wright are appalled that party leaders order a young student named Reachi (Norman Budd) to be beaten to death after he questions the validity of their criticism of the American system at a public rally. Sam is welcomed back into mainstream society by his father, who emphasises how the communists are using the dissatisfaction of black Americans with racial discrimination as a means for cynically manipulating them. There are more slaves in communist countries, his father suggests, than there ever were in the US. Approached by her priest and her mother, Mollie too is persuaded to give up her political allegiance to Stalinism. Dramatically re-entering her parish church, she suddenly rediscovers the deeper meaning of religious faith and undergoes a sudden conversion from political activism. Bill and Nina, meanwhile, have become lovers and decide to leave the party. Believing they need to flee, they drive furiously across the country until they end up exhausted in a small Texas town, whose kindly sheriff patiently explains that they live in a free country and therefore have nothing to fear since they have committed no crime. As they leave the sheriff's office, a little boy informs them that the man is known in town as 'Uncle Sam'. Reviewing the film in *The New York Times*, Bosley Crowther was moved to comment that 'if the local comrades are as corny as they act in this film, then their only likely potential would seem to be to make us laugh ourselves to death'.[8]

Hollywood's Cold War noirs demonstrate a greater variety and political depth than might ordinarily have been expected. In part, this was because the industry had good reasons of its own for strongly supporting with timely productions the vigorously anti-communist policies of first the Truman and then the Eisenhower administrations. The 1947 HUAC investigations of the industry resulted in ten from the filmmaking community being designated as 'unfriendly witnesses' and subsequently convicted on contempt citations, leading to their imprisonment. This widely publicised episode proved unexpectedly harmful and embarrassing, as the industry, its studios headed by some of the nation's most successful and prominent Jewish businessmen, fell under a cloud of suspicion that was never far from contacting the deep anti-Semitism long latent in American culture. Ironically, a special difficulty was raised by Hollywood's participation in government propaganda efforts during World War II, when the Soviet Union had become a de facto ally.

It did not seem to matter to the HUAC investigators that the World War II pro-Russian films had been made with government approval and encouragement. Roosevelt's Office of War Information had been eager to justify to the American public the huge investment in Lend-Lease to the Russian army, and the industry had accommodated the wishes of the administration. In the early years of the Cold War, Hollywood took pains to deny that legacy, with every studio, major and minor (Universal alone excepted), producing at least one anti-communist spy thriller or melodrama. Industry conservatives (including actors John Wayne, Ronald Reagan and director King Vidor) even founded the Motion Picture Alliance for the Advancement of American ideals, with novelist Ayn Rand penning *A Screen Guide for Americans*. This short list of general principles was meant to serve the industry as an informal 'production code' shaping its anti-communist policies.

With its self-consciously realist approach to crime celebrating the virtues and power of law enforcement and of civil institutions more generally, the noir semi-documentary proved an especially useful sub-genre for the establishment of the industry's political *bona fides*, as we have seen in the cases of both *The Iron Curtain* and *Walk East on Beacon*. A 'secular' parallel can be glimpsed in one of the most popular sub-types of film noir, the 'city confidential' films of the era. A notable example is Robert Wise's *The Captive City*, released by United Artists in 1952, which traces the heroic attempts of a newspaper reporter to uncover the workings of a crime syndicate that has seized control of local politics. Senator Estes Kefauver, who in the 1950s headed a Senate committee investigating small-town corruption, appears in the film to preach the need to defeat this menace threatening the American way of life. A significant and popular group of anti-communist films of that era collectively make up a kind of 'national confidential' meant to inform the American public of the deadly conspiracy operating just beneath the apparently benign surfaces of everyday life.

A number of these noirish exposés, to be sure, are only barely politicised, using anti-communist themes merely as an attempt to breathe life into narratives and themes that threatened to become overly conventional. Robert Aldrich's *Kiss Me Deadly*, released in 1955 by United Artists, sinks private detective Mike Hammer (Ralph Meeker) into a ever more threatening whirlpool of intrigue involving a gang of criminals eager to obtain a briefcase – dubbed 'the great whatsit' by Hammer's secretary Velda (Maxine Cooper) – that contains, as it turns out, radionuclide material. In the final scene, the briefcase is opened, revealing its true nature as a Pandora's box that explodes, with the result (only in the film's original theatrical release ending) that something like a world-ending nuclear apocalypse occurs. Aldrich's original notion, later restored in the DVD release, was less earth-shattering, a house fire from which Hammer and Velda escape to apparent safety in the nearby ocean.

In *Pickup on South Street*, directed by Samuel Fuller and released by Fox in 1953, a small-time pickpocket (Richard Widmark) accidentally steals microfilm of secret US government plans stolen by a Communist spy ring. Though the film has become a cult classic because of Fuller's brash visual style and provocative representations of violence and sexuality, *Pickup on South Street* does not deal in any depth with Cold War themes and ideology. Its spies seem no different from ordinary gangsters. So superficial is the anti-communist material, in fact, that when the film was released in France and its politics needed to be sanitised, it proved easy enough to eliminate all reference to the gangsters as spies, converting them instead to drug dealers. An artfully scripted updating of the pre-noir thriller *The Petrified Forest* (1936), *Split Second*, directed by Dick Powell and released by RKO in 1953, also minimally engages Cold War themes. The film explores the reactions under pressure of a diverse group of hostages held by escaped criminals in a ghost town. The only connection to contemporary politics is that the nuclear age provides its ticking clock source of suspense, as the town is the designated site for an upcoming nuclear test, from which the group escapes with barely a minute to spare.

Columbia's 1959 release *City of Fear*, directed by Irving Lerner, only minimally engages global realities. Like Elia Kazan's more justly famous *Panic in the Streets* (1950), this thriller traces the police pursuit of a man evading capture in a large metropolitan area (here Los Angeles rather than New Orleans) who is unwittingly in the process exposing his fellow citizens to great danger (now the radioactive material he has stolen rather than the bubonic plague). An extended pursuit, artfully managed, also forms the centrepiece of *The Atomic City*, directed by Jerry Hopper and released by Universal in 1952. Despite the elaborate security precautions taken with the personnel at

Los Alamos involved in nuclear weapons research, Russian agents manage to kidnap the young son of one of the programme's most important scientists, Dr Frank Addison (Gene Barry), with a view to extorting vital information from him. Though it begins in full semi-documentary style (a stern voiceover plays over actual footage of the semi-industrial New Mexico complex), *The Atomic City* soon abandons any pretence at political relevance; the Russian agents seem little different from standard noir heavies out to collect a ransom rather than a scientific formula.

The most artistically successful of the national confidential films is undoubtedly *Walk a Crooked Mile*, directed by Gordon Douglas and released by Columbia in 1948. The daring murder of an FBI agent who is trailing a suspicious foreigner named Radchek in Lakeview, California (where an important weapons research facility is located) alerts his superior, Daniel O'Hara (Dennis O'Keefe), that something sinister may indeed be afoot. Radchek is trailed to San Francisco, where he is murdered despite twenty-four-hour surveillance. O'Keefe is at this point introduced to British MI5 agent Philip Grayson (Louis Hayward), who has come to the US in order to investigate how a painting shipped from there to London has had ingeniously inscribed beneath the paint a secret formula only recently developed at the Lakeview facility.

The two agents join forces in an investigation that eventually reveals how the most strenuous security precautions have failed to prevent not only this formula, but a continuous series from being transmitted to the painter, who is a member of a communist spy ring. Suspicion then falls on the five scientists involved in the project. Only the persistence, endurance and courage of the two detectives (rather than the impersonal workings of a vast enforcement agency) lead to the eventual discovery of the culprit who, in an interesting twist, is not one of the two 'foreign' members of the group, but its American-born leader, Dr Romer Allen (Charles Evans), who, it is revealed, is the scion of a prominent Boston family with deep roots in American society. In accordance with the noir semi-documentary formula, much of *Walk a Crooked Mile* takes place entirely in the transitory social spaces of the night-time underworld from which everyday society and family life have been completely banished: seedy gyms, dark alleys, cheap apartments and underground railway tracks, where a complex shoot-out is effectively staged. Even O'Hara's office is glimpsed only late at night when empty of other agents and personnel. Instead of the customary chest-thumping portrayal of its huge force of trained functionaries, even the FBI gets the sinister noir chiaroscuro treatment.

Besides being European aesthetes (who else would have conceived the plan to smuggle out vital information copied onto an oil painting?), the communist operatives in *Walk a Crooked Mile* seem little different from typical noir criminal 'masterminds'. And, as in *The Atomic City*, they are served by seemingly brainless thugs who differ not at all from conventional noir heavies (and are

Figure 4.1　American communist meeting, *I Was a Communist for the FBI*.

played by actors prominent in that series, such Raymond Burr, the conscience-less killer in *Walk a Crooked Mile*, who is made to look more 'foreign' by a pasted-on goatee). The film's most political moment comes when a rooming-house domestic, just arrived in the country from Eastern Europe, takes a bullet meant for O'Hara and dies happy, so she admits, because she has played a role in the defeat of this plot to undermine her newly adopted country.

Though it otherwise follows closely the same formulae, Gordon Douglas's *I Was a Communist for the FBI* (released by Warner Brothers in 1951), based on the 'real life' experiences of Matt Cvetic (played by Frank Lovejoy), more interestingly explores the supposed political activities and domestic subversion practised by American communists in the industrial centre of Pittsburgh. One highly placed party member, Jim Blandon (James Millican), works in the personnel office of a local steel mill and makes sure that key positions are filled by fellow communists. At one point Blandon arranges for the local union to strike the plant and then for hired thugs to attack them using steel pipes covered in copies of the local Yiddish language newspaper, hoping to incite an anti-semitic reaction among the general public that the party can manipulate and exploit.

The communists, it is revealed, customarily use both the discontents of minorities and prejudice against them in order to create civil unrest. At one party meeting, the party's legal support of the Scottsboro boys through a series of well-publicised trials is cynically discussed as an inexpensive way of making international news out of American racism.

The party's infiltration of the educational system is also emphasised. Just returned to Pittsburgh, Cvetic is approached by Eve Merrick (Dorothy Hart), a local schoolteacher who has been sent by party leaders to check on his movements. An idealist seduced by the promise of communism to deliver social justice, Merrick is soon thoroughly disillusioned by the party's conscienceless exploitation of social prejudice. She and Cvetic eventually become lovers when she realises that he is working for the FBI; only with difficulty do they escape from the party thugs sent to eliminate them. Rejected by his family for his supposed embrace of communism, Cvetic is finally exonerated when he testifies for the government at the HUAC meeting at which the Pittsburgh party operatives are revealed as dangerous subversives. His true patriotism revealed, the erstwhile true believer reconciles with his son and brother, who had for years become thoroughly disgusted by what they thought was Matt's traitorous behaviour. The 'adventures' of this double agent (now known as Herb Philbrick) were continued, first on radio and then on television, in one of the most popular series of the era: *I Led Three Lives*.

Given Hollywood's fearful experience with their investigations, it is perhaps not surprising that stern and patriotic members of HUAC play a heroic role in *I Was a Communist for the FBI* (interestingly enough, the film also 'earned' an Academy Award Best Picture nomination even though it is clearly not an 'A' production and undoubtedly stood no chance of actually winning). Even more supportive of HUAC, however, is *Big Jim McLain*, directed by Edward Ludwig and released by Warners in 1953. After a brief prologue in which the voice of a ghostly, and deeply worried, Daniel Webster inquires if all is well in the country, the film opens with a HUAC meeting at which an obviously guilty communist (the viewer knows that because he is a shifty-eyed man with a foreign accent) pleads Fifth Amendment protection when asked if he is a communist. Apparently hampered by the freedoms afforded citizens in the Bill of Rights, the committee must turn to less formal (that is, strongarm) methods of getting at the truth. Two massive and hulking investigators, Jim McLain and Mal Baxter (played by John Wayne and Jim Arness respectively), are dispatched to Hawaii, where they are to identify local members of the party in order to foil the subversive activities in which it is suspected they are involved.

Like Matt Cvetic, McLain hooks up almost immediately with a local female member of the party, Nancy Vallon (Nancy Olson) who also by film's end becomes disillusioned with the party's tactics. In his attempts first to identify local communist leaders and then to discover who has murdered Baxter, McLain makes his way through something like the dangerous noir underworld (including a brassy but harmless landlady memorably played by Veda Ann Borg). The only difference is that the lowlifes McLain runs into are largely now disillusioned ex-communists who, formerly taken in by the party's appeal to unionism and egalitarianism, have now realised that its real aim is the destruction of the American way of life. The seriousness of their plotting emerges when, having kidnapped Mal, the communists accidentally kill him with an overdose of truth serum. With the help of the political converts, McLain is finally able to make sure that. Mal's murderers (including the group's cold-blooded leader, Sturak, played superbly by Alan Napier) are brought successfully to justice. But the others, not implicated in any specific act of lawbreaking, only find themselves testifying before a special session of HUAC. They too 'plead the fifth' and must be released from custody. McLain's righteous indignation at this cynical exploitation of American freedoms is assuaged somewhat by his witnessing, at film's end, an Army unit parading through the refurbished docks of Pearl Harbor. This sequence completes the patriotic tour of the base that had begun earlier with a heart-rending visit to the *Arizona* memorial. By the end of the film, the narrator is thus able to answer Webster's question about the state of the republic with a resounding proclamation that all is well.

We Will Not be Driven by Fear into an Age of Unreason

As *Big Jim McLain* and these other films suggest, Hollywood's experience was that the noir semi-documentary could be easily adapted to anti-communist themes, with just enough political content added to provide a topical flavour. Committed to hard-boiled dialogue and action, these releases lack the deeper engagement of less generic productions such as *The Iron Curtain* and *Guilty of Treason* with the difficult social and ideological questions raised by the growth of East–West rivalry, the formation of the Eastern bloc and the contrast in economic and social promise of liberal democratic capitalism, on the one hand, and state socialism based on Marxist theory on the other. This is true as well of the several crime melodramas of the early postwar period that emphasise communist themes, usually in a fairly superficial or predictable fashion. Political commitment and its lasting consequences for an attempted 'fresh start' are the focus in *The Woman on Pier 13* (also released under the more provocative title *I Married a Communist*), directed by Robert Stevenson and released by RKO in 1949. Brad Collins (Robert Ryan), a well-placed executive in a San Francisco shipping company, is actually Frank Johnson, a former dockworker and member of the communist party. On his honeymoon, Collins runs into an old girlfriend, Christine (Janis Carter), who, still an active member of the communist party, tells the party boss, Vanning (Thomas Gomez), that Collins could easily be blackmailed through threats to expose his past, especially since, as Johnson, he had found himself embroiled in a murder.

Approached by Christine, Collins tells her that he has put the foolish political commitments of his youth behind him – and that he also wants nothing to do with her. The blackmail eventually succeeds, however, as Collins cooperates for a time with party thugs in order to shut down the waterfront. Realising his error as his wife finds herself in danger, Collins turns on Vanning and kills him, but is fatally wounded in the process. Before dying, the repentant former communist tells his wife he met her too late to begin a new life.

Figure 4.2 Seductive communist appears, *The Woman on Pier 13*.

In *The Woman on Pier 13*, the fear that the vast communist conspiracy can manifest itself anywhere at any time expresses itself through the noir theme of the 'dark past'. Like many a noir fellow traveller, Brad Collins finds himself trapped between times and between different versions of himself. Such instability renders impossible his coupling with a good woman and the everyday respectability he now eagerly pursues. The noir theme of the dark underside of everyday life figures prominently in another notable crime melodrama of the period with a communist theme: the oddly titled *The Whip Hand*, directed by William Cameron Menzies and released by RKO in 1951. The film opens with a meeting of the Russian military chiefs in Moscow, at which it is most improbably decided that the plan to cripple American society by spreading a killer virus is best served by making a home base in the backwoods community of Winnoga, Wisconsin. A vacationing journalist, Matt Corbin (Elliott Reid), foils the plot when he becomes suspicious that much of the property in the area has been bought up by a group of foreigners (who, somewhat stupidly, are proudly displaying on a bookshelf in the local lodge several books by their leader, a notorious former Nazi criminal scientist, Dr Wilhelm Bucholtz). Bucholtz, it turns out, is living in Winnoga under an assumed name, and he is served by the usual gang of noirish thugs (the reliable heavy Raymond Burr chief among them). With the aid of the local authorities, Corbin manages to prevent Bucholtz from poisoning Chicago's water supply.

In the early postwar era, such narratives had a persistent appeal, even as the political climate began to change. For example, in *The Fearmakers*, directed by Jacques Tourneur and released by United Artists in 1958, Alan Eaton (Dana Andrews) returns home from the Korean War to find that his business partner has mysteriously died. The firm has passed into new hands, a blustery man named McGinnis (Dick Foran), who has moved it into a quite different area of business: conducting public polls to support certain 'special interest' groups. It soon becomes apparent to Eaton that McGinnis is running a communist front organisation whose purpose is to influence public opinion, particularly on the issue of banning nuclear weapons. Despite recurrent flashbacks from the brainwashing he suffered as a North Korean prisoner of war, Eaton manages to collect enough evidence for the police to take action. That communists need to be routed from places of influence by the actions of heroic individuals is a theme that appears also in *The Trial*, directed by Mark Robson for MGM and released in 1955. Only by outing a young Mexican boy's trial lawyer as a communist eager to see his client martyred for the 'cause' does David Blake (Glenn Ford) come to see the 'truth' about prominent liberal organisations supposedly dedicated to social justice (the film's target seems to be a quite thinly disguised American Civil Liberties Union). Blake saves the boy from an unjust sentence with an effective appeal to the very community that had seemed so desperate to see him executed (a lynching is barely averted as the boy awaits arraignment). The film thus makes two related points: that the party does not have the best interests of the poor and downtrodden at heart, despite appearances; and that, properly informed and led, the American people will act justly, showing that the system does work even when strained by prejudice and unreason.

Life in Cold War America, however, was hardly that simple. Based on Richard Condon's notorious novel, John Frankenheimer's *The Manchurian Candidate* (released in 1962 by United Artists) captures the political complexities of the period, of which it wisely never attempts to make sense. There is no doubt that the film is the most artistically successful of the Cold War films, precisely because, adapting an ideologically paradoxical, bitterly sardonic and darkly humorous source, it notably exceeds the usual self-imposed limits of the genre. A platoon of GIs in Korea is led into an ambush, captured, drugged and then flown to Manchuria, where a noted Russian behaviour psychologist subjects them to an intense form of brainwashing. One of the group is conditioned to become a conscienceless assassin, Raymond Shaw (Laurence Harvey), while the others, including their leader Bennett Marco (Frank Sinatra), are conditioned to misremember their 'training' as a combat operation in which Shaw performs with incredible heroism (when in fact he simply 'practises' his technique on his erstwhile comrades). Returned to American society, where he is welcomed as a Medal of Honor winner, Shaw unconsciously assumes the deep cover of his previous identity. His stepfather is a senator, an obvious version of Joseph McCarthy, who, instructed by his wife, has begun an intimidating campaign against government officials he accuses of being communists. In reality, his wife is a Soviet agent, and he her unwitting tool, soon to be nominated as his party's vice-presidential candidate. Shaw's Russian handlers 'test' their pawn by having him murder both his father-in-law and his own wife.

Meanwhile, Marco's conditioning begins to break down as he realises the dim outlines of what happened to him and the others in the platoon. In the film's suspenseful climax, Marco races to find Shaw at the convention hall, where his stepfather is about to be nominated. He fears correctly that Shaw has been programmed to assassinate the presidential candidate, allowing the stepfather to become the party's nominee. But Shaw's conditioning has also deteriorated, and instead of his intended target he guns down both his stepfather and his mother before killing himself. An assassin, a matricide and a suicide, Shaw has finally become the medal winner that his fabricated citation praises through a gesture that completely blurs the lines between heroism and betrayal, summing up the political turbulence of an era.

The Manchurian Candidate is both an indictment of the self-serving fabulations of McCarthyism about some supposed widespread communist infiltration of the federal government and a terrifying dramatisation of how in fact a sophisticated conspiracy, directed by Moscow, might plausibly decapitate American society. Cinematically, the film looks forward to how in the course of the 1960s and 1970s the notion of 'conspiracy' in American life would come to be expressed, particularly in popular culture, as a gaming of the system from within by those who, lacking any scruples, would do whatever might be necessary to seize and maintain power. For American filmmaking, the legacy of the Cold War noir is the political thriller writ large, a narrative form with seemingly endless appeal devoted to exposing the unexpectedly sinister inner workings of a society in which, as film after film continues to suggest, is never what it seems to (or should) be.

Bibliography

Appy, Christian G. (ed.) (2000), *Cold War Constructions: The Political Culture of United States Imperialism 1945–1966*, Amherst, MA: University of Massachusetts Press.
Biskind, Peter (1984), *Seeing is Believing: How Hollywood Taught us to Stop Worrying and to Love the Fifties*, London: Pluto.
Boyer, Paul (1985), *By the Bomb's Early Light: American Thought and Culture at the Dawn of the Atomic Age*, New York: Pantheon.
Caute, David (1978), *The Great Fear: The Anti-Communist Purge under Truman and Eisenhower*, New York: Simon & Schuster.
Ceplair, Larry and Steven Englund (1979), *The Inquisition in Hollywood: Politics in the Film Community, 1930–1960*, Berkeley, CA: University of California Press.
Christensen, Terry and Peter J. Haas (2005), *Projecting Politics: Political Messages in American Films*, Armonk, NY: M. E. Sharpe.
Doherty, Thomas (2003), *Cold War, Cool Medium: Television, McCarthyism, and American Culture*, New York: Columbia University Press.
Engelhardt, Tom (1995), *The End of Victory Culture: Cold War America and the Disillusioning of a Generation*, New York: Basic Books.
Gaddis, John Lewis (1997), *We Now Know: Rethinking Cold War History*, Oxford: Oxford University Press.

Haut, Woody (1996), *Pulp Culture: Hardboiled Fiction and the Cold War*, London: Serpent's Tail.
Haynes, John E. (1996), *Red Scare or Red Menace?: American Communism and Anticommunism in the Cold War*, Chicago, IL: Ivan R. Dee.
Hewison, Robert (1981), *In Anger: Culture in the Cold War, 1945–1960*, London: Weidenfeld and Nicolson.
Hixson, Walter L. (1997), *Parting the Curtain: Propaganda, Culture, and the Cold War, 1945–1961*, New York: Macmillan.
Kuznick, Peter J. and James Gilbert (eds) (2001), *Rethinking Cold War Culture*, Washington, DC: Smithsonian Institute Press.
May, Lary (ed.) (1988), *Recasting America: Culture and Politics in the Age of the Cold War*, Chicago, IL: University of Chicago Press.
——. (2000), *The Big Tomorrow: Hollywood and the Politics of the American Way*, Chicago, IL: University of Chicago Press.
Nadel, Alan (1995), *Containment Culture: American Narratives, Postmodernism, and the Atomic Age*, London: Duke University Press.
Naremore, James (1988), *Acting in the Cinema*, Berkeley, CA: University of California Press.
Radosh, Ronald and Allis Radosh (2005), *Red Star Over Hollywood: The Film Colony's Long Romance with the Left*, San Francisco, CA: Encounter.
Rose, Lisle (1999), *The Cold War Comes to Main Street*, Lawrence, KS: University Press of Kansas.
Sayre, Nora (1982), *Running Time: Films of the Cold War*, New York: Dial.
Schwarz, Richard A. (1998), *Cold War Culture: Media and the Arts, 1945–1990*, New York: Checkmark.
Shaheen, Jack (ed.) (1978), *Nuclear War Films*, Carbondale, IL: Southern Illinois University Press.
Whitfield, Stephen J. (1996), *The Culture of the Cold War*, Baltimore, MD: The Johns Hopkins University Press.

Notes

1. Bosley Crowther, 'It's a Wonderful Life', *The New York Times*, 23 December 1946.
2. Nick Smedley, *A Divided World: Hollywood Cinema and Émigré Directors in the Era of Roosevelt and Hitler, 1933–1948* (Bristol: Intellect, 2011), p. 28.
3. Ibid., p. 37.
4. This doubleness, as James Naremore brilliantly demonstrates, also characterises the viewer's experience with the film's foregrounding of performativity, for the 'performances' of Walter and Phyllis as 'themselves' are managed by MacMurray and Stanwyck as revealing the strain between the need to adopt one's self as a mask and the powerful force of inner expression ('I am not what I seem to be') that defines the characters' psychological states. See James Naremore, *Acting in the Cinema* (Berkeley, CA: University of California Press, 1988).
5. Kennan, George, 'The Long Telegram', online at www.gwu.edu/~nsarchiv/coldwar/documents/episode-1/kennan.htm (accessed 12 October 2009).
6. Ibid.
7. Ibid.
8. Bosley Crowther, 'The Red Menace', *New York Times*, 27 June 1949, online at www.nytimes.com / movie / review ? res = 940DE5DE113CE23BBC4F51DFB0668382659EDE (accessed 7/9/2014).

5. NOIRING THE PITCH: THE CONFLICTED SOUNDTRACKS OF *OUT OF THE PAST*, *THE BLUE GARDENIA* AND *THE LONG GOODBYE*

Krin Gabbard

In Jacques Tourneur's *Out of the Past* (1947) and Fritz Lang's *The Blue Gardenia* (1953), a romantic ballad plays over the opening credits and recurs regularly as it becomes associated with the central characters, but is not heard at the end of the film. Although the scores for both films are otherwise entirely typical of Classical Hollywood, a vanishing love song is unusual. On one hand, the phasing out of a love theme seems well-suited to film noir if only because so many noirs begin with the promise of romance before descending into negativity. I cannot, on the other hand, locate any films from the 'official' years of noir besides *Out of the Past* and *The Blue Gardenia* in which a love song is heard at the beginning but not at the end. Regardless of whether or not these two films are unique in their use of love songs, it is significant that in both films the songs are introduced diegetically by African-American musicians. The songs may disappear from the films because they are associated at the outset with otherness.

We need to go beyond the years of classic noir – usually designated 1942 to 1959 – to find another example of a disappearing love song. Long after Orson Welles drove a stake through the heart of film noir with the perverse revisionism of *Touch of Evil,* Robert Altman revised the Hollywood love song even more perversely with *The Long Goodbye* (1973). Altman commissioned no less than John Williams and Johnny Mercer to write the song 'The Long Goodbye' for his film. The song is heard repeatedly throughout the film, often popping up in extremely unlikely places. But at no time does the audience hear the entire song, either with or without Mercer's lyrics. And instead of hearing the song at the end of the film, we hear an ancient recording of 'Hooray for

Hollywood'. Altman was not merely revising the genre of hard-boiled noir in particular and Hollywood cinema in general. He was also asking audiences to contemplate how popular songs drift in and out of movies and how that music may or may not affect the rest of the film.

Monotheme Cinema

Even before studios began aggressively bundling the promotion of a film with the promotion of a song, it was not unusual for a film to feature the same song from beginning to end. The practice probably begins with Otto Preminger's *Laura* (1944), in which David Raksin's song 'Laura' is first heard over the opening credits.[1] The song is heard throughout the film both diegetically and non-diegetically as it becomes associated with Laura (Gene Tierney) and then with the couple, Laura and Mark (Dana Andrews). As the film ends, the same song plays over the closing credits. Mark's love for Laura is presented at first as vaguely necrophiliac, but the film eventually validates the love affair according to the familiar standards of Hollywood heteronormativity. Jeff Smith has documented the extent to which producers in the 1950s demanded that films promote a single musical theme.[2] He has coined the term 'monotheme score' to describe music that could easily be marketed alongside the film. Smith writes, '*Laura* (1944) is perhaps the paradigmatic example of the monotheme score, but its formula was successfully duplicated in *High Noon* (1952), *Love Is a Many-Splendored Thing* (1955), and *Around the World in Eighty Days* (1956)'.[3] *Out of the Past* and *The Blue Gardenia* begin as monothemed films. *The Long Goodbye* assiduously parodies the tradition.

Unlike the romance between Laura and Mark in *Laura*, the love affair between Jeff Markham/Bailey (Robert Mitchum) and Kathie Moffat (Jane Greer) in *Out of the Past* quickly turns murderous and remains so until the end. The love song that plays behind their romance seems at first to genuinely celebrate the affair, but as the film winds down, it is played in a minor key if at all. Similarly, the song that introduces *The Blue Gardenia* is associated first with the flirtation between Norah Larkin (Anne Baxter) and Harry Prebble (Raymond Burr) and later between Norah and Casey Mayo (Richard Conte). The romance with Prebble ends in his death while the Norah/Casey romance is compromised by Casey's willingness to exploit Norah for the sake of his own newspaper headlines. The conclusion of the film holds out the hope for a rapprochement but, as many critics have pointed out, any real understanding between the two seems unlikely after what has actually taken place between them. The music is more 'realistic' about the possibility of romance than is the script. In *The Long Goodbye*, Williams' and Mercer's love ballad belongs to no one, certainly not to a pair of lovers. We do know that Roger Wade (Sterling Hayden) had an affair with Sylvia Lennox, and we know that Terry

Lennox (Jim Bouton) and Eileen Wade (Nina van Pallandt) are lovers. But neither couple is ever on camera. There is certainly no romantic partner for Phillip Marlowe (Elliott Gould), who appears to be entirely asexual.

Although there are narrative justifications for phasing out the love songs in *Out of the Past* and *The Blue Gardenia*, there were no economic reasons for doing so. Both songs had some success as pop tunes, either before or after the release of the film in which it is heard. The song that begins *Out of the Past* is 'The First Time I Saw You', written by Nathaniel Shilkret and Allie Wrubel. The lyrics to the song are not heard in *Out of the Past*, but both the words and the music were prominently featured in Rowland V. Lee's *The Toast of New York* (1937), where it is played on a harp and sung by Frances Farmer. 'The First Time I Saw You' was widely recorded by jazz orchestras, including those led by Charlie Barnet, Jimmy Lunceford and Bunny Berigan, and by singers Chick Bullock and Seger Ellis. The score for *Out of the Past* is by composer Roy Webb, who worked regularly in Hollywood, frequently for Jacques Tourneur. In his book on movie music, Christopher Palmer holds Webb in great esteem, both for his scores for films noirs such as Norman Foster's *Journey into Fear* (1943), John Brahm's *The Locket* (1946) and Edward Dmytryk's *Crossfire* (1947), and for his compositions for horror films. Palmer calls Webb's score for Tourneur's *Cat People* (1943), for example, a marvel of 'musical chiaroscuro'.[4]

'Blue Gardenia' was written specifically for *The Blue Gardenia* by Bob Russell and Lester Lee. Bob Russell wrote memorable lyrics for several tunes by Duke Ellington, most notably 'Do Nothin' Till You Hear from Me' and 'Don't Get Around Much Anymore'. Lester Lee, who wrote the music for the song 'Blue Gardenia', was a very busy composer for Hollywood and Broadway but left behind little that we remember today, with the possible exception of 'The Pennsylvania Polka', heard more often than anyone could wish in Bill Murray's constantly repeated visit to the park in Harold Ramis's *Groundhog Day* (1993). 'Blue Gardenia' was intended for Nat King Cole, who sings it in the film, but Dinah Washington recorded a more popular version of the song a few years later. Raoul Kraushaar, who wrote the score of *The Blue Gardenia*, began his Hollywood career as a music supervisor and conductor and then went on to write the scores for an endless succession of 'B' movies, including *Abbott and Costello Meet Captain Kidd* (1952), *Bomba and the Jungle Girl* (1952), *Island of Lost Women* (1959) and *Billy the Kid Versus Dracula* (1966). *The Blue Gardenia* may be one of the few films for which he is remembered.

John Williams is today the most successful composer for movies the world has ever known. Even people who have never seen a *Star Wars* film will instantly recognise the theme that Williams wrote for Darth Vader. In the late 1950s, Williams worked as a jazz pianist in groups led by Red Norvo, Ray Anthony and Buddy Collette while also writing a great deal of music for television programmes. He was on the cusp of his triumph as a film composer when Altman hired him to write the music for *The Long Goodbye*. Johnny Mercer, who wrote the lyrics to 'The Long Goodbye', is every bit as eminent in the Great American Songbook as Williams is in music for the movies. Rather than list titles from the many memorable songs with lyrics by Mercer, I offer a single anecdote. Henry Mancini wrote the music for 'Moon River' before he handed it over to Mercer for lyrics and then to Blake Edwards for his *Breakfast at Tiffany's* (1961). Here is what Mancini wrote after he heard Mercer sing his lyrics for the first time: 'Every once in a while you hear something so right that it gives you chills, and when he sang that "huckleberry friend" line, I got them'.[5]

The Tough Guy and the Femme Fatale

Shilkret/Wrubel's 'The First Time I Saw You' would have been ten years old by the time *Out of the Past* was released in 1947, but most of the audience surely recognised it. In Webb's lavishly orchestrated version, the song plays over RKO's signature logo, a radio antenna sitting on a globe, even before the title of the film appears on the screen. Once Webb's score has established the melody of 'The First Time I Saw You' in two different keys, the score segues into the more pastoral music associated throughout the film with the great outdoors. *Out of the Past* is typical of film noir in many ways, but not because of its moments of pastoral beauty. Robert Miklitsch observes that, in the opening sequence, Webb's music is just as effective as Nicholas Musuraca's lyrical cinematography in creating the illusion of an idyllic paradise. Together the music and the photography tell us that, in Miklitsch's words, 'this is God's country'.[6] The film is unusual for its vanishing love song but also for the lovingly photographed lakes and mountains that are so strongly differentiated from the film's conventionally noir urban locations.

After 'The First Time I Saw You' is played over the opening credits, the audience does not hear the song again until several minutes into the film. First, however, the audience sees the arrival of Joe Stephanos (Paul Valentine) in Bridgeport, an actual town in northern California. They then see Jeff with Ann (Virginia Huston), the local woman with whom he has fallen in love, as they enjoy a fishing trip near at a lake. After Jeff meets with Joe and realises that he must revisit his past, he begins the seventy-eight-mile drive from Bridgeport to Lake Tahoe with Ann in the passenger seat. With Jeff's voiceover driving the flashback, the audience sees his first encounter with Whit Sterling (Kirk Douglas), who hires Jeff and his sleazy partner Fisher (Steve Brodie) to find Kathie and bring her back along with $40,000 she has taken from him.

Jeff's flashback continues as he enters an African-American nightclub where he hopes to speak with the black woman who worked as a maid for Kathie.

Fifteen minutes into the film, the audience hears the first diegetic version of 'The First Time I Saw You'. The music begins with a tight close-up of the face of an African-American trumpeter who plays a bracing, unaccompanied jazz cadenza before the orchestra launches into a swing version of the song. The scene features a performance by Theresa Harris as Eunice, Kathie's now unemployed maid. Harris was a very busy actress in the 1930s, 40s and 50s, usually playing maids but almost always with a bit of glamour and sexiness. A few years earlier she had appeared as Bette Davis's maid Zette in *Jezebel* (1938), in which she gives a performance so spirited that Richard Dyer cited it in an important essay on Hollywood's practice of displacing onto African-American characters the emotion that whites are expected to repress.[7] Harris had also worked for Jacques Tourneur, giving what James Naremore (1998) has called 'a fine, unstereotypical performance' in Tourneur's *I Walked With a Zombie*.[8]

After the camera cuts from the trumpeter, it quickly pans across the club to reveal that Jeff is the only white person in the room. As Jeff interacts with Eunice, her boyfriend (Caleb Peterson) and another couple who politely excuse themselves when Jeff begins asking questions, there is a distinct matter-of-factness to the exchanges between the black patrons and the white interloper. The well-dressed black customers are not so much surprised by Jeff's presence as they are intrigued by what he wants to find out. To quote Naremore again, 'the scene as a whole is played without condescension'.[9] Surely one purpose of this scene is to show that Mitchum's private investigator is well schooled in extracting information from people even from people not of his tribe. The scene also reveals that he is hip enough to treat blacks with a degree of respect and solicitude. 'The First Time I Saw You', however, is associated here at its first diegetic hearing with a milieu that was held in contempt by most Americans in 1947 and that the film itself ultimately disparages.

The scene in the nightclub, during which the band never stops playing 'The First Time I Saw You', is the beginning of Jeff's pursuit of Kathie, and it takes him from the exotic underworld of African-American culture to the exotic underworld (as in *under* the United States of America) of Acapulco, Mexico. Only after Jeff has passed through this portal does Kathie walk out of the sun and into his life. William Luhr has suggested that Kathie's character is strongly marked by these essentially racist associations with Harlem and Mexico through which Jeff makes his way in order to find her.[10] Luhr also points to the workings of fate in the film. After his first encounter with Kathie, Jeff goes to the telegraph office to notify Whit. But the office is closed, and he is unable to accomplish what he was being paid to do. By the time the telegraph office has reopened, he has presumably become so besotted with Kathie that he decides to betray his employer. As Luhr suggests, the screenplay implies that Jeff is subject to forces beyond his control, a trope that is common in film noir but that is seldom handled as deftly as in this scene in *Out of the Past*.[11]

Twenty-one minutes into the film, 'The First Time I Saw You' has its second diegetic appearance. As Jeff greets Kathie in Pablo's, the cantina where she tells him she 'sometimes' goes, a violinist begins a version of the tune accompanied by a pianist. At no point during this scene does Jeff acknowledge the coincidence of the same song popping up in two different locales. He does not even appear to be listening. As Claudia Gorbman has suggested in her essential work on film music, the song is essentially 'inaudible' (unless, of course, one is an academic trying to develop a thesis about the music in film noir).[12] But, by this time, 'The First Time I Saw You' has become the official love song for Jeff and Kathie. It plays non-diegetically a few minutes later when Jeff and Kathie share their first kiss. The song is heard again moments after that when they meet in a lyrical day-for-night shot on the beach that is as impressive as the nature scenes that cinematographer Nicholas Musuraca shot in the California mountains. Still supplying the voiceover as he narrates the flashback for Ann, Jeff says that Kathie would 'come along like school is out' as the song plays on the score.

A few moments later the tune moves seamlessly from the diegetic to the non-diegetic register and then back again. For the first time, Kathie has invited Jeff to her bungalow. As they come in from the rain, Kathie walks to her record player and puts the tone-arm onto a disc with still another version of 'The First Time I Saw You'. Kathie briefly resists as Jeff vigorously but playfully applies a towel to her wet hair. As they kiss once again, the camera pans to the front door which suddenly sweeps open to let in the wind and the rain, a conventional metaphor for sexual intercourse. Like every adult in the audience, the censors at the Hays Office knew what the film was saying, but the Production Code was clear: there could be no explicit acknowledgement that anyone had engaged in pre-marital sex. So, as the music on the record morphs into another elaborately orchestrated variation of 'The First Time I Saw You', the audience sees a fully clothed Jeff, his hair combed and dry, closing the door. The music then becomes diegetic once again as Kathie, also fully put back together, lifts the tone arm off the record, and the music stops. At this moment the lovers agree to run off together and forget about Whit.

Two minutes later the audience sees Jeff in his hotel room preparing for his trip back north with Kathie. As he puts items into his suitcase, he actually whistles the melody to 'The First Time I Saw You'. Although he did not appear to be listening when musicians played the tune at the black nightclub or at the cantina in Acapulco, Jeff has apparently picked it up. Or, if we wish to take the film literally, Jeff could be like many in the 1947 audience who had frequently heard the various recordings of the tune on the radio. Jeff's performance of the song, however, is interrupted by the unexpected arrival of Whit and Joe. The song will suffer another significant interruption six minutes later when the lovers meet at the cabin where they are hoping to avoid Fisher,

Jeff's erstwhile partner who correctly believes that he has been cut out of the deal of bringing Kathie back to Whit. Knowing that Fisher is looking for them, Jeff and Kathie have stayed away from each other for several days. When they first re-encounter each other at the cabin, they lock eyes as the song once again becomes part of the non-diegetic score. But when Fisher appears out of the darkness, Webb has written a cue directing the musicians to hold a chord in the middle of the tune. Then tympani provide a crescendo. The song essentially stops dead, as it did when Jeff ended his whistling the moment he saw Whit and Joe outside his hotel room.

Kathie reveals herself to be a murderous sociopath when she shoots Fisher and drives off in his car, leaving Jeff to clean up the mess. The film is approximately halfway through when Jeff's flashback ends. He and Ann arrive at Whit's estate in Lake Tahoe and the audience never again hears Jeff's voiceover. He has even more definitively lost control of the narrative when, to his surprise as well as to that of the audience, he discovers that Kathie has returned to Whit on her own volition. Jeff has, of course, violated his contract with Whit and gone into hiding. And, as Frank Krutnik has convincingly demonstrated in a psychoanalytic reading of film noir, Jeff has violated the Law of the Father by attempting to take 'mother' (Kathie) away from 'father' (Whit).[13]

By the time Jeff re-encounters Kathie with Whit, the audience is made to assume that he no longer loves her and that he has become attached to Ann, a much less problematic object choice. When Kathie and Jeff have a brief moment alone in Whit's house, she tries to convince him that she had no choice but to go back to Whit. Jeff expels her from his room, saying, 'I have to sleep in this room. Let's just leave it where it all is. Get out'. After Kathie leaves the room, the audience hears a version of the song played, for the first time, in a minor key. This version of 'The First Time I Saw You' segues into a brief cue for a theremin that sounds curiously reminiscent of music for the horror cinema. In fact, Roy Webb did the music for all of Jacques Tourneur's horror films, including *Cat People* (1942), *I Walked With a Zombie* (1943) and *The Leopard Man* (1943). Like the vast majority of Hollywood composers, Webb was not above recycling bits of melody and orchestration, and he surely found the theremin cue to be as appropriate for Mitchum dealing with his conflicted memories of Kathie as it was for scenes in which a character in a horror film encounters the uncanny.

After migrating to a minor key, 'The First Time I Saw You' might seem to have served its purpose in *Out of the Past*. But the affair between Jeff and Kathie is not actually over, and the song is heard briefly on two final occasions. First, when Jeff sees Kathie at the party just after he has hidden the body of the attorney Eels in hopes of outsmarting Whit in his attempt to pin the murder on Jeff. Realising that Jeff is aware of a scheme in which she plays a significant role, Kathie desperately tries to convince him that she is innocent and that she

Figure 5.1 Jeff (Robert Mitchum) and Kathie (Jane Greer) in conflicted embrace as 'The First Time I Saw You' plays, *Out of the Past*.

has never stopped loving him. The music is heard on the soundtrack as they kiss. The music now stands for their contaminated romance but also for Jeff's masochistic infatuation with Kathie and even for her manipulative attempts to make him the fall guy.

Finally, audiences can hear a brief phrase from the song after Kathie has killed Whit and coolly told Jeff that she is now in charge. The listener has to pay close attention to hear a few faint phrases from the tune played slowly in a score that is designed to represent Jeff's predicament and the murderous behaviour of Kathie rather than any revival of their love. This is the last time 'The First Time I Saw You' can be heard, and it is barely recognisable.

Of course, Kathie and Jeff soon die together in a spectacularly unromantic fashion. As Luhr points out, Kathie actually shoots Jeff in his crotch.[14] In the film's final moments the love song has vanished. Instead, Webb has recycled the pastoral music associated with the mountains and lakes around Bridgeport and with Jeff's romance with Ann. This is the music of the paradise we saw at the beginning to which Jeff was hoping to return. The music takes on a note of pathos as the audience has one last look at 'The Kid', the young deaf mute played by Dickie Moore, who has apparently lost the one person in Bridgeport who looked after him. As Miklitsch points out, the film ends with the Kid's silent salute to Jeff and with a great deal more silence about what the film cannot say in its last moments.[15] Roy Webb's lush score tells us as much as we are allowed to hear from the film as it winds down.

The Reporter and the Innocent Woman

The Blue Gardenia begins with its love song playing over the opening credits, and as in *Out of the Past*, the melody of the song segues into a new set of motifs that will be heard throughout the film. But *The Blue Gardenia* has no pastoral settings. The film takes place entirely in Los Angeles. Appropriately, over the opening credits, 'Blue Gardenia' gives way to the music of big-city hustle and bustle as newspaperman Casey Mayo (Richard Conte) and his photographer sidekick Al (Richard Erdman) drive through the streets of LA. The audience will soon learn that Casey has an address book full of the names and phone numbers of the many women he has dated while Al can only dream of sexual success. Appropriately, Casey is driving as Al sleeps in the passenger seat.

Just as 'The First Time I Saw You' is not heard until fifteen minutes into *Out of the Past*, the audience does not hear 'Blue Gardenia' until the film has been running for twenty minutes. During the first minutes of the film Harry Prebble (Raymond Burr) gets close enough to telephone operator Crystal Carpenter (Ann Sothern) to get her phone number, and Norah Larkin (Anne Baxter) receives a letter from her fiancé in Korea telling her that he has fallen in love with a nurse and that he is going to marry her. Norah is alone in the apartment she shares with Crystal and Sally (Jeff Donnell) when she sits down to an elaborate dinner with her absent boyfriend, having arranged it as the appropriate setting to read what she assumes is a heartfelt love letter. When Harry calls for Crystal, Norah has just read the letter with its unexpected message. She takes the call intended for Crystal, and in a moment of despair-driven devil-may-care, she accepts his invitation to dinner. They agree to meet at a Polynesian restaurant, also known as the Blue Gardenia.

The entertainer at the restaurant is Nat King Cole, who sings with a small group on camera as well as with an invisible orchestra playing an arrangement written for the film by Nelson Riddle. The scene designer has created an elaborately detailed set for the restaurant that suggests decadence and something less than good taste or, as Tom Gunning has phrased it, '50s bad taste exoticism'.[16] Even Cole and his sidemen are wearing tacky flowered leis. Cole sits beneath a large mirror that seems designed to show the audience his fingers on the keys but adds to the strained exoticism of the mise-en-scène.

Before Cole sings 'Blue Gardenia', Prebble is plying Norah with a drink called a Polynesian Pearl Diver. In the seconds just before Cole begins to sing, the audience hears a bit of the song non-diegetically as the blind woman who sells flowers in the restaurant approaches Norah and Prebble's table. Although Cole endows the song with his usual elegance, 'Blue Gardenia' has already been associated with the inelegance of a restaurant with the same name as his song.

After Cole does a complete performance of 'Blue Gardenia', Prebble takes

Figure 5.2   Nat King Cole, *The Blue Gardenia*.

Norah to his apartment for more drinks, but only after he has placed Cole's recording of 'Blue Gardenia' on the turntable. At first, the music on the record player is standard seduction fare, but it soon provides what Gorbman has called an 'anempathic' background as Prebble becomes more aggressive.[17] Cole goes on singing and the orchestra goes on making romantic music as if it were oblivious to the imminent rape of Norah. But when a desperate and intoxicated Norah strikes at Prebble with a fireplace poker, composer Raoul Kraushaar plays several expressionist variations on the song, taking it from diegetic to non-diegetic. The recording of 'Blue Gardenia' abruptly ends even though there is no indication that the turntable has been bumped or somehow turned off. Instead, the score provides a dissonant version of 'Blue Gardenia' and then various iterations of the melody's first phrase played against a repeated motif from a harp. The music at this point complements images of swirling liquid and animated pinwheels that are superimposed over Norah as she tries to overcome the effects of too many Polynesian Pearl Divers. The expressionist camera work in this scene does not last long, however. Most of the film is dominated by the highly professional, naturalist cinematography of Nicholas Musuraca, who coincidentally also shot *Out of the Past*.

Kraushaar continues to inject the song into his score throughout most of the rest of the film. In fact, there are more cues with fragments of 'Blue Gardenia' in *The Blue Gardenia* than there are cues from 'The First Time I Saw You' in *Out of the Past*. After the scene in Prebble's apartment, the audience next hears 'Blue Gardenia' while Casey interviews the blind woman who had sold the blue gardenia to Prebble at the restaurant. In this scene, much of the song is heard without the lyrics in a fairly straightforward arrangement as the film re-encounters the sweet old woman who was briefly associated with the song even before it was sung by Cole. The romance in the song is now shifted to pleasant feelings for the blind woman.

A few minutes later, motifs from the song are dropped into the score much more discordantly as Norah becomes increasingly paranoid about being discovered as the murderer of Prebble. Lang sets up the sequence by filming each of the three roommates in bed. Sally is shown first, sleeping peacefully with the latest slasher novel by 'Mickey Mallet' resting on the covers of her bed. (Audiences in the 1950s would have had no trouble associating Mickey Mallet with the notorious but widely read Mike Hammer novels of Mickey Spillane.) Crystal appears to be dreaming, smiling and moving suggestively as she mutters the name of her ex-husband Homer, with whom she is presumably having a more active sex life than when they were married. But Norah is surreptitiously listening to the radio to hear the latest news about the murder she thinks she has committed. She then climbs out of bed to burn the dress she wore on the night she was in Prebble's apartment. As Janet Bergstrom has suggested, Norah does not live in a supportive, homosocial woman's world.[18] And Gunning writes, 'The fantasy life of these frustrated and lonely young women consists of sex and violence and perhaps involves an equation between the two'.[19] I would add that the roommates are only minimally attentive to Norah. Meanwhile, Norah sees police everywhere she turns. It is into this environment that Kraushaar inserts several fragments of the song.

'Blue Gardenia' is heard bombastically a few minutes later when Casey writes a newspaper story, 'Open Letter to an Unknown Murderess', in hopes of locating the woman who has become known in the press as 'The Blue Gardenia' because of the flower from the restaurant that was left behind in Prebble's apartment. The music plays prominently over shots of a newspaper printing press. As variations on the song appear in the score, Lang creates a montage with people from various walks of life reading their copy of the *Los Angeles Chronicle* with Casey's headline taking up the entire front page. An oboe plays an eroticised version of a motif from the song as the camera briefly shows a louche blonde woman smoking while she reads the paper in bed. When the montage ends, Norah is alone in her apartment reading Casey's story. As Bergstrom points out, Norah reads the 'letter' written to her by Casey in a camera set-up deliberately designed to recall her position at the table when she read the break-up letter from her ex-fiancé. Bergstrom even produces a passage from *The Blue Gardenia*'s shooting script explicitly stating that the second scene should recall the earlier one.[20] Although Norah believes that Casey is writing to her with sincerity, the film clearly suggests that he is betraying her as surely as she was betrayed by her fiancé.

When Casey actually meets Norah in a diner, he plays the Nat King Cole recording on the jukebox. Practically the entire song with Cole's vocal can be heard behind their conversation. For a moment it seems as if 'Blue Gardenia' might become the love song that unites Norah and Casey, driving out the film's association of Norah with the oleaginous and murdered Prebble. But Casey is motivated almost entirely by his narcissistic need to file a hot story, and he is ultimately responsible for setting up Norah to be arrested. The second-last time the audience hears the 'Blue Gardenia' theme is more than ten minutes before the end of the film. Just the first four notes of the melody are played as the sleazy counterman at the restaurant where Casey and Norah had met acknowledges that he is the one who overheard their conversation and phoned the police. The exact same version of the cue plays a few seconds later when Norah is being fingerprinted at the police station. Appropriately, it is just a smattering of the melody in this farewell to the tune.

As in *Out of the Past*, audiences do not hear 'Blue Gardenia' in the final moments of *The Blue Gardenia*. Rather, they hear several cues in quick succession: the triumphant march that anchors the justice insignia on the floor of the courthouse; the fluid melody that connotes camaraderie among the three female roommates; the music of big-city bustle as the camera cuts back to Mayo; the chromatic descending tones that accompany Casey's address book full of women's names and phone numbers as it flies into the waiting hands of Al; the appropriate wolf-whistle effect as Al pages through the address book; and finally a symphonic gesture of closure that recycles the big-city music that was played over the opening credits. This closing music suggests that Casey and Norah may have a new beginning without the baggage of a murder and Norah's arrest. The certainty of reconciliation and a romance, however, is undermined by a camera set-up in the final scene: 'the insignia of the Hall of Justice appears to descend over Norah's head like a noose'.[21]

Rip Van Marlowe

Many of the films that Robert Altman directed during the heady days of the 1970s were revisions of familiar genre pictures. Like many of his peers in the 'New Hollywood', he was deeply suspicious of the kinds of films that Hollywood had been cranking out for so many years while at the same time he was fascinated by their conventions. Like Martin Scorsese, Francis Ford Coppola and Arthur Penn, he would make films that resembled familiar genre movies, but his films parodied or 'corrected' the old genres.[22] After revising the war film with *M*A*S*H* (1970) and the western with *McCabe and Mrs. Miller* (1971), Altman would have his way with the gangster film (*Thieves Like Us*, 1974), the buddy film (*California Split*, 1974), the musical (*Nashville*, 1975) and science fiction (*Quintet*, 1979). Altman says that he was not determined to revise the hard-boiled detective film, but that he was intrigued by a script that Leigh Brackett had taken from a detective novel by Raymond Chandler, *The Long Goodbye*. Brackett had previously worked on the screenplay for the 1946 classic *The Big Sleep*, also based on a Chandler novel, in which Humphrey Bogart played the definitive Philip Marlowe. Brackett co-wrote the screenplay for *The Big Sleep* with none other than William Faulkner. But Altman may have been more interested in Brackett because she had worked on the 1946 film with Howard Hawks, a director Altman greatly admired.

Altman claims that the Chandler novel was effectively unreadable, but he liked Brackett's ending in which Marlowe kills his friend Terry Lennox because he betrayed their friendship. Altman knew enough about the book to know that this is not how the novel ends. He told Jerry Bick and Elliott Kastner – who owned the rights to the novel – that he would direct the film on two conditions: that they didn't change the ending and that they didn't cast Robert Mitchum as Marlowe.[23] When shooting began, Altman decided to set the film in present-day southern California. But he also decided to make his Philip Marlowe (Elliott Gould) a mostly faithful rendering of the character created by Chandler. Altman saw Chandler's novels as clothes lines on which the author could hang 'little thumbnail essays' about his city and his times even when they were largely unrelated to his mostly incoherent plots.[24] Also more important than the plot was Chandler's character Phillip Marlowe who, as a private eye, was uniquely positioned as an outsider who could resist the corrupting pressures of American institutions. As Terence Rafferty has written, Altman's and Elliott Gould's Marlowe was 'solitary, rumpled, nicotine-dependent, irreverent of power both legitimate (the cops) and illegitimate (the crooks), and weirdly, stubbornly gallant'.[25] Marlowe's integrity leads him to kill Terry Lennox (Jim Bouton), even if Chandler was not willing to take his Marlowe quite that far.

In order to place the 'authentic' Marlowe of the 1940s in present-day Hollywood, Altman created what he has called 'Rip Van Marlowe', as if the private detective had been asleep for thirty years and suddenly found himself in the California of the early 1970s. Elliott Gould's Marlowe drives a vintage car, calls a stray dog 'Asta' (the name of the pet in the *Thin Man* movies of the 1930s and 1940s) and uses the term 'looney tunes' to describe crazy people. He tells the man in the hospital who is entirely covered in bandages that he has seen all of his films, referring to either the *Mummy* films or the *Invisible Man* films, also from the 1930s and 1940s. And Marlowe is the only character in the film who smokes, and he smokes almost as much as the characters in *Out of the Past*.

Altman's 'provocative mash-up of anti-noir and neo-noir'[26] is as aware of Hollywood tradition as is Marlowe, but that tradition is not treated with nostalgic affection. It is mostly about the hucksterism, violence and wasted lives of Hollywood then and now. Appropriately, the film begins with a raucous version of 'Hooray for Hollywood' that announces even before we have finished seeing the United Artists logo that *The Long Goodbye* is profoundly suspicious of American cinema. The scratchy recording of the tune comes directly from one of the lesser films of Busby Berkeley, *Hollywood Hotel* (1938). The opening and closing quotations from that film's soundtrack constitute the only music in the film that is not a version of Williams' and Mercer's 'The Long Goodbye'.

Robert Altman had worked with John Williams in 1964 when Williams wrote the score for a pilot for a television series that went nowhere. Directed by Altman, the pilot was shown as the made-for-TV movie *Nightmare in Chicago*. Altman and Williams would work together a few years later on Altman's Bergmanesque puzzle film, *Images* (1972). By this time, Williams was establishing himself as a more than reliable writer for television series. A year after *The Long Goodbye* he would hook up with Steven Spielberg to make *Sugarland Express* (1974), and he was on his way. So far as I can tell, Altman asked Williams and Mercer to write a legitimate love song that was reminiscent of 1940s noir. He almost certainly did not tell them that only portions of the song would ever be heard. Sheet music for a complete version of the song is in the Altman archives at the University of Michigan. It is indeed a lovely song – much more effective than the clunky songs of Leonard Cohen in *McCabe and Mrs. Miller* – and I am surprised that no one seems to have recorded it after the release of the film.[27]

The song 'The Long Goodbye' is heard only seconds after the burst of 'Hooray for Hollywood' at the very beginning of the film. The song is played softly by the Dave Grusin Trio during a five-minute introductory section in which Gould's Marlowe mostly deals with his cat. The song becomes much more prominent as the opening credits roll and the camera cuts to Terry Lennox in his car. This version of the song, with a vocal by trumpeter Jack Sheldon over the Grusin Trio, seems to be emerging from the radio in Terry's car. For the next several minutes, Altman cuts back and forth between Terry's car with Sheldon singing, Marlowe's car in which the radio is playing a version with female vocalist Clydie King and a store where a syrupy muzak version of the song is being piped in. Still another version, all light and jazzy, plays either diegetically or non-diegetically back at Marlowe's apartment. In less than four minutes we have heard five different versions of the tune. We cannot help but notice the song, if only because each version is constantly being cut short while another suddenly pops up on the soundtrack *in medias res*.

The song continues to reappear in different forms and musical genres. When Marlowe drops Terry off at the Mexican border, the song is played by a flamenco guitar with castanets. After a music-less stretch of about twelve minutes, we hear Jack Riley fumbling with the tune on the piano in the bar where Marlowe picks up his messages. Riley says he is trying to learn it. The first four notes of 'The Long Goodbye' also constitute the sound of the doorbell at the estate of Eileen and Roger Wade. When Marty Augustine's girlfriend (Jo Ann Brody) turns on a car radio, we hear still another vocal version, this time featuring a pop singer named Morgan Ames. Later, an unidentified saxophone player takes on the tune and, after that, Marty himself clumsily sings it a cappella. More than halfway through the film, Marlowe goes to Mexico to look into the supposed suicide of Terry Lennox, and we see the Tepoztlan Municipal Band marching and playing the song as funeral music. Altman even lets us see the sheet music that he has taped to the back of the musicians so that they can read as they march.[28] Late in the film, in a moment that seems intentionally confusing, we hear the song played by the Grusin Trio at an even volume as the camera cuts back and forth between Eileen in her car and Marlowe running after her. Although it does not seem to be on the car radio, Eileen suddenly begins humming along. Near the end, when Marlowe returns to Mexico, we again hear flamenco guitar and then a new wordless version with trumpet and saxophone. As Marlowe walks down the tree-lined path to kill Terry, we hear a slower version of the tune on guitar. Returning to the path after shooting Terry, Marlowe is accompanied by still another guitar version, this time with strings playing in a minor key. Marlowe seems to be celebrating his revenge on Terry by playing his tiny harmonica in a surprisingly musical fashion. Then we get a reprise of 'Hooray for Hollywood'. As the credits roll, we hear more of the version of the song that opens *Hollywood Hotel* (1938), including a feature for the strident tenor of Johnny 'Scat' Davis. We also hear vocal inflections from various members of the Benny Goodman band – Harry James, Gene Krupa and Frances Langford. Only Langford sounds like a real vocalist.

I can't help wondering if Altman was referring to *Out of the Past* when Marlowe goes to Mexico to search for Terry, in the same way that Jeff had gone looking for Kathie in Acapulco. Just as 'The First Time I Saw You' was played by a violinist in a cantina in Acapulco, so Marlowe hears 'The Long Goodbye' played by the Mexican marching band. But Altman has taken the games of the monotheme film much further, eliminating all of the generic background music that plays through *Out of the Past*, *The Blue Gardenia* and the vast majority of classic noirs when the main theme is not on the soundtrack. Jonathan Rosenbaum, one of the few critics who has more than a few words to say about the music in *The Long Goodbye*, compares the music in the film to cinematographer Vilmos Zsigmond's constantly moving camera that is always forcing the audience to focus and refocus on the action. 'We are required, in other words, to improvise our own "Long Goodbye," both figuratively and literally, in order to establish our proximity to all the others'.[29] Writing in 1975, Rosenbaum was right to assert that Altman had gone further than any other filmmaker in asking audience members to enter into the film on their own terms. And of course, this is what Altman would continue to do for the rest of his career.

KNOWING THE SCORE

Except for the vanishing love songs, there is nothing unusual about the music in *Out of the Past* and *The Blue Gardenia*, just as the music for *The Long Goodbye* is nothing special to anyone who is not listening carefully. Both *Out of the Past* and *The Blue Gardenia* are suffused with music for approximately half of their running time, and the constant reappearance of bits of melody throughout the films is standard operating procedure for the Classical Hollywood score. Each time a familiar melody reappears, it seems to have been carefully orchestrated to fit the dramatic circumstances. The rest of the score includes several motifs that are not taken from the opening song but that are similarly designed to 'anchor' the meaning of the action with music.[30] Again, none of this is unusual. Consider the case of Max Steiner, perhaps the most typical composer for Classical Hollywood. As Gorbman has shown in some detail, Steiner regularly recycled themes throughout one of the many films he scored at Warner Bros., Michael Curtiz's *Mildred Pierce* (1945).[31] After identifying five principal themes that dominate the score, Gorbman writes, 'The melodies are treated in conventional ways to fit each narrative context in which they appear. Variations in tonality, register, harmonic accompaniment, time signature, rhythm, and instrumentation alter their sound and mood'.[32] Much the same can be said of countless scores for films, both old and new. Think of the themes by John Williams that we know so well from *Star Wars* films and how they are so clearly designed for specific characters and places. In Altman's film, Williams was just as careful to come up with appropriate versions of 'The Long Goodbye' for a struggling cocktail pianist, the muzak in a grocery store, the radio in a gambler's sports car and a bus trip to Mexico. Of course, Williams may not have anticipated the perverse playfulness with which Altman truncated the various versions and made it difficult for audiences to decide what was diegetic and what is not.

The music for *Out of the Past* and *The Blue Gardenia* functions according to the same rules that Max Steiner was following and that John Williams has always followed. Perhaps as a result, the two older films seem to require that their love songs disappear. On the one hand, the songs have been contaminated by their connection to romances that turn murderous, and there is no place to put the music as the films conclude. On the other hand, one cannot ignore the fact that both songs are introduced diegetically by African-American artists. In this sense it can be argued that they were 'contaminated' from the outset. By no means am I suggesting that the writers, directors or producers of either film were racists who deliberately used black people to connote darkness and crime. Quite the contrary. As Thomas Cripps has exhaustively demonstrated, Hollywood made serious attempts to find work for African-Americans and often to portray them in positive ways.[33] Hollywood liberals were especially determined that movies should strive to integrate blacks into the mainstream of American life. The dignified behaviour of the black characters at the nightclub in *Out of the Past* and the charm and romance projected by Nat King Cole in *The Blue Gardenia* surely testify to the filmmakers' good intentions.

Nevertheless, the filmmakers were creatures of their era, and even though neither Jacques Tourneur nor Fritz Lang was raised in America, they were immersed in the entrenched conventions of Hollywood cinema. Whether they were fully conscious of it or not, they did not shake the boat as they navigated the ideological waters. As I mentioned earlier, William Luhr has argued that in *Out of the Past*, Jeff's journey through the underworld of African-Americans and Mexicans to find Kathie suggests that she belongs to that world much more than to the normative world of white Americans. In this sense, it does not matter how dignified the blacks at the nightclub appear to be or how much respect Jeff grants them. Of course, Jose Rodriguez (Tony Roux) is treated as a mostly comic character out for a quick buck. The important thing is that blacks and Mexicans were consistently othered in postwar American culture, and the codes of the cinema were working according to plan when femme fatale Kathie is associated with them.

Nat King Cole was among the few black entertainers to have real appeal for white Americans in the 1950s. He even had his own television programme on NBC for an entire year in 1956 and 1957. It was the first time that a major network had starred a black performer in a regularly scheduled programme, and there would not be another network television programme with an African-American host until Sammy Davis Jr's brief tenure on NBC in 1966.[34] In spite of Cole's cross-racial appeal, in *The Blue Gardenia* he could easily be associated by whites with the tacky exoticism of the Polynesian restaurant and with the unscrupulous womanising of Harry Prebble. In the popular imagination, black musicians, especially black jazz musicians, lived in a world of drugs, heavy drinking and loose sexuality. Cole's voice is present, after all, at the opening of that extremely paranoid film noir, Robert Aldrich's *Kiss Me Deadly* (1955), which starred Ralph Meeker as Mike Hammer. Harry Belafonte has a prominent role in Robert Wise's late noir, *Odds Against Tomorrow* (1959), but Nat King Cole is surely the single most seen and heard black performer in all of film noir. In *The Blue Gardenia*, Cole is constantly beneath the bizarrely tilted mirror that foregrounds him – he was, after all, an extremely popular entertainer with a long list of hit records. But the mirror also marginalises him, turning him into a part of the commodified and suspect exoticism of the restaurant.[35]

No one associated with *Out of the Past* or *The Blue Gardenia* was objectively trying to slow the progress of African-Americans towards full equality. They invited talented black artists into their films and let them display their talents in full. They did not ask Theresa Harris, Nat King Cole or any other black performer to act out minstrel stereotypes. But on a deeper level, the filmmakers were unable to free themselves from myths that were still present in postwar America. And they were certainly unwilling to assault the prejudices of the many whites in their audiences. Ultimately, the love songs in *Out of the Past* and *The Blue Gardenia* were contaminated at least in part by race, and therefore they had to vanish, even in an industry that was almost as interested in promoting popular songs as in promoting popular films.

The situation is different with *The Long Goodbye*. The otherness of Mexico and the corrupt officials that covered up the disappearance of Terry Lennox hardly rubs off on Lennox's character. I would not argue that the film's portrayal of Mexican poverty and seediness is part of some racist subtext. Terry Lennox is a creature of the amoral culture of Los Angeles in the 1970s, and the plot mechanics that lead him to kill and be killed are straight out of the film noir handbook. The otherness in the film comes from Hollywood itself. Altman's critique of Hollywood has driven him to interrupt even a song as lovely as the one John Williams and Johnny Mercer wrote for *The Long Goodbye*.

Notes

1. For what it's worth, the novel on which *Laura* is based was written by Vera Caspary, who also wrote the short story that is the source for the plot of *The Blue Gardenia*.
2. Jeff Smith, *The Sounds of Commerce: Marketing Popular Film Music* (New York: Columbia University Press, 1988).
3. Ibid., p. 17.
4. Christopher Palmer, *The Composer in Hollywood* (New York: Marion Boyars, 1990), p. 169.
5. Henry Mancini, excerpt from *Did They Mention the Music?* (1989), in Mervyn Cooke (ed.), *The Hollywood Film Music Reader* (Oxford and New York: Oxford University Press, 2010), p. 196.
6. Robert Miklitsch, *Siren City: Sound and Source Music in Classic American Noir* (New Brunswick, NJ: Rutgers University Press, 2011), p. 20.
7. Richard Dyer, 'White', *Screen* 29(4) (1988), 44–65.
8. James Naremore, *More than Night: Film Noir in its Contexts* (Berkeley, CA: University of California Press, 1998), p. 240.
9. Ibid., p. 240.
10. William Luhr, *Film Noir* (Malden, MA: Wiley-Blackwell, 2012), p. 114.
11. Ibid., p. 113.
12. Claudia Gorbman, *Unheard Melodies: Narrative Film Music* (Bloomington, IN: Indiana University Press, 1987), p. 73.
13. Frank Krutnik, *In a Lonely Street: Film Noir, Genre, Masculinity* (New York: Routledge, 1991).
14. Luhr, *Film Noir*, p. 105.
15. Miklitsch, *Siren City*, p. 254.
16. Tom Gunning, *The Films of Fritz Lang: Allegories of Vision and Modernity* (London: British Film Institute, 2000), p. 400.

17. Gorbman, *Unheard Melodies*, p. 24.
18. Janet Bergstrom, 'The mystery of *The Blue Gardenia*', in Joan Copjec (ed.), *Shades of Noir* (New York: Verso, 1993), p. 109.
19. Gunning, *Films of Fritz Lang*, p. 403.
20. Bergstrom, 'Mystery', p. 108.
21. Ibid., p. 107.
22. The term '"corrected" genre movie' was coined by Robert B. Ray in *A Certain Tendency of the Hollywood Cinema, 1930–1980* (Princeton, NJ: Princeton University Press, 1985), p. 327.
23. Michael Wilmington, 'Robert Altman and *The Long Goodbye*', in David Sterritt (ed.), *Robert Altman: Interviews* (Jackson, MS: University of Mississippi Press, 2000), p. 137. Mitchum was cast as Philip Marlowe in *Farewell My Lovely*, a 1975 remake of *Murder, My Sweet* (1944). He would reprise the role in the 1978 retread of *The Big Sleep*. I'm guessing that Altman knew something about Mitchum being up for the role a few years before filming began on *Farewell My Lovely*.
24. Ibid., p. 135.
25. Terence Rafferty, 'Revisiting Altman's *The Long Goodbye*', *New York Times*, 13 April 2007, online at www.nytimes.com/2007/04/11/arts/11iht-chandler.1.5233762.html?pagewanted=all&_r=0
26. Jeremy Kaye, 'Hard-boiled nebbish: The Jewish Humphrey Bogart in Robert Altman's *The Long Goodbye* and Woody Allen's *Play It Again, Sam*', in Rick Armstrong (ed.), *Robert Altman: Critical Essays* (Jefferson, NC: McFarland, 2011), p. 132.
27. My search through Tom Lord's online *The Jazz Discography* turns up several recordings of tunes called 'The Long Goodbye.' See www.lordisco.com/tjd/TuneDetail?tid=1577. But one is by pianist Alan Broadbent, and another is by the jazz composer and conductor Butch Morris. If there are recordings of the Williams/Mercer song, they can only be on obscure labels because I could not locate a single one on iTunes.
28. Altman reveals this information in the featurette that accompanies the 2002 DVD release of *The Long Goodbye*.
29. Jonathan Rosenbaum, 'Improvisations and interactions in Altmanville', *Monthly Film Bulletin* 44(2) (1975), 95.
30. Gorbman has taken the term 'ancrage' from Roland Barthes's comments on how captions beneath photos in magazines anchor polysemous images to specific meanings. Similarly, movie music 'enforces an interpretation' of a complicated set of images. See Gorbman, *Unheard Melodies*, p. 32.
31. Ibid., pp. 91–8.
32. Ibid., p. 95.
33. Thomas Cripps, *Making Movies Black: The Hollywood Message Movie from World War II to the Civil Rights Era* (New York: Oxford University Press, 1993).
34. Krin Gabbard, *Jammin' at the Margins: Jazz and the American Cinema* (Chicago, IL: University of Chicago Press, 1996), p. 245.
35. I thank Robert Miklitsch for suggesting this reading of the scene.

6. SPLIT SCREEN: SOUND/MUSIC IN *THE STRANGER/CRISS CROSS*

Robert Miklitsch

Robert Siodmak and Orson Welles are both central figures in the history of sound film. As Deborah Lazaroff Alpi observes, all of Siodmak's early sound films such as *Abschied* (1930) 'are distinctive for their exceptionally sophisticated use of sound'.[1] The same, of course, could be said about Welles' early films. For example, with its expressive deployment of 'lightning mixes' and overlapping audio, 'pan' and 'deep-focus' sound, *Citizen Kane* (1941) is the prototype of the modern sound film.[2] Siodmak and Welles are also central to the history of film noir. Siodmak not only helmed a number of seminal proto-noirs such as, in Germany, *Der Mann, der seinen Mörder sucht* (1931), *Voruntersuchung* (1931) and *Stürme der Leidenschaft* (1932) as well as, in France, *Pièges* (1939), but the ten films noirs that he directed in the United States between 1944 and 1949 – *Phantom Lady* (1944), *Christmas Holiday* (1944), *The Suspect* (1945), *The Strange Affair of Uncle Harry* (1945), *The Spiral Staircase* (1945), *The Dark Mirror* (1946), *The Killers* (1946), *Cry of the City* (1948), *Criss Cross* (1949) and *The File on Thelma Jordon* (1950) – 'are regarded by many film critics and scholars as the quintessence of the genre'.[3]

Although Welles' contribution as a director to the genre is not nearly as voluminous as Siodmak's, his films noirs encompass almost the entire history of the genre, from *Citizen Kane*, arguably the Ur-American film noir, to *Touch of Evil* (1958), for many the baroque culmination of the classical period. At the same time, if it's true that Siodmak is more closely associated with film noir than Welles (Welles, like Hitchcock, tends to retain a certain genre-transcendent status), none of Siodmak's films has received the sort of critical attention, especially with regard to their soundtracks, that *The Lady from Shanghai* (1948) or *Touch of Evil*,[4] not to mention *Citizen Kane*, has.

For this last reason, my attention in this chapter is split between subject (Welles/Siodmak) and topic (sound/music). More specifically, given the aforementioned critical literature on Welles, the first part concentrates on the play of silence and ambient sound in what has traditionally been considered both a minor Welles film and marginal film noir, *The Stranger* (1946). Reversing track, the second part rack-focuses on what is arguably Siodmak's most accomplished film noir, *Criss Cross*, as a way to engage a more inclusive notion of 'music'. Here, instead of bracketing the score to map the sonic landscape as I do in the first part, I bracket the use of ambient sound or acoustic effects in order to explore the notion of music understood not simply as 'background' or 'source' music but as voiceover narration.

Sound: Mapping the Sound 'Score' of *The Stranger*

While Welles remains one of the most innovative sound directors in Classical Hollywood cinema, he later claimed to have made *The Stranger* in order to 'prove to the industry that [he] could direct a standard Hollywood picture'.[5] Critics, not surprisingly, have taken the director at his word. Thus, in *Hello, Americans* (2006), Simon Callow writes that the use of sound in *The Stranger* is 'negligible'.[6]

However, since Welles' pronouncements are famously unreliable, the absence of what Callow calls a 'sound score'[7] for *The Stranger* should be taken *cum grano salis*. In fact, as Gene D. Phillips observes in *Out of the Shadows* (2012), 'The picture is a good deal better than Welles was prepared to admit'.[8] Although *The Stranger*, originally titled *Date with Destiny*, was subject to extensive pre- and post-editing, it has not only 'found a niche in the canon of film noir'[9] but, as a 'close listening' to it suggests (the recording was supervised by Corson F. Jowett, who also worked on *The Chase* (1946) and *Kiss the Blood off My Hands* (1948)),[10] *The Stranger* possesses a remarkably sophisticated soundtrack.

After an opening credit sequence scored by Bronislau Kaper, *The Stranger* opens with the sound-image of a woman closing the door on a meeting of the Allied War Crimes Commission in Czechoslovakia. The film then dissolves to a high-angle shot of the back of a man's head. The man, who is gesticulating with his pipe as he speaks ('Leave the cell door open'), is Inspector Wilson (Edward G. Robinson), and he wants to release an ex-Nazi prisoner named Konrad Meinike (Konstanin Shayne) in order to locate another ex-Nazi, Franz Kindler (Welles), the originator of the 'theory of genocide'.

While the other members of the commission prevaricate ('It might entail the most embarrassing repercussions'), Welles uses the concert of their voices ('*Exactement*', 'Certainly') to set up the film's first decisive sound effect. Passionately arguing that 'this obscenity must be destroyed!' Wilson breaks his pipe in two while gesturing violently towards a wooden table, a dramatic gesture that is emphasised – simultaneous with a sharp downward tilt of the camera – by a stinger on the soundtrack.

In the succeeding disembarkation scene set in South America,[11] a customs official asks Meinike, 'Your business in this country?', and Meinike repeats the answer he has been practising as if it were a prayer, 'I am travelling for my health'. When the customs official asks Meinike what country he is from, Meinike replies, 'Poland' as the camera rapidly cranes up to a shot of Wilson standing next to a woman – his face obscured, like the woman's, by a concrete slab – and knocking his pipe against a guardrail.[12] The message is clear as Morse code: Wilson, whose 'wide-brimmed hat and rumpled coat' are reminiscent of the 'typical film noir detective',[13] is trailing the 'little man' like a shadow.

The final scene of the extended opening sequence foreshadows the later 'projection' scene that constitutes the audiovisual centrepiece of *The Stranger*. While the passport photographer tells Meinike to 'Hold it', Meinike's unsmiling face sans hat is reflected, juxtaposed to the photographer's animated one, in the camera lens.

Meinike utters the name of Franz Kindler and, in a striking point of synchronisation, the photographer clicks off his light, eclipsing Meinike's image. The photographer claims that 'Franz Kindler is dead', but Meinike announces, 'I have a message for you from the All Highest', at which point the photographer hands him a postcard, phonetically pronouncing the address written on the back, 'Con-nec-ti-cut', as if it were some exotic country. When Meinike turns the postcard over, the front shows a picture of a clock tower and the film cuts

Figure 6.1   Konrad Meinike (Konstanin Shayne) captured in the lens, *The Stranger*.

on a live match shot to 'Harper, CT, USA', a dissolve that effectively 'eliminates any perception of distance between the noir landscape of Europe and South America and the life-as-usual happiness of small-town Connecticut'.[14]

The first distinctive sound effect in Harper acts as a segue from the first to the second part of *The Stranger*. A Grayline bus arrives in downtown Harper, and as Meinike gets up and reaches for his luggage, the man behind him knocks down a pipe, which lands with a light thud on the seat. Although the man, Wilson, says 'Excuse me', Meinike knows it is no accident. This tense moment is followed by a classic passage of Wellesian comic relief: after Meinike enters Potter's Drugstore as Wilson approaches the outside service window, the owner, Solomon Potter (Billy House), is heartily laughing along to a comedy programme on the radio: 'The hotel room was so small every time I closed the door the knob got into bed with me. You know how cold brass knobs are on a winter night'. In another Wellesian acoustic touch, Potter's laughter is mixed with a distinct, bell-like sound, the ring of his cash register. It's a sly but provocative bit of sound montage: another ex-Nazi has arrived in the sleepy, picture-perfect town of Harper, Connecticut, but business continues as usual, regular as clockwork.

Meinike's subsequent escape with Wilson in hot pursuit is articulated via various sound effects: a honking car as Meinike runs across a street, a slamming door as he enters the Harper School for Boys (based on the Todd School that Welles attended as a boy) and a swinging practice weight that Meinike, standing on a balcony overlooking the gymnasium, sends thudding into Wilson's head, knocking him down and, momentarily, out. Meinike is now free to contact Franz Kindler, aka Charles Rankin, a history instructor at the Harper School for Boys. To highlight Meinike and Kindler's reunion, Welles employs counterpoint: Meinike, hidden in some bushes, calls out to his former superior as Rankin is walking across the town square and, for the first time in the film, ambient 'colour' – bird song – becomes audible. The thematic subtext of the scene, natural innocence versus human experience, is reinforced on the soundtrack by the boyish cries of Rankin's students who, catching up with him, invite him on a 'paper chase'.

The 'paper chase' sequence is a bravura passage in *The Stranger*. While the young men's voices carry offscreen in the crystalline autumn air, Rankin leads Meinike out of the open sunlight and into the dark of the woods, along the way bragging about his 'camouflage':

> Guess what I'll be doing at six o'clock tonight? Standing before a minister of the gospel with a woman's hand in mine, the daughter of a justice of the United States Supreme Court, a famous liberal ... Who would think to look for the notorious Franz Kindler in the sacred precincts of the Harper School surrounded by the sons of America's first families?

The peroration of Rankin's monologue ('I'll stay here [in Harper] until we strike again') is marked by one of the most suggestive, albeit subtle, sound effects in *The Stranger*. After Meinike asks, 'There will be another war?' and Rankin answers 'Of course', a train can be heard whistling offscreen. The significance of this 'locomotive' sound only becomes apparent *après coup* – after, that is, the subsequent 'projection' sequence during which Wilson screens documentary footage of the concentration camps.

If the sequence set at Potter's Drugstore comments on the closed society of Harper and the 'paper chase' on Rankin's double nature (his collegial relationship with his students versus his murderous past as a former Nazi leader), the third soundscape of *The Stranger* involves his wife Mary's (Loretta Young) golden retriever, Red. At a dinner party to celebrate the married couple's return from their honeymoon, Red comes whimpering up to the table and, as Mary feeds him, her father Adam Longstreet (Philip Merivale) says, 'Good thing you're back. That dog of yours has been inconsolable'. That night, Mary and Charles return to their new house and Charles, despite her protestations, takes Red out for a walk in the woods. However, when Red starts scratching at Meinike's fresh grave, Charles starts chasing him. The ensuing straight cut – an arresting piece of audiovisual montage – recollects one of the director's seminal influences, Eisenstein. After Rankin viciously kicks Red because he won't stop pawing at the grave, the film cuts to Wilson sitting bolt upright in bed, as if the kick has awakened him. (In actuality, Wilson has suddenly remembered a telling comment that Rankin made at dinner, 'Marx wasn't a German, he was a Jew'.)

In a scene that both mirrors and contrasts with Wilson's awakening, Rankin returns home and steals into the bedroom where his wife is fast asleep, his body casting an enormous shadow on the wall above her headboard. Mary wakes, like Wilson, with a start: 'I was dreaming about that little man'. After she recounts her dream to her husband ('Wherever he moved he threw a shadow, but when he moved away the shadow stayed there behind him'), Red starts barking, then yelping, offscreen. When Charles explains he has put him in the cellar, Mary responds, 'I don't believe in dogs being treated like prisoners. Red's my dog', but Charles overrules her, leaving her wide-eyed and awake in bed while Red continues to whine offscreen.

The various noises that Red makes – barking, yelping, whimpering – are retrospectively reaccentuated when we see Mary's brother, Noah (Richard Long), walking out of the woods with the dog dead and silent in his arms: 'Poor old Red. He heard my whistle I'll bet, but he couldn't bark or anything'. Noah and Wilson proceed to Dr Lawrence's office, located above Potter's Drugstore, where we learn (the men's voices, heard behind glass, are naturalistically muffled) that Red was poisoned. As Noah and Wilson sombrely exit the doctor's office, a passing cyclist rings his bell, as if tolling Red's passing, then, as

Figure 6.2 Mary (Loretta Young) watches concentration camp footage, *The Stranger*.

the men cross the square, Noah asks Wilson, 'What does the law say about this kind of murder? Is it the same as killing a man?'

Noah's question convinces Wilson that it is finally time to confront Mary with the truth about her husband. After Mr Longstreet calls his daughter at home (the ringing phone interrupts Charles' confession to Mary that he's willing to turn himself in to the police for killing Meinike),[15] she goes to her father's house where, in his study, Wilson shows her a photo of Meinike – the 'commandant in charge of the one of the more efficient Nazi concentration camps' – after which he screens 'some films' for her. While the 16mm projector whirs and the projection light flickers on Mary's face, Wilson describes the images on the screen: massed dead bodies, a gas chamber, a lime pit.[16]

'All these things you're seeing,' he tells Mary, are the 'product of one mind, the mind of a man named Franz Kindler'. Wilson goes on to explain that Kindler disappeared after the war, so the only way to locate him was to release his 'one-time executive officer', Meinike: 'He led me here, and here I lost him – until yesterday. Your dog Red found him for me'. Welles caps Wilson's exposé ('Now in all the world there's only one person who can identify Franz Kindler') with a startling audiovisual effect: the sound of the film running out and clacking loudly against the reel.[17]

In *Audio-Vision* Michael Chion writes that 'with film we can . . . say that the image is projected and the sound is a projector in the sense that the latter projects meaning and values onto the image'.[18] There is perhaps no better example of this phenomenon than the above 'projector' sequence from *The Stranger* in which the running projection underscores, like some abstract, atonal music, the terrible black-and-white images on the screen. The clacking of the film represents not only the stuttering of Mary's consciousness, her inability to come to terms with the truth about her husband's identity, it also marks an impasse or *aporia* at the very heart of *The Stranger*, a lacuna that no sound or image, no sound-image, can adequately represent.

The last part of *The Stranger*, at least in terms of its sound arc, is the densest and revolves around the antique bell imported from Strasbourg that Rankin has been busy repairing throughout the course of the film. (Wilson's only real clue to Rankin's identity has been the latter's 'mania for clocks'.) The clock tower where the bell is housed can first be seen in the title sequence, and Rankin himself comments at one point on the 'incongruity of a Gothic clock in a Connecticut clock tower'. Indeed, the initial 'freeze frame' of Harper suggests that the town has 'stayed fixed in time',[19] a reading that's reinforced by Mary's passing remark in the original script about the effect that the running clock will have on Harper: 'the whole character of the town might undergo a change. I'm sure it's not very different from the Harper of the eighteenth century. Perhaps that's because the clock hands have never moved'.[20]

In the immediate wake of Wilson's demonstration of Rankin's secret life, Mary flees from her father's arms to the clock tower[21] where she climbs the ladder to join her husband in the belfry. Rankin announces, 'It's striking' and, offscreen, the residents of Harper can be heard running up excitedly to look and listen as the formerly still automatons – a gilded angel, sword in hand, and a grimacing demon – start to move, the angel chasing the devil across the face of the clock. 'That angel started marching,' Potter exclaims, 'and it was a sight to behold'. From this point on, the town of Harper begins to wake from its slumber (Potter observes, 'If it's gonna strike all night, how's a body to get any sleep?'), a transformation that is paralleled on the audio track by the proliferating sound of bells.

Mary, suddenly concerned about the 'sunlight', is drawing the living room curtains in her home when the doorbell rings ('That time already?'), signalling the arrival of guests for her tea party. At the party, a woman complains to Rankin, 'I wish you'd left that clock alone. Harper was a nice quiet place until it began banging'. Later, after Mary's father warns the housemaid that his daughter's life is in danger, the film cuts to a rapidly rising crane shot set to a sawing sound succeeded by a low-angle deep-focus shot of Rankin – 'like a distant spider spinning its web'[22] – sawing away at the clock-tower ladder. The bell chimes and the camera cuts (in an echo of the earlier sonic 'shock' effect) first to Wilson in his hotel room smoking his pipe, looking out of a window, then to Mary in bed, fitfully trying to sleep.

As Rankin plots to eliminate his wife, bells continue to dominate the soundtrack. The next day Rankin is crossing things off a to-do list ('3:25 Phone Mary') when a bell rings in the background, marking the beginning of his German history class at the Harper School for Boys. At 3:25 p.m., he places a coin in the phone at Potter's Drugstore and a small bell rings. While he's waiting for the connection and Potter is ringing up another sale on the cash register, Rankin is simultaneously humming 'Deutschland über alles' and drawing a swastika on the notepad next to the phone. Having completed his phone call, Rankin, still humming, walks over to where Potter is playing checkers just as, offscreen, Peabody drops some firewood he has brought in for the stove, a sonic reminder that Rankin's infernal plan is now underway: when Mary reaches the top of the belfry ladder, the rung will break and she will fall to her death.

At 3:45 p.m., Rankin leaves Potter's Drugstore and returns home, the location of two rhyming offscreen sound effects. The first occurs when he enters the house and Mary calls out to him from offscreen, a sign his plan has failed. (In the meantime, Mary has asked Noah to go in her stead to meet her husband at the clock tower, and we have seen Wilson climb the ladder and survive the sawed-off rung.) The second rhyming effect occurs when Noah enters his sister's house and calls out to her from offscreen. Hearing her brother's voice, Mary faints,[23] the only sound a swinging door as Rankin makes his escape.

The final clock-tower sequence dramatically illustrates the chiming effects that animate *The Stranger* (and, for that matter, Welles' films as a whole).[24] In another sonic rhyme, we see Mary wake up in her bedroom to the sound of a tolling bell. Having acknowledged her complicity in her husband's crimes, she resolves to do something. Secretly making her way through the cemetery to the clock tower (a scenario that invokes both the 'Dracula' and 'female gothic' story),[25] she climbs the ladder and joins Rankin in the belfry. What the script refers to as the 'rhythmic grinding of the works' is particularly audible here.

While the townspeople gather loudly in the square below, Wilson belatedly comes to Mary's aid and knocks the gun from Charles's hand. Then, in an extremely elliptical passage, Mary picks up the revolver and shoots at her husband, accidentally hitting the clock mechanism and 'sending it spinning wildly out of control [and] instigating the collapse of Kindler's ordered universe'.[26] As the floor gives way, Rankin falls onto the ledge of the clock tower where he makes a sudden volte-face, stumbling straight into the archangel's sword before plummeting like Satan to his death.[27]

Wilson's parting line – 'Good night, Mary, pleasant dreams' – is at once cheering and cautionary. For Welles, dreams are the royal road to the political unconscious, and the only defence against the ever-present threat of fascism, even or especially in 'America', is a perennial vigilance. As for Mary, it may be 'V-E day in Harper', according to Wilson, but as the now silent soundtrack and the 'shattered, nearly blank look' on her face intimates,[28] she is henceforth condemned, not unlike Rankin, to be a stranger in a strange land.

'Music': Miklós Rózsa, Esy Morales and Voiceover Narration in *Criss Cross*

Although the most memorable 'criss cross' between Welles' and Siodmak's careers occurred when Welles appeared as the Emperor Justinian in Siodmak's final film, *Kampf um Rom* (1968–9), both directors were 'especially suited' in 1940s Hollywood to 'expressionist genres such as the thriller' or film noir.[29] In his revised edition of *The Magic World of Orson Welles* (1989), James Naremore revisits 'two memorable Hollywood thrillers', *The Stranger* and *The Lady from Shanghai*, and his analysis pivots on the 'montage' between sound and image.[30] As Naremore observes, we will never know how the play between sound and image would have been realised in these films if Welles had been allowed 'final cut', but *Criss Cross*, perhaps because it was a sequel to *The Killers*, not only offered Siodmak the 'chance to fully realize [his] artistry'[31] but represents, according to Raymond Borde and Étienne Chaumeton's *Panorama of American Film Noir*, 'the summit of Siodmak's career'.[32]

As in the Mark Hellinger-produced *The Killers*, *Criss Cross* features a heist, a romantic triangle and a protagonist played by Burt Lancaster. Like *The Killers*, it also features a score by Miklós Rózsa,[33] a 'source music' set piece, and voiceover/flashback narration. (The script was composed by Daniel Fuchs, a working-class writer who adapted Don Tracy's novel and who had an 'acute sensitivity to the tastes and the vernacular of city people'.)[34] But as opposed to *The Killers* in which Kitty Collins (Ava Gardner) croons 'The More I Know of Love' to piano accompaniment, the musical set piece in *Criss Cross* is an instrumental one and showcases Esy Morales and His Rhumba Band.[35] Moreover, the flashback narration in *Criss Cross* is not a product of various voices, as it is in *The Killers* and its prototype, *Citizen Kane*; instead, it's relayed, as Siodmak himself put it, 'from one character's point of view'.[36]

This character is Steve Thompson (Lancaster), a man who, after having drifted around the country for the better part of a year trying to exorcise the memory of his ex-wife, still only has eyes for her. Consequently, when we first see Anna (Yvonne De Carlo) – a fur slung over one shoulder, her lustrous dark hair swept back and held with a hair slide, arched eyebrows setting off her full lips and high cheekbones (this, after the opening aerial shot that descends upon the lovers like enemy aircraft) – it is easy enough to believe her when she tells Steve:

> All those things that happened to us, everything that went before, we'll forget it, you'll see, I'll make you forget it. After it's done, after it's all over and we're safe, it'll be just you and me, you and me, the way it should have been all along from the start.

And right from the start, from the moment that the spinning planet in the Universal-International logo appears, Rózsa's score dramatises the lovers' plight, rising to a crescendo complete with crashing cymbal before unspiralling to a simple melodic line whose plangent lyricism suggests the mutability of all things. So when Anna tenderly puts her left hand on Steve's face, the ensuing kiss becomes a *coup de théâtre*, foreshadowing the mortal consummation that is their final embrace. In the beginning is the end.

The 'hot' Latin sound of Esy Morales and His Rhumba Band percolating in the background is, however, a reminder that such grand passion tends to originate not in the heavens but in the flesh. In fact, Steve and Anna are meeting in the parking lot rather than inside the Rondo (where at this very moment Slim, debonair in a white tux with rose buttonhole, is angrily searching for his suddenly absent spouse) because they're rehearsing a script which, if it comes off as planned, will not only reunite them with the heist money but will also leave Slim holding the proverbial bag. Cut to Steve en route to the heist driving an armoured truck, Pop (Griff Barnett) in the windowed cabin behind him.

Up until this point in time, *Criss Cross*'s tone, like that of Hellinger's other films noirs, is more sociological than existential, an effect that can be attributed to Siodmak's use of real exteriors such as Union Station and the crisp black-and-white cinematography of Franz Planer. The first flashback, though, retroactively colours this apparent objectivity. As Steve drives, he is haunted by Anna's parting remarks in the parking lot: 'After it's done, after it's all over and we're safe, it'll be just you and me'. When Steve's own thoughts do become audible ('From the start, from the beginning'), the film dissolves to a shot of Steve – dressed in a white shirt and tie, a suitcase in one hand, a dark coat and hat in the other – getting off a trolley in the Bunker Hill section of Los Angeles:

> It all happened so fast. It was only eight months ago that I came back home. The Los Angeles sun was shining the way it's always supposed to. The old trolley looked the same, the old street, the old houses. I was glad to be back.

There is real music here, Fuchs' lyrical language and Lancaster's muted but emotive line readings allowing us direct, unmediated access to Steve's conflicted state of mind.

If the first part of Steve's voiceover is nostalgic, the second part is tinged with regret. As Steve climbs the steep sidewalk to his mother's house, past the cars baking in the sunshine (a visual allusion to the film's opening sequence), we begin to learn why he left in the first place and why, despite his misgivings, he has come back: 'I didn't come back on account of her. It had nothing to do with her. I wasn't going to go looking for her. I didn't expect to run into her. I didn't particularly want to see her. I was sure of that if I was sure of anything'.

The force of all the negative constructions here points to only one thing: Steve can't get 'her', Anna, off his mind.

Accordingly, when he jogs up the steps to his mother's house, his thoughts abruptly change tack: 'Then from the start it all went one way. It was in the cards or it was fate or a jinx or whatever you want to call it. But right from the start'. Steve's sudden invocation of fate is ostensibly due to the fact that his mother is not home, but Siodmak underscores the fatalistic nature of the flashback via mise-en-scène: while Steve is sitting on the top step of the front porch, rough-housing with the family dog, the 'criss cross' grillwork on the screen door behind him visually complicates his brief moment of joy.

In the subsequent scene – Steve is standing in a phone booth trying to call former friend Pete Ramirez (Stephen McNally) – the aura of predestination is even more conspicuous and highlights Siodmak's masterful orchestration of the audiovisual elements of Classical Hollywood cinema, elements that have retrospectively become associated with the semantics of film noir. Steve's gloomy voiceover is only one part of this *Gesamtkunstwerk*, which, as written by Fuchs, is suffused with the poetry of the quotidian:

> I went down to the drugstore to call up Ramirez, Pete Ramirez. I thought I might drop over and kill an hour, but it all went one way that sunny afternoon – in the cards, he was out. His wife told me he was away somewhere working on the job. Pete always had the night shift, but this afternoon he was on day duty. This particular afternoon.

Here, sound and image – music and voiceover and composition – coalesce to produce a charged moment: while Steve stands facing us tightly framed inside a phone booth that is itself located inside a drugstore, the 'criss cross' wire mesh on the glass catches the late afternoon sunlight as Rózsa's score rises inexorably on the soundtrack.

This music – expectant, slightly apprehensive, with an undercurrent of sexual *tristesse* – forms an acoustic bridge to the ensuing scene at the Rondo. The camera is set at the back of the nightclub and, as Steve enters, the bright California sunlight spills into the dimly lit interior. It's a perfect, Hopperesque moment – a woman in the right foreground, a bartender in the middle and two men drinking at the end of the bar. In fact, the place looks like any other joint, but for Steve it is alive with the sort of memories that keep one up at night:

> Then somehow there I was in the Rondo, the old place, the old hangout. There I was alright looking for her whether I felt like admitting it to myself or not. A little strange to see the place in the daytime – empty, quiet, dim.

Steve makes small talk with the bartender, then, nickel in hand, heads straight towards a telephone booth when he is interrupted by a Chinese cook (Lee Tung Foo) – 'Hot tip, hot tip' – who wants to place a bet on a horse race. When the bartender comes over to continue the conversation ('If it turns out that you are a snooper, then I want an apology'), the cook passes by, complaining about his bad luck: 'too late, too late'. This bit of comic relief is a prelude to a shot from Steve's point of view of the now empty phone booth, which, as lit by Planer, looks like the loneliest telephone booth in the world. But before Steve is able to call Anna, the door opens and Ramirez, who is now a cop, walks in with the light and proceeds to interrogate Steve with a jocular insistence bordering on sadism about why he has returned to Los Angeles, then insists on driving him home.

Home at last, Steve has dinner with the family – his mother (Edna Holland), his brother Slade (Richard Long), his brother's fiancée (Meg Randall) and a friend of his mother's, Pop. Although Steve talks up his job prospects ('I'll go down to Horten's in the morning'), Siodmak's staging of the scene indicates his mind is elsewhere. When Slade whispers in his fiancée's ear, Steve retreats to the living room where, after turning down offers to go to the movies, bowling and ice-skating, he lies on the couch pretending to read the newspaper. Finally, after Slade threatens to hit his fiancée, then kisses her, Steve, dragging on a cigarette stuck like a toothpick in his mouth, begins to reminisce again:

> Anna, we were married about two years ago. A man eats an apple, gets a piece of the cork stuck between his teeth, you know? He tries to work it out with some cellophane off a cigarette pack. What happens? The cellophane gets stuck in there too. Anna, what was the use?

As in the telephone booth scene, Rózsa's score plays continuously under Steve's voiceover, forming a musical bridge to the next climactic scene: his return, at night, to the Rondo.

According to Eddie Muller, Siodmak in *Criss Cross* 'infuses the drama with an urgent dreaminess that gets under your skin like a narcotic'.[37] Perhaps no other scene in all of Siodmak's oeuvre epitomises this dreaminess better than the one where Steve watches mesmerised as Anna dances to a rhumba band. The fusion of music and montage is so hypnotic that it resembles nothing so much as what Freud calls a 'dream wish'. In *Criss Cross*, Anna's dance is equivalent to Kitty's song in *The Killers*,[38] except that Steve possesses and is possessed by Anna in a way that forever eludes the Swede.

At the Rondo, it is not Steve's first pristine vision of Anna but his *revision* of her that is indelibly impressed on our psyches like a burn. When Steve, having fled his mother's house, walks towards the back of the Rondo – past the bartender with the funny voice (Percy Helton) and the female lush (Joan Miller)

Figure 6.3 Yvonne De Carlo seductively dances with Tony Curtis, *Criss Cross*.

who gaily waves to him – he knows deep down inside that he is going to see Anna 'this particular evening'.

The rhumba sequence proper commences with a slight low-angle shot of Morales playing the flute before the camera pans out to Anna dancing with a darkly handsome partner (played by Tony Curtis). While the focus appears to be more on the band than Anna – it's as if Morales is a snake charmer and she is the cobra (he trills and she twirls) – we only see Anna, like Elvis, from the shoulders up. Indeed, Anna's dancing is intensely erotic precisely because it is photographed so indirectly. As in a Tourneur film, suggestiveness is all.

Anna, dancing in place, blinks. Has she seen Steve, somehow felt his gaze, or is she merely trying to find the rhythm of the song, appropriately titled 'Jungle Fantasy'? The camera eventually cuts away to Steve who, unlike the people moving to the music around him, is standing impassively at the edge of the dance floor, the 'criss cross' screen that blocks the right part of his body reflecting his increasing entrapment. Anna turns in a circle, moving away from Steve's ardent gaze, then, showing off her stuff (De Carlo began her career as a ballet dancer), spins again, a hint of a smile momentarily animating her otherwise serious demeanour, her hair whipping in the air like a lash. After another rhyming shot of Steve watching from the sidelines, dancers' shadows moving on the ceiling above him, Siodmak turns his attention back to the band.

The piano player (René Touzet, the world-renowned Cuban pianist and composer) begins to mimic the beat, while the percussion section – bongos, congas, maracas, castanets –picks up the tempo. The rapid editing mirrors the music, the camera dynamically cross-cutting between the pianist's hands hammering the keys and Anna spinning, 'absorbed in the music and her own being'.[39] The concluding shot of the sequence – a determined Anna dropping her head and dancing past Steve – punctuates the theme of sexual triangulation like a gunshot.

Gutted, Steve is about to beat a hasty retreat when Anna sees him across the dance floor and calls out his name, taking him by the hand to her table where they reminisce about the bad old days. Anna: 'All the fun we used to have in this place, Steve, remember?' Steve: 'Yeah, and all the fights. Boy, we sure used to go round and round'. Then Slim shows up and Steve lets Anna know just how little he thinks of her new beau: 'You running around with *him*?' Steve starts towards the door, promising to give her a ring, although it is Anna who makes the first move, calling him at home. (It's not lost either on her or on the audience that 'good' girls don't do this. One can almost hear the disgust in Mrs Thompson's voice when she realises it is Anna on the other end of the line.)

Despite the fact that Anna, according to the bartender, has been seen consorting with a 'known criminal', Steve agrees to meets her at the corner drugstore. A new cigarette pack in his hand, he tries to break it off – 'Why don't we just let it go and call it a day' – but she lingers at the counter and he relents, asking her to go swimming with him that Saturday at Zuma beach. The only noise is the sound of traffic outside, which beckons like another, less constrained world where things do not 'go round and round'.

While we never do see Steve and Anna resume their relationship, going, as he says, to the 'races and shows', it is clear some time has elapsed when the film cuts from the drugstore to Steve's bedroom where he's getting ready to go out for the night. Steve's mother knows he has been seeing Anna ('Of all the girls in Los Angeles, why did you have to pick on her?') and, when he won't listen, throws a hanky at his head, barking, 'Wipe your nose!'

Esy Morales's band is playing in the background when Steve saunters into the Rondo, the name of which evokes a 'musical form that's linear but also circular'.[40] After Steve jokes with the female lush whose solitariness reflects his own divorced status, the bartender deals Steve the ultimate losing hand, informing him – as he pours him a drink on the house (a bad omen, this) – that Anna has married Slim. The outside world falls away and Steve's voice-over resumes where it left off, Rózsa's music now ebbing then surging on the soundtrack: 'He kept on talking, jabbering away. I didn't hear a word of it, I couldn't think ... so she married Slim Dundee. Of course, he had all the dough, that's all she wanted. I told myself fine, it was a lucky break, probably the best thing that ever happened to me.'

Needless to say, Steve's luck does not hold, and by the time he realises how bad things have become, it is too late to do anything. It is as if he is already a dead man, like Joe Gillis (William Holden) in *Sunset Boulevard* (1950), telling his story from the other side of paradise. The aura of otherworldliness becomes even more pronounced when Steve's narration carries over from one sequence to another, as in the transition from the scene at the Rondo to the one at Union Station. Time and place dissolve like a landscape in the fog, and we are left with only the sound of Steve's voice, pensive, vincible:

> A month went by, a second, a fourth ... I was all finished, done with, water over the dam, only it wasn't. You know how it is. You don't know what to do with yourself, you want to travel, get away, anywhere. Every place you go you see her face, half the girls you pass. Did it ever happen to you?

The direct address – a brilliant touch on Fuchs' part – is perfectly timed, eliciting our sympathy just when Steve has almost completely retreated into himself. Indeed, the tone of Steve's voice, more so than its non-diegetic status, confers a profound, preordained causality on the action. In such moments, audio dominates vision, Steve's score-enhanced voice carrying us along as on a swift current, transporting us – whether we like it or not – into the future, looming ahead like Niagara Falls. Accordingly, when Steve sees Anna at Union Station, the 'music' comes not from an external source – say, a house band – but from the motion of his mind, which keeps returning over and over again to that sublime object he cannot bear to have lost.

Anna herself is a vision of loveliness, immaculately attired in a white dress and, despite the white fur stole (this in high summer!), looking impossibly cool in the midday heat. Doomed as ever, Steve keeps descanting even as the noose is being slipped over his head: 'If I hadn't been hanging around Union Station that day, if the clerk at the newsstand hadn't picked that moment to run out of cigarettes, to reach down for a pack'. Steve sees Anna, then before he can recover from the shock, watches her join Slim as they hurry towards the departing trains. Momentarily disabused of the notion Anna is on her own again (and no doubt figuring that she has made her bed and can sleep in it), Steve decides to split.

But if Steve is always leaving Anna, Anna always seems to reappear when he least expects it. And, true to form, no sooner is he back outside than she ends up standing right next to him, waiting to cross the street. Since Slim's driver will be along in a moment to take her home, Anna pleads with Steve not to make a scene and, for once in his life, he complies: he's not only done fighting *with* her but also *for* her. Then, in another twist of fate in a film full of such fateful twists (nothing, it seems, is accidental in *Criss Cross*, such is the universe as created by Siodmak), Vincent drives off and Anna has to fend for herself.

Siodmak's direction of the conclusion of the Union Station sequence (set in the blazing sunlight) and the beginning of the subsequent one (set in the cool darkness of Anna's apartment) epitomises 'the Siodmak touch'. In the first exterior shot, Anna does not return to her previous spot, standing next to Steve, but instead walks over to a taxi stand: while she waits in the left background, Steve remains fixed in the right foreground. When the camera cuts to Anna's apartment, Steve is now standing near a window in the right background while Anna is in the left foreground sitting at a piano. The 'symbolism' may be 'disguised',[41] but the 'criss cross' formed by the editing speaks volumes about Steve and Anna, whose intertwined destinies have brought them to just this place, at just this moment. Put another way, if Anna's and Steve's characters can be said to be subject to the byzantine ruses of the unconscious, Siodmak crosses chance with necessity, destiny with determination, investing their behaviour with a phantasmagorical objectivity.

In a musical echo of *Christmas Holiday*, *Phantom Lady* and *The Killers*, the song that Anna is playing on the piano, and humming as she plays, is 'I'll Remember April'. Anna appears to be mourning her lost relationship with Steve or her abusive one with Dundee, but Steve lays into her, calling her a 'tramp' or, more precisely, a 'cheap little no-good tramp'. He is about to snatch his jacket and leave when she replies, 'Stick around. You make it all so nice and sad'. After Steve finally asks Anna what's really on his mind ('Why did you do it?'), she abruptly stops playing 'I'll Remember April' and, giving back as good as she got, blames Steve's mother and his brother and his 'lovely friend', Pete Ramirez.

By the time she stands up to show Steve the welts on her back ('Look at the way he treats me!'), her 'Woe is me' lament has become a 'What are we gonna do?' plea. Like Kitty in *The Killers*, Anna doesn't have to run after Steve because he isn't going anywhere. It has always been 'too late', as the Chinese cook forecast, and it's going one way, not 'straight down the line' – as another doomed couple, Walter Neff (Fred MacMurray) and Phyllis Dietrichson (Barbara Stanwyck), intone in *Double Indemnity* (1944) – but straight downhill, like Sisyphus in reverse.

Before the flashback ends, a lot of water goes over the dam: Steve returns to the Rondo and picks a fight with Pete ('I'm gonna see her any time I want'), visits with Anna in his bedroom at home (a rendezvous that confirms Steve has chosen Anna over his mother, transgressive sexuality over maternal fidelity) then, after going downstairs to see Slim and his gang sitting in his mother's living room as if they lived there, tells Slim about his plan to hijack one of Horten's armoured trucks. Later, Steve meets with Dundee's gang at a boarding house near Angels Flight where a shot of Anna fast asleep on a bed, Slim's sports jacket thrown over her body, indicates – like a similar shot of Kitty in *The Killers* – that she is the 'real prize'.[42]

A fanfare of horns on the soundtrack announces Steve's final reflections as, driving, he nears his destination: 'This is it now, the payoff. Another five minutes and we're across the bridge. Another five minutes to San Rafael, to Vincent and the ice cream wagon'. Although Steve is right on time (he's the 'inside man' on the job, so is in the driver's seat in more ways than one), the extraordinary constriction of Siodmak's framing – the cabin very nearly fills the frame – counterpoints Steve's apparent freedom of movement. After what can only be called a jump cut to an overhead shot of the truck making a 'criss cross' as its path intersects with a passing train, we watch – as in the opening fateful shot, from above – as the truck makes its way towards its destination. The score dies down, and we appear to be nearing the light at the end of the tunnel. What could possibly go wrong?

The heist sequence is a tour de force, positively 'balletic' in its pacing and choreography.[43] The 'men at work' leisurely finish their lunch; two businessmen, briefcases in hand, cross the path of a milkman dressed in white. Suddenly, there is an explosion. The play of guns, smoke and gas masks – plus, on the soundtrack, people coughing, Rózsa's pounding score and the steady racket of alarms – imbues the scene with a surreal air, as if it is happening underwater. Is this the stuff of Anna's dreams? If it is, it soon becomes a nightmare when Pop is shot, Steve, retaliating, takes a bullet and the screen fades to black as he passes out.

Siodmak reserves a special irony for his post-heist protagonist. Steve wakes up, trapped in traction, to learn that although Pop is dead, he has been proclaimed a 'hero' for saving half the payroll. But what little relief he feels is short-lived since his 'lovely friend' Pete Ramirez is perfectly willing to leave him alone and defenceless in his hospital room at night. (In this, as Michael Walker observes, he is Slim's 'alter ego'.)[44] Sure enough, a hardware salesman named Nelson (Robert Osterloh) who Steve has turned to for help turns out to be one of Slim's henchmen and, brutally severing the wires that keep Steve's arm in traction (the pain is so intense it knocks Steve out), kidnaps him.

When Steve comes to in a car, he thinks he has outwitted Dundee, having bribed Nelson to take him to Palos Verdes where Anna is waiting for him. Anna, however, knows that Nelson has gone right back to Dundee and gives her former husband the not-so-long goodbye. Steve: 'You going away? You going to leave me here?' Anna: 'How far could I get with you? What kind of a chance would we have?' Steve protests, invoking that other four-letter word, 'love', while Anna continues to pack her bags, spelling out her philosophy of life, one that does not include naive dreamers like Steve:

> Love, love. You have to watch out for yourself. That's the way it is. I'm sorry. What do you want me to do? Throw away all this money? You always have to do what's best for yourself. That's the trouble with you, it always was, from the beginning. You just don't know what kind of world it is.

The light of the moon glinting on the lake in the window frame behind him, Steve, still dressed in a hospital gown and using his right arm to hold up the other, useless one in the blouson-like cast,[45] muses out loud about what went wrong:

> I am different. I never wanted the money. I just wanted you. After we split up, I used to walk around the streets in strange cities at night. I used to think about you. I just wanted to hold you in my arms, to take care of you. It could have been wonderful, but it didn't work out. What a pity it didn't work out.

Anna apologises, then turns and walks out of Steve's life. There is the sound of a car outside. Lights flash across the open door and the screen goes black. Into this momentarily empty space, Slim appears like an apparition, his body halved in shadow, a cane in one hand, a gun in the other. Anna backs up into Steve's embrace and, in one of the most perfectly unhappy endings in all of film noir, Slim, like a director, calls out the action, 'Hold her, hold her tight', before he pulls the trigger. When the smoke clears, Steve – just as he dreamed ever since Anna first entered his eye's fantastic orbit – is holding her tight in his arms, forever.

The Wagnerian echoes in Rózsa's score hint that, at heart, '*Criss Cross* is nothing less than a gangland Tristan and Isolde'.[46] In fact, compared to *The Killers* (which ends on a comic note when Kenyon gives Reardon (Edmond O'Brien) the weekend off after dryly observing that the 'basic rate at the Atlantic Casualty Company, as of 1947, will probably drop one-tenth of a cent'), the dénouement of *Criss Cross* is pitiless and all the more exhilarating for being so. Even the majestic ending of Jacques Tourneur's *Out of the Past* (1947) seems positively upbeat by comparison. For Siodmak, romance is a disaster waiting to happen. In *Criss Cross*, thanks to Fuchs, Rózsa and Morales, it is ambient.

Recommended Reading

Alpi, Deborah Lazaroff (1998), *Robert Siodmak*, Jefferson, NC: McFarland.
Harvey, James (2000), *Movie Love in the Fifties*, New York: Knopf.
Heylin, Clinton (2005), *Despite the System: Orson Welles versus the Hollywood Studios*, Chicago, IL: Chicago Review Press.
Miklitsch, Robert (2011), *Siren City: Sound and Source Music in Classic American Noir*, New Brunswick, NJ: Rutgers University Press.
Naremore, James (1989), *The Magic World of Orson Welles*, Dallas, TX: Southern Methodist University Press.
Palmer, R. Barton (1994), *Hollywood's Dark Cinema*, New York: Twayne.
Phillips, Gene D. (2012), *Out of the Shadows*, Lanham, MD: Scarecrow Press.
Shadoian, Jack (2003), *Dreams and Dead Ends: The American Gangster Film*, Cambridge, MA: MIT Press.
Walker, Michael (1992), 'Robert Siodmak', in Ian Cameron (ed.), *The Book of Film Noir*, New York: Continuum, pp. 110–51.

RECOMMENDED FILMS

Abschied (Siodmak, 1930)
Christmas Holiday (Siodmak, 1944)
Citizen Kane (Welles, 1941)
Criss Cross (Siodmak, 1948)
Kiss the Blood off My Hands (Foster, 1948)
Phantom Lady (Siodmak, 1944)
Pièges (Siodmak, 1939)
The Chase (Ripley, 1946)
The Killers (Siodmak, 1946)
The Lady from Shanghai (Welles, 1948)
The Stranger (Welles, 1946)
Stürme der Leidenschaft (Siodmak, 1931)
Touch of Evil (Welles, 1958)

NOTES

1. Deborah Lazaroff Alpi, *Robert Siodmak* (Jefferson, NC: McFarland, 1998), p. 32.
2. For an introductory account of 'lightning mixes' and overlapping sound montage, see David Cook, 'Orson Welles and the modern sound film', in David Cook, *A History of Narrative Film* (New York: Norton, 2004), pp. 330–1. On 'pan' and 'deep focus' sound respectively, see James Naremore, *The Magic World of Orson Welles* (Dallas, TX: Southern Methodist University, 1989), pp. 41–3 and Rick Altman, 'Deep focus sound: *Citizen Kane* and the radio aesthetic', in Ronald Gottesman (ed.), *Perspectives on Citizen Kane* (New York: G. K. Hall, 1996), pp. 94–121. On the use of sound and space in Welles, see Phyllis Goldfarb, 'Orson Welles's use of sound', in Morris Beja (ed.), *Perspectives on Orson Welles* (New York: G. K. Hall, 1995), pp. 107–15.
3. Alpi, *Robert Siodmak*, p. 6.
4. On *The Lady from Shanghai*, see, for example, Robert Miklitsch, 'Stereophone siren', in Robert Miklitsch, *Siren City: Sound and Source Music in Classic American Noir* (New Brunswick, NJ: Rutgers University Press, 2011), pp. 241–50. On *Touch of Evil*, see, for example, Jill Leeper, 'Crossing musical borders: The soundtrack for *Touch of Evil*', in Pamela Robertson Wojcik and Arthur Knight (eds), *Soundtrack Available: Essays on Film and Popular Music* (Durham, NC: Duke University Press, 2001), pp. 226–43.
5. Gene D. Phillips, *Out of the Shadows: Expanding the Canon of Classic Film Noir* (Lanham, MD: Scarecrow, 2012), p. 198.
6. Simon Callow, *Hello, Americans* (New York: Viking, 2006), p. 273.
7. Ibid., p. 273.
8. Phillips, *Out of the Shadows*, p. 197.
9. Carl Macek, 'The stranger', in Alain Silver and Elizabeth Ward (eds), *Film Noir: An Encyclopedic Reference to the American Style* (Woodstock, NY: Overlook, 1992), p. 269.
10. On sound in *The Chase* and *Kiss the Blood off My Hands*, see Miklitsch, *Siren City*, pp. 65 and 70.
11. What Welles referred to as the 'great long sequence in Latin America' – 'much the best thing in the picture' – was cut by producer Sam Spiegel's hired hand, 'supercutter' Ernest Nims. On the pre- and post-editing of *The Stranger*, see Clinton Heylin, *Despite the System: Orson Welles versus the Hollywood Studios* (Chicago, IL: Chicago Review Press, 2005), pp. 173–97.

12. In the original script, Wilson's female agent dies, having been savaged by dogs, an incident that foreshadows Red's 'hunting' role later in the film. It's also worth quoting the script here as it illustrates Welles' interest in the soundtrack: 'As the men set the stretcher and its burden upon an empty table, there is a small thud as some object drops to the floor' (cited in Heylin, *Despite the System*, p. 178). The object is a gold hooped earring, and the sound it makes hitting the floor prefigures two acoustic incidents in *The Stranger*: first, when Wilson's pipe lands on the bus seat after he and Meinike arrive in Harper; and, second, when Mary, near the end of the film, hands her husband Charles a fire poker with which to kill her and, before he flees, he drops it, sending it thudding to the floor.
13. Phillips, *Out of the Shadows*, p. 190.
14. R. Barton Palmer, *Hollywood's Dark Cinema: American Film Noir* (New York: Twayne, 1994), p. 119.
15. On this backstory (Rankin claims Meinike was blackmailing him over the accidental boating death of Meinike's sister, who was Rankin's girlfriend at the time), see Phillips, *Out of the Shadows*, p. 204.
16. In an interview with Welles, Peter Bogdanovich remarks that '*The Stranger* was the first commercial film to use footage of Nazi-concentration camp atrocities' (Orson Welles and Peter Bogdanovich, *This Is Orson Welles* (New York: Da Capo, 1998), p. 189).
17. There is a similar moment in *Citizen Kane* when the 'theme music that concludes the "News on the March" is distorted by the sudden stopping of the projector' (François Thomas, '*Citizen Kane*: The sound track', in James Naremore (ed.), *Orson Welles's Citizen Kane: A Casebook* (New York: Oxford University Press, 2004), p. 176).
18. Michel Chion, *Audio Vision*, trans. Claudia Gorbman (New York: Columbia University Press, 1994), p. 144.
19. Heylin, *Despite the System*, p. 118.
20. Welles, cited by Heylin, *Despite the System*, p. 81.
21. The original script again illustrates Welles' attention to the sonic register: 'There is the sound of running feet . . . then the slam of a car door . . . the grinding of a starter . . . the clash of gears . . . the motor racing as [Mary] speeds away' (Heylin, *Despite the System*, p. 191).
22. Peter Cowie, *The Cinema of Orson Welles* (New York: A. S. Barnes, 1973), p. 95.
23. In the original script, an 'impressionistic montage' edited out by Nims would have reintroduced the ladder imagery as well as Mary's dog, Red: 'Red howls furiously and claws at the foot of the shaft . . . His baying echoes and merges strangely with the music' (Heylin, *Despite the System*, p. 185).
24. Consider, for example, the 'barely audible tinkling of small bells' after Kane (Orson Welles) whispers the word 'Rosebud' at both the beginning and end of *Citizen Kane* (Thomas, '*Citizen Kane*: The sound track', p. 181). More generally, I am thinking as well of Welles' *Chimes at Midnight* (1965).
25. Palmer, *Hollywood's Dark Cinema*, p. 126.
26. Ibid., p. 142.
27. Phillips, noting the resemblance between Rankin's fall in *The Stranger* and Welles' fall from a fire escape in *Hearts of Age* (1954) – 'a silent short [Welles] made at the Todd School for Boys' – writes: 'Welles' contention that *The Stranger* is an impersonal film, and that there is nothing in it, seems more an exaggeration than ever' (Phillips, *Out of the Shadows*, p. 200). On Rankin as Satan 'hurled down to earth' by the 'avenging angel, St. Michael', see Phillips, *Out of the Shadows*, p. 205.
28. Palmer, *Hollywood's Dark Cinema*, p. 128.
29. Naremore, *The Magic World of Orson Welles*, pp. 122–3.

30. Ibid., p. 271.
31. Alpi, *Robert Siodmak*, pp. 5–6.
32. Raymond Borde and Étienne Chaumeton, *A Panorama of American Film Noir, 1941–1953*, trans. Paul Hammond (San Francisco: City Lights, 2002), p. 79.
33. Rózsa's American career as a film composer changed over time, evolving from the 'Oriental' phase of *The Four Feathers* (1939), *The Thief of Bagdad* (1940) and *The Jungle Book* (1942) to the historical-epic period of *Quo Vadis* (1951), *Ivanhoe* (1952) and *Ben Hur* (1959). Rózsa's immediate, post-'psychological' work – he won an Academy Award for *Spellbound* (1945) – encompasses the first, classic cycle of film noir: *Double Indemnity* (1941), *The Strange Love of Martha Ivers* (1946), *Brute Force* (1947), *The Secret beyond the Door* (1948), *The Bribe* (1949) and *The Asphalt Jungle* (1950). As Rózsa himself remembers in his autobiography, *A Double Life* (whose title references his other career as a concert composer), these films noirs, which dealt with 'American urban low life and the underworld', 'demanded a new approach' (New York: Wynwood Press, 1989, p. 152).
34. Joseph Greco, 'Criss Cross', in Joseph Greco, 'The file on Robert Siodmak in Hollywood: 1941–1951', unpublished dissertation, p. 124.
35. Morales was born in Puerto Rico and had just organised his Latin Rhythm Orchestra, having previously worked with Xavier Cugat and the Brothers Morales Orchestra. As John Storm Roberts observes, Noro Morales –who, like Touzet, played the piano – became 'one of the major names of downtown Latin music' in the 1940s (*The Latin Tinge: The Impact of Latin American Music on the United States* (New York: Oxford University Press, 1999), p. 103). As with Esy Morales' piano-and-rhythm sound in *Criss Cross*, Noro's music shows 'highly effective contrasts between busy Afro-Cuban percussion and [an] always interesting piano style that occupies a very personal space between "international" Latin and more traditional Cuban playing' (pp. 103–4).
36. Greco, 'The file on Robert Siodmak', p. 124.
37. Eddie Muller, *Dark City: The Lost World of Film Noir* (New York: St. Martin's Griffin, 1998), p. 101.
38. Michael Walker, 'Robert Siodmak', in Ian Cameron (ed.), *The Book of Film Noir* (New York: Continuum, 1994), p. 141.
39. Greco, *The File on Robert Siodmak*, p. 127.
40. Jack Shadoian, *Dreams and Dead Ends: The American Gangster Film* (Cambridge, MA: MIT Press, 2003), p. 316.
41. I am drawing here on Greco, who notes that Siodmak reshot this scene in order to accent the 'criss cross' effect (*The File on Robert Siodmak*, pp. 121–2).
42. Walker, 'Robert Siodmak', p. 143.
43. Palmer, *Hollywood's Dark Cinema*, p. 69.
44. Walker, 'Robert Siodmak', p. 144.
45. For a very suggestive reading of the symbolic relation between the white blouson sleeves of the Latin band-members' traditional costumes and Steve's cast, see Sean McCann, 'Dark passages: Jazz and civil liberty in the postwar crime film', in Frank Krutnik, Steve Neale, Brian Neve and Peter Stanfield (eds), *'Un-American' Hollywood: Politics and Film in the Blacklist Era* (New Brunswick, NJ: Rutgers University Press, 2007), p. 124.
46. Carlos Clarens, 'Shades of noir', in Carlos Clarens, *Crime Movies* (New York: Da Capo, 1997), p. 201.

7. GENDER AND NOIR

Elisabeth Bronfen

Thinking of film noir, we immediately summon up the image of a hard-boiled detective in a trenchcoat wandering along a dark alley, ready to combat corruption come what may; or a group of reckless gangsters driving along the nocturnal streets of a big city, willing to risk everything for the thrill of a heist. And we think of those modern-day sirens singing in glitzy nightclubs, who use their feminine allure to seduce gullible men and draw them into an intricate web of clandestine transgressions. As Mary Ann Doane notes, because the classic femme fatale is never really what she seems, she gives voice to a threat which is not entirely legible, predictable or manageable. The danger she poses to the infallibility of the noir hero – be he on the side of the law or its rogue opposite – thus emerges as a secret which must aggressively be disclosed, while her eradication involves 'a desperate reassertion of control on the part of the threatened male subject'.[1] Like the ruthless gangster he combats, the tough private eye, in turn, is self-reliant and invulnerable. Playing Philip Marlowe in *The Big Sleep* (1946) or Sam Spade in *The Maltese Falcon* (1941), Humphrey Bogart, as Frank Krutnik puts it, remains 'the manipulator of the scenario, rather than its victim'.[2] While he may get caught up in the femme fatale's manipulations, he never fully succumbs to her fatal charm.

Although unequivocal masculine inviolability becomes rarer in the course of the 1940s, John Huston's adaptation of Dashiell Hammett's novel sets the tone for the gender trouble around which this film genre so consistently revolves. Preoccupied with the cigarette he is in the process of rolling, Sam does not initially look up when his secretary Iva enters his office, explaining that a girl named Wonderly is waiting outside to see him. Beaming radiantly, she adds, 'you'll want to see her anyway, she's a knock-out'. The elegant woman who cautiously enters the room seems to be distraught, yet appears demure and soft spoken as she spins her tale about a sister whom she needs to find. Spade's partner, Archer, interrupting this first meeting, insists on taking on the case himself, as smitten by the femme fatale's startling beauty as by the two $100 bills she has left as a retainer. In response to his claim that while his partner may have seen her first, he spoke first, Bogart cynically replies, 'you've got brains, yes you have'. Archer will be shot that very night while throughout the film narrative Sam Spade will be the one who is both unfailingly witty in conversation and clever in his strategy. Although he is taken by the woman who soon admits that she is not who she claims to be, he is not taken in and instead repeatedly laughs away any betrayal she may have in store for him. Brigid (Mary Astor) soon admits that she is a liar and everything but innocent, yet continues to play her part. Appealing to his strength, she insists that her dangerous secret is one she cannot yet disclose while he openly lauds her for her acting skills.

Put another way, even though she soon realises that both know she is putting on an act, she remains elusive about what it is she really wants. Sam, in turn, aware from the start that he cannot trust her, is nevertheless willing to protect her against the small-time crooks she has double-crossed. He gives in to her seduction not despite but because of his realisation that she is deceiving him, while she, fully aware that he has seen through her, enjoys playing the part of a secretive woman in distress. Indeed, precisely because they know that each is trying to dupe the other, there is a lighthearted rapport (not a tragic bond) between this detective and the femme fatale, their repartee closer to the sophisticated comedies than the gangster films of the 1930s. However, even though Sam remains loyal to Brigid during their final confrontation with her shady partners in crime, he will not protect this murderess from her just punishment. His infallible poise thrives on his loyalty to the law. Although his self-reliance sometimes brings him in conflict with the police, he repeatedly calls on his friend, detective Tom Polhaus, to make sure that in the end all criminals are brought to justice. His ability to regain control over a dangerous situation even when his assailants seem momentarily to have the upper hand is predicated on the fact that he knows his cause is justified.

It is easy to see why critics have used Brigid O'Shaughnessy as a prime example for the way the femme fatale can be taken as a symptom of the noir detective. Even more alluring than her appearance is the secret Brigid embodies. Sam Spade takes on her case, because, in that she poses a challenge to his cleverness, by solving her he can not only overcome the dangerous sexuality she poses but can also prove how good he is at detecting. Everything revolves around this wonder-inspiring woman and yet she seems to be without any substance beyond the effect she has on others. Indeed, precisely because she remains elusive throughout the film narrative, without a backstory to explain her actions, she is first and foremost a narrative necessity – the assignment the hero must accept, the obstacle he must confront and the temptation he must relinquish. Thus, while subsequent films noirs tend to present less infallible heroes, *The Maltese Falcon* sets the generic tone regarding the sacrifice of the woman who knows how to tap into a hero's transgressive desire. During their last conversation, while the police are already on their way, Sam bullies Brigid into confessing that it was she who shot his partner, Miles Archer. The mise-en-scène initially has Bogart towering over Mary Astor, so as to visually endorse not only her depravity but also his moral superiority.

The emotional violence enacted during the conversation that follows, in which he assures her that she will take the fall so that his name can be cleared, is legitimated by the fact that she is, indeed, guilty. When she, revising her act one last time, accuses him of having been toying with her affection, he replies, 'I don't care who loves who, I won't play the sap for you'. Expressing a sinister hatred which we have not previously seen, he adds, 'you killed Miles and you're going over for it'. Then, while Brigid continues weeping, he, once more looming over her, explains the strange logic of self-defence at issue: 'I've no earthly reason to think I can trust you, and if I do this and get away with it, you'll have something on me that you can use whenever you want to. Since I've got something on you, I couldn't be sure that you wouldn't put a hole in me some day'. The fact that they may love each other cannot outweigh the lack of trust between them. They have no language in common and it is this gendered miscommunication which also serves as a template for subsequent films noirs.

While *The Maltese Falcon* leaves open whether, in proffering her love to Spade, Brigid is simply playing yet another role or telling the truth, she emerges as his symptom in a twofold sense. She not only embodies a love that is transgressive because it requires of him to break the law were he to decide not to give her up to the police, but is also the embodiment of what must be sacrificed so as both to cleanse him of this dangerous desire and to prove that he can resist temptation. Once Detective Polhaus has turned up, Sam, without any sign of hesitation, names her as the killer of his former partner. Huston gives us one final close-up of his femme fatale. Her eyes still filled with tears, Brigid stands behind the bars of the elevator which cast a shadow on the right side of her face before the door closes and she descends, disappearing completely from sight: a *mater dolorosa* to his resurrection.

The restitution of the detective who prefers to take the stairs down is, however, troubled by the fact that he also has come to be disclosed in the process. In this scenario of masculine self-reliance, the toughness he puts on display is as much a role he has assumed as is the alluring distress of the femme fatale. Regarded by critics as the first of the classic films noirs, *The Maltese Falcon* installs the gender trouble at the heart of this genre: while the two key players may share the act of seduction, they do not have a fantasy in common. The noir hero's erotic temptability may offer an insight into masculine weakness, yet the fact that Spade is willing to sacrifice this love if that is what survival requires points to the duplicity inscribed in his pose of infallibility. If the femme fatale's sacrifice reaffirms the very masculinity she threatened, the insecurity she engendered, however brief, is as seminal to the hero's restitution as is her demise. Only by virtue of her punishment can he prove his worth. Typical for the negotiation of gender in this film genre, noir narratives put the dangerous power of feminine sensuality on display so as to articulate concerns regarding the threat of women's agency. If, however, the femme fatale ultimately loses her power and disappears from sight, the disturbance she embodies remains until the end. Her play with masculine authority tarries in our memory. Sylvia Harvey notes: 'Despite the ritual punishment of acts of transgression, the vitality with which these acts are endowed produces an excess of meaning which cannot finally be contained. Narrative resolution cannot recuperate their subversive significance'.[3]

Equally significant for a reading of the closure offered in the final scene of *The Maltese Falcon*, however, is the historical context. The film premiered in 1941, just as the United States was about to enter World War II. Humphrey Bogart would soon join in Hollywood's war effort and, one year later, would reunite with Sydney Greenstreet and Peter Lorre in Michael Curtiz's *Casablanca*, with all three actors fighting for the allied cause.[4] In Huston's film noir, Sam Spade's fallibility must be acknowledged, then, as something that can be overcome. Along with the femme fatale, who brings the sought-after falcon with her from Hong Kong (a foreign place already implicated in what was about to become the Pacific theatre of war), that part of American masculinity which might waver and derail is vanquished. Important to note further is that, if Bogart's detective is always in control, then his judgement is never clouded, even when he seems to be making a false move. Indeed, he relinquishes the femme fatale precisely because he is aware of the power of his urge to transgress the law for her sake. By giving her up to the police he consciously renounces an emotional ambivalence that psychoanalysis aligns with fetishism – knowing that something is not what it seems to be, yet desiring it nevertheless. What is surrendered along with the femme fatale is, thus, the willingness to entertain a desire which one knows to be bad. While the woman, whose tears no longer compel, disappears forever, the man who proved capable of resisting her charm walks off the stage, about to re-emerge unequivocally valiant on a different set. Everything is again straightforward.

Triangulation of desire

While in *The Maltese Falcon* both the detective and the femme fatale are shown to be self-reliant players in an intrigue of their own making, far more typical for film noir are fated heroes and heroines, driven by a blind desire for happiness, prosperity and personal freedom. They think they are in control of the shady deals they are prepared to accept only to discover in the end that they have been fortune's fools. They realise too late that they are nothing more than pawns in a claustrophobic world, imprisoned in sombre machinations well beyond their personal reach, with either their past crimes or the law ultimately catching up with them. Joan Copjec also suggests reading the femme fatale as a double of the noir hero, created to indemnify himself against the dangerous risk he has been willing to embark upon. By surrender to her the *jouissance* he cannot himself sustain, he tries to split himself between knowing what is bad for him and giving in to this fatal desire: 'Giving up his right to enjoyment, the hero contracts with the femme fatale that she will henceforth command it from him, as levy'.[5] Yet if classic film noir continues to fascinate us today, then it does so in part because it troubles this easy alignment of gender positions. Even while the femme fatale serves as a projection for the noir hero's emotional ambivalence she commands the screen as a subject in her own right. If she is not what she seems to be then it is because, in this world of crisscrossed desires, the hero is unable or unwilling to recognise any fantasy beyond his own. The distance he seeks by projecting his dangerous enjoyment onto another is a form of self-delusion which the femme fatale ultimately forces him to acknowledge, proving to be the more resilient of the two, even if she brings death to both.

In Jacques Tourneur's *Out of the Past* (1947) a blurring of gendered positions of empowerment corresponds to the murky transgression into which the femme fatale lures the vulnerable detective. Jeff Bailey (Robert Mitchum), a former private eye seeking to distance himself from all obligations that tie him to the gangster Whit Sterling (Kirk Douglas), goes to visit his former employer at his home in Lake Tahoe only to find that Kathie Moffat (Jane Greer) has returned to the fold. Years earlier he had been sent to find her and bring her back because she had robbed Whit of $40,000, but instead fell in love and betrayed his boss. Trying once more to seduce him, Kathie explains, 'I couldn't help it, Jeff'. While both know that she enjoys pretending to be powerless in the face of any unexpected turn events happen to take, Jeff (and therein he radically differs from Sam Spade) prefers to give up any responsibility for his actions by taking this forced return to her as a sign of fate, not a question of personal choice. He knows she will double-cross him and yet, when she asks him to believe in her love, he doesn't resist. Instead, he laconically replies, 'Baby, I don't care'. Like the femme fatale in *The Maltese Falcon*, she too is introduced into the narrative by virtue of a cryptic allusion to her alluring appearance. Whit, having contracted the private detective, had assured Jeff that, once he had seen Kathie, he would understand everything, thereby triggering the hired man's own transgressive desire. And indeed, the minute Kathie walks from the bright sunlight of Acapulco into the dim interior of a café where Jeff has been waiting for her, an ominous romance sets in.

Even though this femme fatale does not seek him out on purpose, she captivates the private eye who has found her and the stolen money, and they embark on a clandestine love affair that takes them back to San Francisco. There, she will kill his partner Fisher, who, having discovered their illicit relationship, has come to blackmail them. Crucial to the scene in which (again in contrast to Sam Spade) Tourneur's hero is a horrified witness is the way it casts Kathie as a ruthless woman, willing to destroy everyone who attempts to cross her. Insisting that necessity compelled her to kill Fisher, she pits her drive for survival at all costs against Jeff's delusion that their romance could be sustained against all odds. While she is willing to admit that they will sacrifice each other should their interests prove to be at cross purposes, Jeff retains an emotional ambivalence. Once she has abandoned him, he convinces himself that he wants to be released from the past and tries to jettison all transgressive desire by projecting it onto the woman who betrayed him. He takes on a new identity as the owner of a gas station in Bridgeport, a small town outside Los Angeles, where he hopes to set up a home and family with the kind-hearted Ann. Yet when Whit sends for him so as to involve him again in dark machinations orchestrated by the femme fatale, he finds himself once more helplessly enthralled.

We thus have a constellation of characters typical for a large subset of films belonging to the noir genre. These place the hard-boiled yet dupable hero between a dangerously manipulative woman who acts outside the law and a faithful woman on the side of domesticity. This romantic triangulation, in turn, is reduplicated by virtue of the fact that Jeff desires a woman tied to an illicit figure of paternal authority (Witt), who is willing to have him take the fall to protect himself, while the vulnerable hero is also opposed by a licit representative of the police (Sheriff Douglas), who, because he himself loves Ann, has personal reasons to have him arrested. The hero is thus torn not only between two opposed female love objects, but also between two sides of the law. Typical also for this subset of film noir is the fact that the more powerful older man is supported by a set of fellow gangsters and their morally dubious dames, while the hero has friends (like the boy helping him at the garage) who, along with Ann, belong to the world of the ordinary everyday. Finally, if Jeff articulates a masculinity in crisis, unable to resist the act put on by the femme fatale, Kathie's duplicity primarily involves allowing men to dupe themselves. As she moves from one lover to the next she is unabashedly looking out for herself, using her sexual allure in a self-styled pursuit of freedom and prosperity.[6]

Poignant for the specific gendering of the players in *Out of the Past* is the way Jeff's clandestine affair with Kathie is presented as a flashback while he is driving Ann through the night in the hope of reaching Whit's villa at Lake Tahoe by dawn. The past may have caught up with him, but he needs Ann as his compassionate listener to make his confession. During this nocturnal narration, his voiceover casts Kathie as the destroyer of an illicit romance even while he is as yet unwilling to accept his own culpability regarding their transgressions. Given her unconditional trust in him, Ann argues against his narrative of fated love, confident that a peaceful resolution may still be found, even while she will not believe that Kathie is purely evil since he once loved her. In *Out of the Past*, the femme fatale thus initially emerges onscreen out of the darkness of the night through which Jeff is driving, a projection meant to embody the shady deals of the past that have caught up with him. In that his confession is addressed to a second woman who refuses to accept her rival as being nothing more than the hero's nemesis, the mise-en-scène debunks the very framing of the femme fatale which the voiceover confession seeks. We are meant to recognise that Jeff remains caught up not only in the world of criminal intrigues but also in the unfathomability of his own desire.

By casting Kathie as the dangerous double-crosser who fatefully changed the course of what would otherwise have been an ordinary life, he is deluding himself not only about the woman whom he continues to be charmed by but more importantly also about himself. Making her the exclusive hoarder of a transgressive desire that was from the start a joint venture allows him not to acknowledge that perhaps he does not really want the ordinary domesticity Ann could offer him. Given the disjunction between his voiceover and the subsequent scenes of seduction and double-crossing that unfold on screen without any further voiceover commentary once he has arrived at Lake Tahoe, we are able to read his nocturnal confession against the grain and recognise in the femme fatale a dark inversion of justice. She undercuts the power of all the male figures, playing one man off the other while repeatedly eluding the police. But, most pointedly, she stands for an ethical stance beyond narcissistic self-delusion when, in her final confrontation with Jeff, she insists, 'I never told you I was anything other than I am. You just wanted to imagine I was'. Pitting her self-image against the one he has come up with in order to screen out his own complicity in their mutual crimes, Kathie forces him to recognise that, in contrast to his willingness to give himself up to the coincidences of fate, she, actually, could help it all along.

Working against the misogynist encoding of his voiceover narrative, Kathie forces Jeff to realise that the past will always haunt him because it is the very motor of his desire. 'You're no good and nor am I,' she calmly assures him.

'We've been wrong a lot, and unlucky a long time. I think we deserve a break'. With his retort, 'We deserve each other', Jeff indicates that he no longer wishes to separate his transgressive enjoyment from his knowledge of himself, recognising this to be tragic self-delusion. The only card left for him to play involves turning what he had chosen to read as fatal necessity into an act of conscious choice – accepting the punishment of the law he has transgressed and ceding the desire that prompted him to do so. In contrast to the narrative resolution *The Maltese Falcon* offers, for him relinquishing love is tantamount to accepting both his guilt and his just punishment. He is the one to call the police, but only after Kathie has compelled him to acknowledge the emotional ambivalence on which his transgressive desire was predicated. They will die together during a shoot-out at the roadblock the police put up in answer to his call.

Tragedy, as Stanley Cavell argues, not only offers proof that our actions have consequences 'which outrun our best, and worst intentions'. Rather, 'the reason consequences furiously hunt us down is not merely that we are half blind, and unfortunate but that we go on doing the thing which produced these consequences in the first place'. To break loose from this self-engendered cycle of fatality what is needed is 'the courage, or plain prudence, to see and to stop'.[7] For the world of film noir, predicated as it is on vengeance and retaliation, this means asking what it takes to maintain that tragic delusion which draws everything into a net of fatality. And it means asking what it would take to abdicate from all shady dreams of prosperity. Cavell adds, 'Tragedy is about a particular death which is neither natural nor accidental'. However, the death which could not be averted need not have happened. 'So a radical contingency haunts every story of tragedy'. This raises the question of whether these contingencies could have been prevented; tragedy is also haunted by a radical necessity. 'It is the enveloping of contingency and necessity by on another', Cavell concludes, that produces the fatality. The death at the end of a tragedy, 'strikes us as inexplicable: necessary, but we do not know why; unavoidable, but we do not know how'.[8]

For the hero in Tourneur's film to stop and to see means acknowledging the self-delusion so key to his desire, but also the fact that it overrules all survival instincts. In contrast to Sam Spade, he allows himself both to violate the moral laws and to lose his clear judgement because he does not want to view the world in terms of the ordinary. He prefers his benighted fantasies. Going along with the illicit plans the femme fatale has in store for them both proves to be as much an impossibility as any return to the licit world of the everyday Ann promises. Instead, by turning to the law, Jeff puts an end to the cycle of fatal repetition. His courage consists in refusing to continue acting in a way that produces tragic consequences. Instead, he brings the fatality of such action to light, along with the responsibility he carries for his actions, which includes a responsibility for the outcome of his fate. *Out of the Past* is unusual in that it has Jeff ultimately revise his self-conception, while, as the following discussion will show, noir heroes more often than not die while clinging to their self-destructive fantasies, or are saved by others just before their blind obsession could become fatal. Indeed, film noir often distinguishes between a catastrophic turn of events predicated on self-engendered delusions that abdicate all personal responsibility to the forces of fate, and the recognition that one is responsible for one's actions and thus can determine their consequences, even if this means death. And this distinction is usually gendered.

To underscore the lack of a shared fantasy, many films noirs, like *Out of the Past*, make use of a voiceover confession by the hero, whose point is to clear himself of the desire a woman inspired and the guilt this entailed. The hero not only does not recognise the woman who has enthralled him as being anything other than his projection, but also refuses to heed the message about the fragility of luck she brings him. Noir heroines, in turn, rarely take centre stage and more often than not have no say in how their story is told. Nevertheless, they are the ones who most often stop and see, pitting tragic choice against the necessity of fate, even if – in contrast to Kathie – they are not always able to compel the hero to do the same. These women are fatal not only because they draw the hero into risky adventures that end in failure and death but also because they know that the illegal pursuit of power and money is inevitably thwarted. And they know that one can never rid oneself of the consequences of one's actions by shifting all the blame onto a partner in crime. Precisely because these film narrations are often focalised by the confession of a hero who wants to be duped, the noir heroine does not only mirror the desire and anxieties of her deluded lover. Given that the visual enactment of her story exceeds what the male voiceover has to say, she often functions both as the symptom *within* a male fantasy as well as a subject *beyond* this male fantasy. She is the catalyst of the narrative even while she is never fully contained by it.

WAR AND CRIME CULTURE

The vulnerability of the hero in *Out of Past* explains why the crisis of masculinity at the centre of film noir has come to be read as a cinematic negotiation of the cultural anxieties prevalent during the historical moment when this genre emerged. As Vivian Sobchack pointedly notes, 'it is now a commonplace to regard film noir during the peak years of its production as a pessimistic cinematic response to volatile social and economic conditions of the decade immediately following World War II'.[9] While the narrative resolution of women's melodramas from the home front, such as *Mrs Miniver* (1942) or *Since You Went Away* (1944), celebrate the reunion of the family, film noir highlights how precarious the veteran's homecoming can be. Indeed, as Sobchack goes on to argue, film noir can be seen as 'playing out negative dramas of post-war masculine trauma and gender anxiety brought on by wartime destabilization of the culture's domestic economy and a consequent "deregulation" of the institutionalized and patriarchally informed relationship between men and women'.[10] If, then, the world of crime emerges as a particularly useful trope for the continuation of war in peacetime, the frontline between those who had remained on the home front and those returning from the battlefields overseas is refigured as a domestic war zone. For the veteran, the ordinary world of peacetime America turns dark because he has not yet been able to fully shed his soldier self and has brought unfinished business from the war back home. He may need to do battle with these ghosts before he can successfully reclaim his position in a world of restored peace so radically different from the one he left behind.

Yet his enemy need not only give body to traumatic war events which prevent him from fully adjusting upon his return but can also take the shape of the women waiting for him at home. It has, thus, also become a commonplace to read the femme fatale as a cinematic negotiation of the widespread discontent among American women, who, having achieved economic independence and self-esteem during the war period, were forced to give up their workplace for the homecoming veterans and limit themselves once again to the domestic sphere. In the very home in the name of which soldiers had gone to battle, a new combat came to be played through. If the women who had remained on the home front could never be sure that the veterans had curbed the lust to kill for which war had trained them, the veterans had to contest with a feminine insistence on self-empowerment that had emerged while they were away. Yet the gendered miscommunication around which film noir revolves not only pertains to the femme fatale, embodying anxieties invoked by the image of the independent working woman who had as much trouble readjusting to the peacetime domesticity as the veterans themselves. It also speaks to the way those who had remained at home were willing to vehemently screen out the war in order to move on with their lives, while those who returned from war zones could not help but confront the phantoms of that very past.

Fred Zinnemann's *Act of Violence* (1948) plays through the repercussions of war trauma in postwar America by using the noir genre as a way to discuss the terrible moral stakes of survival. The film serves as a paradigmatic example of the way the fantasies of the women who remained at home prove to be at cross purposes with those of the men who went away as well as of how an attempt to repress a crime committed overseas invariably returns in the shape of a double to haunt the present. As such, this film brings the experience of war explicitly into focus which is only obliquely encoded in films such as *Out of the Past*. In contrast to Tourneur's film, at issue is not the dangerous consequence of transgressive desire called forth by the seductions of a manipulative woman but rather the equally lethal desire an unresolved war trauma can unleash.

The film narrative revolves around a former bombardier, Joe Parkson (Robert Ryan), the sole survivor of a thwarted attempt to break out of a Nazi prison camp, who, in order to avenge the horrible death of his comrades, seeks out the senior officer, Frank R. Enley (Van Heflin), who had informed on them. He has travelled all the way from New York to California to shoot his former comrade in arms. In this battle between one veteran's attempt to repress all knowledge of his past crime and another's obsession with retribution, Joe assumes the position of the classic femme fatale. Cast as the symptom of his superior officer, he is shown to be hoarding the murderous aspect of a survival instinct from which the other man tries to distance himself. Both veterans are indelibly marked by the nightmare of war they share. The difference lies in the fact that Frank has deluded himself into believing he could screen out his secret past, while Joe insists on having him take responsibility for the consequences of his actions. By suddenly resurfacing out of the past, he forces Frank to acknowledge a guilt he can neither forget nor openly admit, which is tantamount to recognising that his prosperous postwar existence is predicated on self-delusion.

The film uses Frank's wife, Edith (Janet Leigh), to represent the ordinary everyday, which, as in *Out of the Past*, marks a space which the noir hero can never fully inhabit. Her reluctance to confront the ugly realities both veterans confide in her because she wishes, at all costs, to hold on to her idea of an intact home and family life, is shown to be as sinister a gesture of denial as her husband's attempt to cover up his former culpability. First Joe invades her living room, justifying his desire for vengeance by describing for her the bullet-riddled bodies and tormented moans of the men who were shot by the prison guards after her husband had betrayed their plan. Several hours later, Frank launches into his own rendition of this fateful event that culminates in a confession of the true horror of his deed: 'They were dead and I was eating. And maybe that's all I did it for. To save one man. Me'. What the appearance of Frank's double brings into the open is thus more than the terrible death of those who failed to escape from a war camp. At issue above all is the moral ambiguity at the heart of the very will for survival on which postwar culture is predicated. This instinct itself emerges as the root of the crime committed in a war zone overseas but implicitly also as the dark kernel hidden beneath suburban prosperity, where self-knowledge and desires one knows to be bad can be safely kept apart.

In *Act of Violence*, the world of crime becomes the one site where war's unfinished business can be played through because, in contrast to the suburbs where the Enleys live, moral ambiguity is its explicit motto. Frank thus flees to the underworld of Los Angeles in search of an assassin and, once he has found one, sets up a meeting with Joe at the train station in Santa Lisa. If the sombre point of this noir narrative consists in disclosing how readily both veterans, sick with war, can be criminalised, the professional killer emerges as the new common enemy, once more placing them on the same side of the fight. To prevent a murder which he, in this case, has explicitly ordered, Frank goes to the train station that night to warn Joe, who has arrived with his gun in his hand, while the gangster looks out at both of them from inside his car. What follows is an act of prudent courage. By turning a fateful cycle of violence into a conscious choice, Frank's intervention (like Jeff's call to the police) is tantamount to accepting responsibility for both past and present actions, including a responsibility for the outcome of his fate. Seeing that the gangster has begun to take aim, Frank runs to the car in order to put a stop to what he, in a moment of moral blindness, set in motion. He takes the bullet meant for Joe, and, though wounded, jumps onto the car as the gangster tries to flee, causing a crash that will leave both dead. By drawing the act of violence onto himself, he not only prevents the death of his former bombardier but also saves himself from becoming a murderer.

The film's dramaturgy, however, requires a fourth position, namely that of a heroine who neither denies the tragic force of the past nor refuses to give in to the necessity of its fateful replaying in postwar America. Throughout the film, Joe's lover, Ann (Phyllis Thaxter), argues against his blind revenge, and, having followed the obsessed veteran to the site of the nocturnal showdown, meets up with him as he hovers over the corpse of his former comrade. In clear conscience he can assure her that he did not go through with the killing he had intended. Although what prevents Joe from becoming a criminal is not Ann's voice of reason but Frank's willingness to take death onto himself, Ann's presence is necessary for the symbolic rehabilitation of both war-sick men. She is the witness who can attest to the fact that all temptation to transgress the law has successfully been averted. For the police, finding the killer and his victim lying next to each other on the pavement, the case is closed. Yet the restitution won by virtue of Frank's self-sacrifice is painted in shades of black. At the end of *Act of Violence*, Joe and Ann, unable to screen out the double death on which their survival in postwar America is predicated, walk side by side back into the night, on their way to Mrs Enley to tell her of her loss.

A second manner in which film noir conceives of American crime culture as a continuation of war concerns the battle between police, politicians and gangsters, as this came to be fought out in urban centres once peace had been re-established. At issue here is not only the fallibility of members of the police, who can be bribed to cross the thin line into the realm of illegality, but above all the vulnerability of the law itself that becomes visible when a detective takes it into his own hands. Fritz Lang's *The Big Heat* (1953) is again taken as a paradigmatic example because in the film, the gendering of this fault line is everything but straightforward. The film discloses the criminals (and those implicated in their transgressions) to be the uncanny inversion of the very law that seeks their punishment. Analogous to the classic femme fatale, the gangster is cast as the hoarder of a dangerous *jouissance* which the detective projects onto him so as to distance himself from his own transgressive desire. At the same time, the femme fatale ultimately proves not only to be on the side of the law, but to be the one to save the detective fighting in its name from his own deluded sense of justice. She will take the fall not because she is compelled by others to do so, but because, having seen where the cycle of violence leads, she has the prudent courage to put a stop to it.

Four women accompany police detective Dave Bannion (Glenn Ford) on his journey through the underworld that brings him to the brink of lawlessness. While they are not the agents of the illegal transactions he seeks to disclose, they are the ones to prompt him on in his fury for finding justice at all costs. They are all fated in that they are the ones who bear the consequences of his decision to take the law into his own hands. The first of these dark women is the widow of a respected police officer. Her husband had committed suicide one night after having written a confession to the district attorney, giving evidence to the extent to which Mafia bribes control his police force. Motivated by greed, Bertha Duncan (Jeanette Nolan) holds back this letter, hoping to blackmail the Mafia boss, even while, in order to protect her own interests, she sends him after everyone who threatens to expose her secret. Her first victim is Duncan's mistress, Lucy Chapman (Dorothy Green), who gave him the idea of confessing his crimes in the hope that he might extricate himself from his criminal alliances. After his death, she confides what she knows about the treacherous game the widow is playing to Bannion. In the web of corruption he is seeking to penetrate, any disclosure can only engender more murders, because no one is willing to stop doing the things that produce this violence. The detective does not keep this knowledge to himself and instead uses it as collateral in his dealings with the Mafia, unwittingly causing the death of his informant.

This first feminine sacrifice is necessary in that it brings to light the widow's ruthless self-interest but also in that it reveals the equally blind obsession which drives the investigating detective. In order to avenge her murder, Bannion will go behind his superior's back and take the case into his own hands, which gets him suspended from the police force. Even his wife Katie (Joselyn Brando) is not safe from the effects of the single-minded pursuit of justice that follows. With her patient, mild gaze, she may represent the safety of a home to which the detective can return after his daily battle against crime. Yet Lang's film – far harsher than *Out of the Past* – insists that even in the ordinary world there can be no room for Katie's unflinching trust because it, too, stands under the influence of the dirty enmeshment of politics and criminality which her husband is seeking to uncover. One evening, while Bannion is reading a bedtime story to his daughter, Katie gets into his car and becomes the victim of the bomb intended for him. This accident also serves a narrative necessity;

Katie's sacrifice has a function. In death, she will direct her husband's revenge, giving him a cause to plunge ever more vehemently into the world of crime.

Bannion finally meets Debbie (Gloria Graham), the carefree girlfriend of the gangster Vince (Lee Marvin), who enjoys the luxuries of his illegal wealth, even while she never dupes herself about the dangerous alliance she is part of. After her lover, in a bout of jealousy, burns the left side of her face by throwing boiling coffee at her, she turns into a two-faced figure of retribution.

The bandage covering up her scar (recalling the destructive aspect of all transgressive desire) sharpens the alluring beauty of the untarnished side of her face (signifying seduction). This sudden impairment of her beauty causes Debbie not only to see through the vanity of a life of crime but to stop the cycle of violence she is implicitly part of. She decides to take down the treacherous widow, thus triggering the 'big heat' that will finally blow the cover on the entire network of political corruption as well. Yet she also realises that she alone is allowed to perform the retribution Bannion seeks. He had confessed to her that he had almost strangled Bertha Duncan in anger, and she had responded by pointing out to him that were he to do so, he would no longer be any different from the men he hates. She decides to take on the role of his double, performing his act of retribution in his stead, which is to say, take on his murderous desire, so as to protect him from the consequences. As in *Act of Violence*, legitimate justice can only prevail if she makes certain that the detective, its representative, will not cross the fine line into illegality.

Debbie visits the widow in her home, and, assuring her adversary that under their mink coats they are both sisters, she pulls out her gun and shoots. Just like her face, her revenge is both beautiful and terrifying, the expression of pure justice absolved from all compassion and self-interest. By drawing death

Figure 7.1   Vince (Lee Marvin) brutalises Debbie (Gloria Graham) before throwing scalding coffee into her face; note the coffee carafe below Vince's elbow, *The Big Heat*.

onto herself, she can bring about the demise of her criminal accomplices while averting the detective's downfall. Debbie returns one last time to Vince and, in order to deliver her fatal message, she makes use of her own disfigured beauty. She takes off her bandage as she informs him of the death of the widow (whose husband's confession will now come into the open). The scar on her cheek serves as visual evidence of all the illegal actions for which he will now have to answer. Vince shoots his nemesis. To the end, he is unwilling to stop doing what had produced the fateful consequences in the first place. Together with the police, Bannion shows up several minutes later and finally brings the man he has so viciously sought to justice. Then the detective tenderly places Debbie's mink coat under her head, while she turns her disfigured side away from him into this pillow, displaying only her immaculate face in profile before closing her eyes.

This last sacrifice is also a narrative necessity. Over her dead body, justice is reinstalled and the detective's reintegration into the ordinary everyday achieved. When Debbie had initially asked him about his wife he had not been willing to tell her anything. Kneeling beside her corpse, he is able to make good on this omission, assuring her that Katie would have liked her. In death, these two women merge into a double portrait of loss, signifying Bannion's redemption from his unbridled lust for revenge. The narrative logic is the same as in *The Maltese Falcon*. Feminine sacrifice undoes the hero's temptability. And yet the difference is as crucial. While Brigid, who may well get the death sentence, is compelled to give herself up to the police, Debbie calls death upon herself so as to put an end to a tragic cycle of violence. She is no one's symptom and instead the subject of a story whose outcome she has in her control. Though she manipulates the hero by taking his illegitimate revenge onto herself, she does so in his interest; and in the interest of the world of the ordinary he represents. There is a new day for Bannion, and, in contrast to *Act of Violence*, in the closing sequence of *The Big Heat*, we see him back in the police station the next morning. Only a small shadow hovers on the fringe of the film frame that shows him sitting again at his desk.

Billy Wilder's Noir Stars

If, in the course of the 1940s, the infallibility of the noir hero becomes ever more troubled, the femme fatale is consistently shown to exceed the frame his narrative devises for her. The films discussed so far offer a reassessment of the relationship between the masculine hero and the women revolving around him, tempting him into a situation from which there is no escape or seeking to save him from the destructive force his transgressive desire unleashes. The noir heroine proves to be as much a subject in her own story as a symptom of his fantasy. By way of closure, two films by Billy Wilder are used to illustrate a further aspect of why noir heroines have had such a resilient survival in our cultural imaginary. If Wilder's fatal women are elusive, then it is because they stand in for the allure of the cinematic medium itself. The ambivalence of emotion they command is comparable to the projected film image that draws us into its charm, even though we know it to be nothing other than the result of light, projected on a screen in the dark.

Double Indemnity (1944) plays through a similar triangulation of desire as *Out of the Past*, in that, here too, the seductive Phyllis Dietrichson (Barbara Stanwyck) entices a younger man, the insurance agent Walter Neff (Fred MacMurray), to trick her husband into signing a life-insurance policy with a double indemnity clause and then help her murder him to get the money. She spins a tale about an unbearable marriage and he falls for it, not because he wants the money or the woman, as he claims in the voiceover confession that once again serves as the film's narrative frame. Instead, he has been obsessed with finding a way to trick his company and thus prove he is cleverer at fraud than the clients who have tried to deceive him. Decisive about the fatal contract Phyllis and Walter agree upon is that they do not share the same fantasy. While the femme fatale allows the insurance agent to delude himself regarding her neediness and project his transgressive desire onto her, she is at no point herself deluded. She stands apart from him and recognises her own manipulation. To underscore his heroine's self-determination, Wilder offers us a series of close-ups that run counter to the misogynist confession his hero offers as a voiceover commentary throughout the film. This disjunction between Stanwyck's face and MacMurray's voiceover pits the specific power of the cinematic image against a narrative technique inherited from literature and, to a degree, anachronistic to this new medium.

We see Phyllis standing on the threshold to her home lost in thought after her husband has unwittingly signed his own death warrant, her eyes sparkling. Then again, when Walter strangles Mr Dietrichson from the back seat of his car a few weeks later, we are given a close-up of her face, as sober pensiveness slowly turns to an expression of quiet joy.

On the evening of the inquest and after the judge has declared the death of her husband to have been an accident, Phyllis visits Walter but hesitates in front of his door because she hears the voice of his supervisor coming from inside the apartment. Charged with investigating the Dietrichson claim, Keyes (Edward G. Robinson) vociferously states his desire to hand the widow over to the police. In her face we see signs of trepidation at the thought that the law might catch up with her after all. We also understand that she is privy to the fact that Walter will sacrifice her to protect himself. A few days later, she calls him to a rendezvous in the supermarket they have chosen as their clandestine meeting point. She takes off her sunglasses as she declares that she will not withdraw her claim. 'We went into it together and we are getting out

Figure 7.2 Phyllis (Barbara Stanwyck) experiences the joy of her husband's strangulation, *Double Indemnity*.

together,' she solemnly assures him. 'It's straight down the line for both of us, remember'. Her uncompromising gaze signals to us that she will not cede to his refusal to assume responsibility for their shared action.

Like so many noir heroes, Walter foolishly believes that he can absolve himself of his guilt by killing the woman who inspired his murderous fantasy. They meet one last time in the darkened living room of her home. Because she astutely anticipates that he has come to kill her, she has placed a gun beneath the pillow of her couch and with it fires the first shot, dropping her weapon, however, before firing a second time. As her wounded lover approaches, we see her face in a close-up one last time. Embracing him, she confesses: 'I never loved you, Walter, not you or anybody else. I'm rotten to the heart. I used you, just as you said ... until a minute ago when I couldn't fire that second shot'. Having seen through her own deception, she stops her act, yet, like Sam Spade before him (though far less invulnerable but also far more murderous than Bogart's private eye), Walter tenaciously holds on to his mistrust and instead fires his gun twice. We see a flicker of astonishment on Phyllis's face, then she winces briefly at the pain she has begun to feel. This close-up draws our attention to the fact that Phyllis has accepted her tragic fate with open eyes. Privileging her visual self-expression over his dialogue, the mise-en-scène attests to her acknowledging responsibility for a death she has chosen. As such, this final close-up forcefully contradicts and overwrites the cliché story of the spider woman Neff comes up with in the frame narrative to indemnify himself for both murders he has committed.

Sunset Boulevard (1950) offers a different spin on the noir triangulation of desire, providing a scathing critique of the dream factory Hollywood itself. The silent movie star, Norma Desmond (Gloria Swanson), has entrapped the young screenwriter, Joe Gillis (William Holden), in her magnificent old villa and contracted him to rewrite her script for a film about Salome. As in *Out of the Past*, the figure of paternal authority is doubled. Norma hopes that she can convince Cecil B. DeMille (playing himself), still making epic melodramas in Hollywood, to bring about her comeback on screen by casting her as the biblical princess. Max (Erich von Stroheim), in turn, takes on the obscene inversion of this role. As her former director and lover, he now oversees a fatal drama staged to sustain her insistence on living a celluloid life which is predicated on the fantasy that she will again move into the public eye. He does everything to help her delude herself even while – and therein the gendering is reversed – he is never deluded himself. On the side of the ordinary everyday, we find Betty Schaefer (Nancy Olson), a Hollywood insider successfully working her way up in the script department at Paramount. In her, Joe sees a way out of the stifling situation he got himself into when, giving in to Norma's temptation, he pretended to revise a script he knows to be unsalvageable because he thought this would produce quick cash. Yet, as the code of the noir world dictates, once he has embarked on his shady scheme, it's straight down the line for everyone involved.

The special twist Wilder comes up with in *Sunset Boulevard* consists in the fact that the male voiceover, casting the silent movie star as the femme fatale to a vulnerable screen writer, is spoken by a dead man. When Joe, having realised the futility of his own dream, tries to leave Norma, she shoots him in the back and he falls, face down, into the pool behind her villa, where the police find him the next morning. As in *Double Indemnity*, the femme fatale, in turn, is again the one associated with the special power of the cinematic medium, making people present to us whom we know are not physically there. Early on in the film we see Norma sitting next to Joe, watching one of her old films projected onto a screen in her darkened living room. Wilder uses her passionate attack against those producers who chose to forget the dramatic qualities of the face that made her one of the greatest silent movie stars, so as to draw attention to what lies behind the duplicity of the projected image. With the help of the projection of light onto a white screen, she can incessantly emerge as a film image, beyond any existence in the real world. At first, while she looks at her celluloid self and invokes her return to the screen, Norma stands with her back to the projector and is illuminated from behind. Then she provocatively turns toward her screenwriter, and in so doing faces the projector as well. While the back of her head and her body dissolve into the darkness of the room, we now see the profile of her face with utmost clarity. The projected beam of light draws out a white line protruding from the rest of her face even while doubling its contours.

Sunset Boulevard ends not with a showdown between the noir hero and the woman who ensnared him, but between the two modes of narration they represent. Significantly it is Max who comes up with the ruse that will compel

Norma to leave her dressing-room and go downstairs, where the police car is waiting for her. Given that the Paramount news cameras have arrived, he lets Norma believe that the shooting of *Salome* is about to begin, and, from the bottom of the stairs, directs one last time the benighted fantasy in which she perfects the role she has designed for herself. While the cameras begin to turn, she descends the main staircase of the villa, while Joe's voiceover offers his last comment: 'Life, which can be strangely merciful, had taken pity on Norma Desmond. The dream she had clung to so desperately, had enfolded her'. This is the last we hear of him, but the sequence is not yet over. As Gloria Swanson glides down the stairway, surrounded by police, newspaper men and fascinated onlookers, the fetish magic of cinema is perfected. Swanson plays both Salome and the deluded silent movie star, once more returned to the public eye.

We know that this celluloid woman is not what she seems to be and we are taken in not despite but because of her duplicity. Norma interrupts her performance once she has reached the foot of the stairs, compelled to confess her joy: 'You see, this is my life. It always will be!' she proclaims, adding, 'There's nothing else. Just us and the cameras and those wonderful people out there in the dark'. We can read this as an ominous commentary on the power of the cinematic image itself. Demurely announcing, 'All right, Mr DeMille, I'm ready for my close-up', she undulates toward the Paramount New cameras. As she moves ever closer, she dissolves in the white light of the film image – in the extreme close-up of her face. The white circle once more fills up with shades of grey, which draw all the light with them and leave behind a completely black screen.

The flowing reversal from white to black can be read as a cipher for the self-reflexivity of film noir. This genre draws on shades of darkness to bring to the screen a world in which nothing is quite like it seems. Over and beyond the mutual duping played out between a silent movie star and her screenwriter, the confrontation at the end of *Sunset Boulevard* thus pertains to the two modes of cinematic narration – the battle between image and sound – which, on the level of the film's diegesis, is targeted as the reason for Norma's fall from celebrity, but which also proves to be at cross purposes in the film's mode of narration. If the voiceover, belonging to the vulnerable noir hero, is pitted against the close-ups aligned with the femme fatale, it is the latter that wins out in the end. Once Norma has embarked on her final act, no one dares speak a word to interrupt or correct her, watching instead in awed pity. Her fatal charm is the very stuff that the dreams of cinema are made of – a play of shaded light. Joe's commentary stops before she has reached the bottom of the stairs, while we never see her arrested by the police and thus never arrested in her movement. Instead, her close-up dissolves into pure light so that we can imagine her dancing Salome's seduction for ever. In a rare spin on the genre, Wilder's fatal movie star, as fully enveloped in her self-delusion as she is in the light that brought it on screen, has consumed the very film frame that consumes her, leaving us, as it were, in the dark.

Filmography

Act of Violence (Fred Zinnemann, USA, MGM, 1948)
Double Indemnity (Billy Wilder, USA, Paramount Pictures, 1944)
Out of the Past (Jacques Tourneur, USA, RKO Radio Pictures, 1947)
Sunset Boulevard (Billy Wilder, USA, Paramount Pictures, 1950)
The Big Heat (Fritz Lang, USA, Columbia Pictures, 1953)
The Maltese Falcon (John Huston, USA, Warner Brothers, 1941)

Bibliography

Bronfen, Elisabeth (2012), *Specters of War. Hollywood's Engagement with Military Conflict*, New Brunswick, NJ: Rutgers University Press.
——. (2013), *Night Passages. Philosophy, Literature, Film*, New York: Columbia University Press.
Cavell, Stanley (1987), 'The avoidance of love. A reading of King Lear', in Stanley Cavell, *Disowning Knowledge in Six Plays of Shakespeare*, Cambridge: Cambridge University Press.
Copjec, Joan (1993), 'The phenomenal nonphenomenal', in Joan Copjec (ed.), *Shades of Noir*, London: Verso.
Cowie, Elizabeth (1993), 'Film noir and women', in Copjec (ed.), *Shades of Noir*.
Doane, Mary Ann (1991), *Femmes Fatales. Feminism, Film Theory, Psychoanalysis*, London: Routledge.
Harvey, Sylvia (1980), 'Women's place: The absent family in film noir', in E. Ann Kaplan (ed.), *Women in Film Noir: Both Sides of the Camera*, London: British Film Institute, pp. 22–34.
Krutnik, Frank (1991), *In a Lonely Street. Film noir, Genre, Masculinity*, London: Routledge.
Place, Janey (1980), 'Women in film noir', in Kaplan (ed.), *Women in Film Noir*, pp. 53–62.
Sobchack, Vivian (1998), 'Lounge time: Postwar crises and the chronotope of film noir', in Nick Browne (ed.), *Refiguring American Film Genres: Theory and History*, Berkeley, CA: University of California Press.

Notes

1. Mary Ann Doane, *Femmes Fatales. Feminism, Film Theory, Psychoanalysis* (London: Routledge, 1991), p. 3.
2. Frank Krutnik, *In a Lonely Street. Film Noir, Genre, Masculinity* (London: Routledge, 1991), p. 95.
3. Sylvia Harvey, 'Women's place: The absent family in film noir', in E. Ann Kaplan (ed.), *Women in Film Noir* (London: British Film Institute, 1980), p. 31. See also Janey Place, 'Women in film noir', in the same volume.
4. In *All Through the Night*, released in 1941, Bogart plays a gambler who becomes patriotic once he has stumbled upon Nazi saboteurs, while in Huston's *Across the Pacific* (1942), his lack of loyalty to his home country emerges as an intelligence ploy. Once the Americans entered the war, Bogart also famously appeared in shorts advertising the sale of war bonds. Greenstreet and Lorre make an appearance in

Hollywood Canteen (a film about soldiers' home entertainment) with a routine that cites their sinister play in *Maltese Falcon*; see Elisabeth Bronfen's discussion of war entertainment in *Specters of War. Hollywood's Engagement with Military Conflict* (New Brunswick, NJ: Rutgers University Press, 2013).
5. Joan Copjec, 'The phenomenal nonphenomenal', in Joan Copjec (ed.), *Shades of Noir* (London: Verso 1993), p. 193.
6. Variations on this triangulation of desire can place a woman, who only plays at being a femme fatale, between two men, as in *Gilda* or *The Big Sleep*, or she could, as in *Laura*, be oblivious to the violent fantasy she has inspired both in the older man, who will commit a crime of passion, and the detective called in to clear the case. Or there could be a doubling of the transgressive woman, as in *Kiss me Deadly*, where one is the victim and the other the perpetrator of a deadly secret. See Elizabeth Cowie's 'Film noir and women', in Copjec (ed.), *Shades of Noir*, pp. 121–65.
7. Stanley Cavell, 'The avoidance of love. A reading of King Lear', in Stanley Cavell, *Disowning Knowledge in Six Plays of Shakespeare* (Cambridge: Cambridge University Press 1987), p. 81.
8. Ibid., p. 112.
9. Vivian Sobchack, 'Lounge time: Postwar crisis and the chronotope of film noir', in Nick Browne (ed.), *Refiguring American Film Genres: Theory and History* (Berkeley, CA: University of California Press, 1998), p. 130.
10. Ibid.

8. THE SUBVERSIVE SHADE OF BLACK IN FILM NOIR

Charles Scruggs

In the American context, there being no way for him to get to the *nigger*, he [Fritz Lang] could use only that other American prototype, the criminal, *le gangster*.

James Baldwin, 'The devil finds work'[1]

Just how subversive was film noir? For Paul Schrader the answer is obvious: the anxiety after World War II over the Bomb, the war's disruption to middle-class domesticity and the Red Menace resulted in films that 'took a harsh uncomplimentary look at American life'.[2] Even before the end of World War II films like John Huston's *The Maltese Falcon* (1941) and Billy Wilder's *Double Indemnity* (1944) tied the unholy trinity of greed, lust and murder to the American Dream, turning a valorised myth upside down. Yet there is one segment of American society that film noir failed to analyse, according to its critics: the caste system that Gunnar Myrdal called *An American Dilemma* (1944). Published a year before World War II ended and film noir (supposedly) began, his famous study investigated the 'dark corner' of American life.[3] Myrdal ruthlessly exposed the contradiction within a social system whose America Creed said one thing, equality and justice for all, and whose practice towards African-Americans said another. Black life, he argued, remained at a standstill, bogged down at the bottom of the social system with no place to go. Although critics such as Eric Lott, Paula Rabinowitz, Julian Murphet, E. Ann Kaplan and Manthia Diawara have written brilliantly about film noir, they all agree, in their different ways, that film noir does not do what Myrdal did in his famous study. The directors of these films either recycled the same stereotypes from other genres, or they used the 'Negro' (male or female) as a negative foil to whiteness (Lott)[4] or as a 'fall from whiteness' (Diawara).[5] Kaplan suggests that the white femme fatale connects the 'darkness of the psyche ... with the literal darkness of racial others',[6] and Julian Murphet ingeniously associates her, in terms of the 'racial unconscious', with the frightening prospect of black masses flooding American cities after World War II.[7] Rabinowitz perceptively sees Kathie Moffat's black maid in *Out of the Past* (1947) as her double but categorises that connection as 'Kathie's aura – another type of literal femme noire'.[8]

James Baldwin's observation about Fritz Lang's *You Only Live Once* gives us another perspective. It reminds us that although directors like Lang and others were hamstrung by the Hollywood system and the Hays Code, they found a way of speaking in 'code', confiding secrets to those in the audience willing to listen and observe. One revelation would be their use of the *doppelganger*. Consider, for instance, the image of the fugitive in film noir in which a white character can mirror a black condition such as the consequences of the Fugitive Slave Law (1793, repealed in 1850). That historical moment would find its appropriate cinematic metaphor in the outsider or the man on the run. Examples here are plentiful: *I Am a Fugitive from a Chain Gang* (1932), *Fury* (1936), *You Only Live Once* (1937), *They Live By Night* (1947), *D.O.A.* (1950), *Dark Passage* (1947), *Out of the Past* (1947), *The Killers* (1946), *High Sierra* (1941), *The Fugitive Kind* (1959). All these films express a sympathy for the fugitive caught in a web of surveillance (for example, *Dark Passage*) or systemic corruption (*I Am a Fugitive*, *You Only Live Once*, *High Sierra*) or in a world with no place to hide. As Jeff Markham (Robert Mitchum) said memorably to Kathie Moffat (Jane Greer) in *Out of the Past*, 'Is there some place left to go?' This doubling of white with black is explicitly made in *Out of the Past* when director Jacques Tourneur links Kathie with her black maid Eunice Leonard (Theresa Harris). Kathie is a fugitive who mirrors Eunice's previous condition, for she is at first pursued by Jeff as though he were a slave catcher.[9]

Fritz Lang had earlier explored this theme of the double in *Fury* (1936), his first American film. Mistaken for a kidnapper, white Joe Wilson (Spencer Tracy) is captured in a small town and subjected to a vigilante lynching which fails. Lang documents both the mindless fury of the mob and Wilson's own transformation into a monster in his desire to wreak revenge upon the lynchers. Lang's primary focus, however, is upon the celebrated American small town as the setting for racial violence. At first, the film seems to indict only the moral myopia of the individuals in the town, but as the movie progresses, Lang's real target is the capitulation of individual will to group hysterics. The trial is the scene in which racism surfaces as the film's major theme. For much of the trial, the ringleaders of the mob remain anonymous as is the case

Figure 8.1 Eunice Leonard (Theresa Harris) suspicious of Markham (Robert Mitchum) in the nightclub scene, *Out of the Past*.

with most southern lynchings of African-Americans, but when the prosecutor shows a newsreel of the event, the ringleaders' alibis are exposed as lies. They are not only captured on film but are shown to be figures driven by the Furies, dehumanised and capable of any monstrous act. Behind this cinematic moment is the truth of American history, especially the exposure of an American political system that has failed to pass an anti-lynching law. The moment is also self-reflexive in that Lang implies that film itself, especially film noir, can present a better history lesson than official history.[10]

A similar theme is explored in Sidney Lumet's *The Fugitive Kind* (1959), a title that refers to a southern literary magazine called *The Fugitive* and a group of white intellectuals known as 'the Nashville Fugitives'. In *I'll Take My Stand* (1930) this group of twelve white men defended the South's agrarian, organic culture (with blacks in their place) against Northern capitalism and its machine culture.[11] The film decimates the myth of the harmonious southern town, exposing its mean pettiness and vicious, xenophobic attitudes, when an outsider, a white blues singer named Val Xavier (Marlon Brando), enters its borders. Ironically, Val is looking for refuge, fleeing the corrupt city (New Orleans) in search of pastoral space. He takes a job as a salesman in a small store and gets involved with an older, married woman, the daughter of an Italian immigrant, another outsider. Her jealous, crippled husband convinces the townspeople to kill them both, the two dying in a fire that the citizens refuse to extinguish. Based on a play by Tennessee Williams (*Orpheus Descending*), *The Fugitive Kind* critiques the town's racism indirectly. Lady Torrence (Anna Magnani), Val's lover, tells him that her own father was murdered and his wine bar burned down because he had served blacks.[12]

This pattern of cinematic subterfuge would also be used in *The Phenix City Story* (1955), a pseudo-documentary which claims to be an exposé of a 'syndicate' that is responsible for crime in a small Alabama town. The movie, however, is a coded analysis of the town's racism, the primal crime that not only supersedes all others but is their source. The unmistakable revelation of what the film is about comes with a shocking scene in which a young, dead 'coloured' girl is thrown from a car like so much garbage, with a note that says to the white authorities that if they don't cease their investigations into the mob's activities, 'this will happen to your kids'. In a sense, it already has. They will grow up to be just like their parents – soulless, racist automatons.[13] It is not by accident that the film's co-screenwriter, Daniel Mainwaring, wrote the screenplay for *The Invasion of the Body Snatchers* (1956).

The theory that underlies my argument in this chapter is Freud's famous essay, 'The Uncanny', which among other things investigates the psychological implications of the German word *heimlich*. Freud is fascinated by its etymology, its double meaning of both 'familiar' and 'unfamiliar', referring to the home both in terms of familiar spaces like kitchen and parlour and as hidden spaces like attic and basement, those spaces 'concealed from sight'.[14] Furthermore, as Anthony Vidler notes, the noun *Heimlichkeit* suggests 'the fundamental propensity of the familiar to turn on its owners, suddenly to become defamiliarized, derealized, as if in a dream'.[15] Film noir, we might say, 'turns' the familiar American Dream embodied in most Hollywood movies into a Gothic nightmare.[16] Film noir is also a dream, as John Irwin notes, in which the familiar/unfamiliar paradox creates a doubling in which the first term, the familiar, can either quietly shade into the second term, the unfamiliar, or precipitously fall into it.[17] For instance, film noir often opens with ordinary life and then shows us, as Foster Hirsch says, 'the precariousness of the normal everyday world'.[18] Hence 'normal' white life, which on the surface seems solid, safe, and expansive, can suddenly find itself falling into an abyss usually reserved for African-Americans.

In addition, as Brian McCuskey has observed, Freud's 'uncanny' can apply to 'members of the household but not the family – specifically, servants and other residents who are both insiders and outsiders'.[19] This last insight has a particular relevance to Lottie (Butterfly McQueen) in *Mildred Pierce*, the black maid who represents a hidden history of hard labour that stands in contrast to characters in the film who try to escape it.

Indeed, the thread that connects the three films I will discuss is the theme of work, done either by African-Americans or by a white working class. Leftist directors of film noir often connect the two, suggesting that what is 'concealed from sight' through comic caricature – or, more specifically, through the pastoral myth of happy darkies picking cotton – has a relevance to white life at the bottom, or wage slavery. For instance, historian James Oakes has debunked the plantation system in the anti-bellum South as pastoral space. He exposes that system as 'factories in the field', an early form of agribusiness, noting

Figure 8.2   Lotte (Butterfly McQueen) and Mildred (Joan Crawford) making home-made pies, *Mildred Pierce*.

that the inhumane managerial system that we associate with the industrialised North was already firmly in place in the South.[20] This historical truth echoes Toni Morrison's perceptive insight that 'an Africanist presence complicates [literary] texts, sometimes contradicting them entirely'.[21] That insight has specific relevance to *Double Indemnity* (1944), *Mildred Pierce* (1945) and *The Set-Up* (1949).

Of the seven scripts for the film version of James M. Cain's novel *Mildred Pierce* (1941), it was William Faulkner's that transformed the white Letty in the novel into the black Lottie in the film, a transformation that was kept in the shooting script. That shooting script was disapproved of by Cain, not because of the substitution of a black maid for a white one, but because the script reduced his novel to 'a murder story not very different from every "B" picture that has been made for the last forty years'.[22] As Cain told the film's producer, Jerry Wald, his characters are not nasty enough to be murderers: 'they are not that kind of people'.[23] And yet that is precisely the film's major theme–most of them are nasty enough to be murderers, the only question being, which one? My point here is that by changing the maid's racial identity to black, the murder committed in the film is not the one emphasised in the plot. Black Lottie's presence also 'complicates' the film's ending. Although the novel ends comically with Bert and Mildred getting 'stinko', the film's final shot, with its foregrounding of scrubbing ladies on their knees in the Halls of Justice, underscores Lottie's significance and as such subverts the film's happy ending.[24]

In the novel, Cain's white female domestic servant, Letty, is a perfect vehicle for his social satire. When Blanche Engel and her husband come to Ray's funeral (Kay in the film), Blanche is upset when she discovers that she was greeted at the door by a maid whom she mistook for being a friend of the family. She feels, as Cain wryly observes, that 'Letty had compromised her social position'.²⁵ The comedy here is that unless Letty is wearing her maid's habit, she can be mistaken for anyone. In the movie, however, there is no mistaking Lottie for anything but the mudsill of society, for it is the colour of her skin, not her uniform, that separates her from the others. In the film (as in the novel), Mildred's (Joan Crawford) divorce from her husband forces her to take work as a waitress, thus beginning a career that will catapult her into the position of successful businesswomen with a chain of restaurants. At first, however, her waitress uniform is a badge of disgrace to Veda (Ann Blyth), her snooty, social-climbing daughter. When Veda makes Lottie wear the uniform, that disgrace is racial, not social. Thus when Mildred tries to defend herself – 'I became a waitress so that you and your sister can eat' – Veda retorts, 'I'm really not surprised. You've never spoken of your people – who you came from – so perhaps it's natural. Maybe that's why father –'. 'Who you came from' implies an ancestry far more shameful than a descent from white trash, though Veda in her malice seems oblivious to the fact that if her insinuation is true, she too would be tainted by the tar brush. It is precisely at this point that Mildred tells Veda, as she does in the novel, that she is thinking of opening a restaurant, implying that the waitress uniform was only a trial run for something bigger.

But here is where Lottie 'complicates' the cinematic text. The film condemns the snobbish Veda for scorning hard work, but the film also praises Mildred for rising above the menial work done by black Lottie. Eric Lott sees the film's depiction of Mildred's 'hard labour' as a waitress as 'nigger work', but it could be argued that 'nigger work' is what is valorised in the film since the film's major characters – Monte Beragon (Zachary Scott), Wally Fay (Jack Carson) and Veda – have a contempt for work of any kind.²⁶ Mildred herself undergoes a sea change when she becomes an adventure capitalist. Indeed, that transformation from waitress to entrepreneur points to a key theme in the film, that of racial masquerade.

Racial masquerade indicates a flight from race rather than class, a theme emphasised in a scene not in the novel in which Kay (Jo Anne Marlowe) does her Carmen Miranda imitation with 'a heavy coating of lipstick and mascara on'. The moment, of course, is right out of vaudeville, its more distant ancestry being the minstrel show. Thus when Mildred tells Lottie to take Kay upstairs 'and wipe that goo off her face', the implication is that Kay can get the 'goo' off her face but Lottie can't.²⁷ 'Blacking up', as Michael Rogin has observed of Al Jolson in *The Jazz Singer* (1927), implies that you can take it off.²⁸

Although racial masquerade implies that wiping 'the goo off' reveals a white identity underneath, the film argues that this identity is both fragile and fictional. For instance, the mask and the reality become the same when Veda, wearing almost an exact replica of Kay's exotic outfit, becomes a stripper (in Hays Code terms) in a seedy bar. Veda's masquerade as a 'native' dancer reveals her to be the tramp that she has always been. That is, she wears a ceremonial dress removed from one culture and transferred in a debased version to another, the stripper bar, but it ironically exposes the true Veda.

The theme of racial masquerade occurs again when Wally and Lottie are doubled in the grand opening of Mildred's first restaurant. Adorned with an apron, Wally complains that he is 'an executive', and Mildred retorts that he's 'now vice-president in charge of the potatoes'. But the most incisive comment upon his 'uniform' comes from Lottie when she tells him 'you look very pretty, Mr Fay'. When Wally attempts to wither her with a contemptuous 'thank you', Lottie, living in a space all her own, is unflappable: 'Not at all'. Like the fool in *King Lear*, Lottie penetrates the fiction of a 'white' social identity. What truly offends Wally is that he will be mistaken for Lottie, but he should be flattered – the film depicts him as being considerably lower on the moral scale than black Lottie.

All that we know from the published script of the film is that Lottie is 'not too smart', but Butterfly McQueen makes her so much more than a mindless dingbat. Donald Bogle's observation on the effect she has on him in general is telling: 'With her large expressive eyes, her bewildered and perplexed stare, and her quivering tremor of a voice, she seemed almost otherworldly'.[29] Bogle's splendid observation, when applied to her character in *Mildred Pierce*, changes what is satiric in Cain's novel to a Gothic subtext embedded in the film. Her strange behaviour – the sense that she doesn't live on this planet – calls attention to a hidden history, one that could only surface as the familiar made unfamiliar. In *The Politics and Poetics of Transgression*, Stallybrass and White argue that the family circle within a capitalist economy attempts to insulate itself from the rest of the world but that the domestic servant, often female, brings contamination into the 'social purity' of the house.[30] Black Lottie is both inside and outside the house. On the one hand, she is 'otherworldly' in the sense of having no social existence within the family, but on the other, her literal presence as a 'worker' makes her like Mildred, as compared, for instance, with spoiled Veda, the indolent Monte and sleazy Wally.[31]

Nowhere is that identification between Lottie and Mildred more apparent than in the scene in *Mildred Pierce* when Lottie compares the excitement of the opening night of Mildred's restaurant to her 'wedding night'. The entire context for this phrase helps to explain the full impact of Lottie's comic non-sequitur. In the chaos of the evening, a waitress tells Mildred that she'll never 'make any money' if she's too generous with her food, and Mildred responds, 'It's all right, as long as the customers are satisfied'. And then out of left field comes Lottie's remark: 'This is just like my wedding night. So exciting!' At that moment the two women are linked by work as a joy in itself, Marx's non-alienating work or work as *homo faber*: man (in this case, woman) the maker, the creator. The two women in this scene participate as equals in the joyful creation of the new restaurant.

Yet Mildred abandons this creative happiness for high capitalism (cloning her restaurants) and high society (in her attempt to win back Veda), thereby returning Lottie to her place as having no social identity. That 'crime' is related to other crimes in the film besides the murder of Monte Beragon, the film's whodunit. Joyce Nelson observes that the murder investigation obscures Wally's cut-throat business practices or 'crimes of the marketplace', as Nelson calls them: 'I didn't mean to cut up your business the way I did', Wally whines to Mildred, 'I just got started and couldn't stop . . . I can't help myself. I see an angle and right away I start cutting myself a piece of throat. It's an instinct'.[32] That there may be more than one crime in the film eludes Inspector Peterson (Moroni Olsen), the detective in charge of the case who insists upon making the act of murder both literal and linear: 'We look at the corpse . . . and we say why? What was the reason? And when we find the reason, we find the guy who made the corpse'. This rational approach focuses upon one murder and one reason, Veda's hurt vanity, and hence all other crimes are erased, including the hint at the movie's beginning through the use of 'false suture' that Mildred herself might have killed Monte.[33]

Indeed, 'false suture' may be the reason why Lottie is cast as an African-American. As Nelson points out, the film's opening murder scene leaves out the 'reverse shot' that would have revealed the murderer. We see Monte being shot, but we are not supplied with the missing 'reverse shot' until the movie's end in which everything is neatly wrapped up in a conclusion that leaves Mildred free to return to her first husband Bert (Bruce Bennett). The movie ends with Bert and Mildred leaving the Halls of Justice in the dawn, but within a mise-en-scène that depicts two scrubbing women on their knees keeping the floors of the Halls of Justice clean. It is the false cleanliness of the neatly resolved ending that disturbs the feminist critics, as well it should. Not only is the patriarchal system back in place, and Mildred back in the kitchen (in her home, not in her restaurant), but the history of the scrubbing women disappears in Bert and Mildred's return to middle-class domesticity.

Yet there is a hidden history that both links those scrubbing women to Lottie and makes her history distinct. Although it was customary for Irish, Scandinavian and German immigrant women to enter domestic service in the nineteenth century, this job was rarely seen as a permanent form of employment, since it was assumed that once married they would leave their employers' houses for homes of their own. In contrast, there was often no such escape for black women. They could not use domestic service as a 'way-station prior to marriage' or a 'stepping stone' to a better job, and they would not, as a rule, become householders. Better jobs were not open to them, and even if they were married, they usually had to supplement their husbands' meagre incomes.[34]

Thus, according to David M. Katzman, 'by 1920 black women comprised 40 percent of all domestic servants', and it was usually a job for life.[35]

Moreover, whether 'living in' or 'living out', domestic service for black women up to the Civil Rights movement of the 1950s and 60s was often nasty, brutal and endless. Also, as Jacqueline Jones notes, domestic service 'undermined the black woman's own role as mother and homemaker'.[36] Thus there was a kind of uncanny truth about the white-focused depiction of the black maid in Hollywood movies: she had no life of her own outside the white family. If she was a 'mammy', she was familiar like a piece of furniture, sometimes a source of pragmatic wisdom but always a version of the American pastoral – sexless, ageless, childless – whose only duty in life was to ensure the well-being of the white house.[37]

If we see slavery as the primal crime of the Republic from which all other crimes flow, then Lottie's social death connects her to the scrubbing women in the film's final shot. They represent the non-sequiturs of history (Lottie's remarks consisting almost entirely of non-sequiturs). They exist as 'clues' to a Gothic mystery story that remains unsolved, for they do not fit into the film's neat melodramatic pattern. Like McQueen's Lottie, the scrubbing women are 'otherworldly' in the sense of being outside the cinematic text itself. They are clues to a murder mystery involving American greed, to the mystery of laissez-faire capitalism run amok.

Film noir becomes the perfect vehicle to express this theme because its distinctive style, especially its expressionistic lighting and distorted perspectives, reflects the instability of an 'American' identity. For instance, Wally is a masher whose mashing involves money, not sex; Monte is an aristocrat whose tenuous charm masks his penury, vulgarity ('one man's poison is another man's meat') and viciousness; Veda is a snob whose playacting slides effortlessly into the pornographic gyrations of the showgirl; and, finally, Mildred is both a domestic housewife and an ambitious capitalist entrepreneur – one restaurant is not enough. The film insists that she return to her place as housewife, but not to the position of the scrubbing women in the film's last shot, those 'little people' whom she has now transcended. It is Lottie's murder as a human being that is the real crime in the movie. She and women like her are the corpses of history that have resurfaced like Lazarus to destabilise a plot that tries to assure us that there is such a thing as 'normal' capitalism and a new day a-dawning.

Double Indemnity also sets black labour against a white world of shady dealings but in a different way. Although Eric Lott reads the presence of black characters in the film as an indication of Walter Neff's (Fred MacMurray) descent into moral blackness, I would argue that just the opposite is true. In the film's opening shots (before the flashback), Lott argues that the 'darkened' office building is 'tended almost wholly by black janitors and custodians', a 'racial space *Double Indemnity* constantly links with black deeds'.[38] What should be noted, however, is that these people are all working, women as well as men, whereas Neff's plans to bilk the Pacific All-Risk Insurance Company is an attempt to escape work for a shortcut to the big bucks – the jackpot of 'double' your money. It is not by accident that director Billy Wilder includes other scenes in which blacks are seen working. Charlie (Sam McDaniel) washes Neff's car while Neff and Phyllis (Barbara Stanwyck) are off to murder Dietrichson; a red cap tries to help Neff (disguised as Dietrichson) get on the train; a Pullman porter makes up his compartment. In conversation, Neff tells Phyllis that a coloured woman cleans his apartment twice a week.[39]

Why is all this black work significant? In the screenplay, the word 'work', when used by the white characters, is not associated with labour performed to produce, make or accomplish something. Rather, the word is associated with deception as though 'work' means energy expended in terms of a confidence game. Insurance investigator Barton Keyes (Edward G. Robinson) tells Neff that 'something has been worked on us . . . I don't claim to know how it was worked, or who worked it, but I know that it *was* worked'. This process began, he says, because his 'little man' began 'acting up' on him, warning him that the insurance company had been deceived. Neff then tells Phyllis that Keyes has 'figured out how it was worked'. Phyllis tells Neff that one reason she has spent time with Nino Zachetti (Byron Barr), Lola's (Jean Heather) boyfriend, was that she 'was working on him' – i.e., trying to find out what he knows. So ubiquitous is the word that Neff asks Phyllis, the second time they meet, if she has a 'beer that is not working'. In other words, every time a white character uses the word it never appears in a context in which someone is doing an honest day's work. These characters live in a world in which it is assumed that everyone practises some kind of trick to get what they desire.[40]

And there is a reason for this. As a salesman, Neff does not produce a product but sells fear and desire. Moreover, he is employed by a company that, as Cain says in the novel, is 'the biggest gambling wheel in the world' in which the odds are always in favour of the wheel. The wheel wins more times than it loses because the insurance company has the statistics and knows how to use them. It may pretend to be 'the friend of the widow, the orphan, and the needy in time of trouble', but it has the edge and it ruthlessly uses it to play the game for profit.[41] Neff (Huff in the novel) wants to 'crook the house', because he knows how it works: 'You're like the guy behind the roulette wheel, watching the customers to make sure that they don't crook the house'.[42] Knowing all the company's 'tricks', he believes he can even out-trick the company's prize trickster, Keyes, who, he tells Phyllis, knows all the tricks.

Much has been made of Neff's hubris in trying to best Keyes at his own game, but critics usually assume that Neff's crime and Keyes' integrity are as different as night and day. After the Greek-American immigrant Sam Garlopis (Fortunio Bonanova) signs a confession that he burned down his truck for the insurance money, Keyes tells him 'now you're an honest man again'.[43] Lott's reading of Garlopis' attempted fraud highlights Keyes' Anglo-Saxon incorruptibility,[44] but we should be reminded of James Naremore's observation that Keyes is primarily 'a loyal agent of industrial rationality'. The ending not used in the film, Neff in the gas chamber with Keyes present, would have brought Keyes 'face-to-face' with the final product of 'industrial culture: the California gas chamber'.[45]

I would go a step further. That 'industrial culture' is a rational capitalist system that keeps Charlie washing cars and black women emptying waste baskets. They may be doing honest work, but it is work defined by a system that never takes 'risks'. In this sense, Keyes and Neff are not different – they are doubles. Keyes works one side of the system, Neff the other, but both are defined by the system, as illustrated by the fact that they are both detectives. Neff's meticulous plotting to 'crook the house' is mirrored by Keyes' own rational investigation to show how the murder was 'worked'. Alan Spiegel claims that Keyes 'is not out "to crook" the house, but to correct it'.[46] True enough, but Keyes remains blind to the injustices of the system itself. He can only see Norton Jr (Richard Gaines), his boss, as a pale imitation of his father who competently ran the company. He doesn't see the system itself as the problem.

Much has been made of Keyes as Neff's surrogate father. In the film's poignant ending, Neff says that Keyes was 'too close' to him to see the truth, and Keyes responds, 'closer than that, Walter', suggesting that we read the relationship as a love story. That may be, for the ending is emotionally powerful, but I want to suggest that in the film's ending the familiar shades into the unfamiliar. The two men are 'too close' to the 'industrial culture' to see how it has corrupted both of them.

Keyes's own 'work' exposes the 'industrial culture' that he is part of. He is at his best (and funniest) when he gives his actuarial account of the multiple ways people commit suicide, gloating to Mr Norton, after delivering his impressive statistics, that he knows of no one who killed himself by jumping off an observation car going at fifteen miles an hour. He wins the day, because he has done his homework, but we should not overlook his grim data of deaths that pile up like cords of wood or like slaves cast overboard a slave ship.[47] It is a reminder that Keyes sees the particulars but is blind to the moral implication of the deaths he is describing. It is no accident that the director of this film, Billy Wilder, was an Austrian Jew who fled Hitler's 'Final Solution', a 'rational' answer to the 'Jewish problem'. To Keyes, these suicides are only numbers in an actuarial table.

The movie reminds us of this by the repetition of the phrase 'the end of the line'. Keyes thinks it refers to the murderers who are on a one-way trip to the cemetery, but, as Naremore suggests, the cemetery may be awaiting capitalism itself, so caught up in its own success that it doesn't see that it is committing suicide. The presence of African-Americans 'working' in the film is a reminder of both the terror of history and a lost America in which hard work was supposed to be the solid rock upon which the Republic stood.

The dilemma Robert Wise faced when he made *The Set-Up* (1949) was how to retain the racial themes of the film's literary source, a narrative poem by Joseph Moncure March, when the film's protagonist would be white. Wise wanted Canada Lee for the part of Bill 'Stoker' Thompson, because March's boxer was black, but RKO wanted a 'name' and chose Robert Ryan who was also a former intercollegiate boxing champion. This, of course, was a great choice, because Ryan is one of film noir's best actors, but it left Wise with the problem of linking Stoker with Pansy Jones, March's aging black boxer now reduced to fighting club fights in seedy, racist venues. He solved the problem by making Thompson a working-class stiff, condemned to a chain gang of hellish club fights in sordid small towns. In his DVD commentary on the film many years later, Wise described Stoker carrying his little bag to the boxing arena as a man 'going to work', but it is work that is draining the life out of him, as it is doing to so many others in the dingy locker room of the Paradise City arena. His name, Stoker, implies that he and the other fighters are proles who are only so much meat on the hoof to their owners and whose existence to the mob that watches them is savage entertainment. By 1959, when *Odds Against Tomorrow* was released, director Wise could be more explicit in connecting racial tensions to class and caste. In that movie, two desperate, working-class men who should be friends, one black (Harry Belafonte) and the other white (Robert Ryan), fight to the death, as in a boxing ring. It is not by accident that one character in this heist film refers to the job they are to do as 'the set-up'. The real set-up is the society that defines them and the racist ideology that imprisons them.[48]

The Set-Up is one of the great noirs, a film that Martin Scorsese called a 'masterpiece', one that influenced his own *Raging Bull* (1980) and John Huston's *Fat City* (1972). March's poem 'The Set-Up' (1928) is clearly a poem of its time. Pansy Jones is named after a famous black middleweight in the 1920s named Tiger Flowers, who had the distinction of twice defeating Harry Greb in 1926 for the middleweight crown. Greb was known as the dirtiest fighter in the business, and that aspect of the sport, along with its racism and corruption, became the basis of Hemingway's great short story 'Fifty Grand' (1927). The historical background of March's poem, however, involved what happened to the sport after Jack Johnson was defeated by Jess Willard in 1915. Because the flamboyant Johnson thumbed his nose at white folks, his legacy put a curse upon black fighters in the 1920s who had a difficult time getting bouts with white contenders.[49]

Pansy is one such fighter who in his prime was unbeatable, but no white fighter of importance would fight him. He lands in jail on a trumped-up charge and emerges ten years later a step slower and a few pounds heavier and finds himself fighting in boxing dives. His managers see him as only another bum in their stable of bums, and so when an opportunity to throw a fight presents itself, they take the money and don't tell Pansy that the fix is in. Pansy fights the fight of his life and wins. His opponent, Sailor Grey, and his owner-thugs believe that Pansy has pulled a fast one, follow him to the city's subway and shove him onto an ongoing train.

March's verse moves with the speed of the subway train that kills Pansy and has the same kind of visceral power. The setting of the poem is the lower depths, the literary naturalism of Zola, Norris, Crane and Dreiser, but expressed in a verse that reads like a furious, embittered Ogden Nash. March admitted, however, that the settings and situations in his poetry were often 'cinematic', and a close look at his poem 'The Set-Up' shows the influence of German Expressionism:

> The Star Arena reeked with age:
> It smelled like the bottom of a monkey cage.
> Dark,
> Stark,
> It stood immense
> Between small shops and tenements:
> Gloomy,
> Dim,
> Sinister looking,
> Grim.
> A glittering white
> Arc light
> Glared against the black night,
> Making great shadows sprawl
> Over the crumbling brown wall,
> And bringing out the rigid shapes
> Of long, slanting fire escapes.[50]

The 'crowd' appears as figures out of Dante's *Inferno* or Eliot's *The Waste Land* (1922). They are 'ghostly,/Blurred', the walking dead: 'Mouths were holes./ Eye-sockets/Looked like deep, black pockets'.[51] They move into the arena like Eliot's zombies: 'I had not thought death had undone so many'.[52]

In his film, Wise converted that waste land world into a kind of allegory of modern life in which those fighters at the bottom recapitulated the working lives of slaves on a plantation. Thus the pastoral, used to defend slavery as a benevolent institution, is reshaped in Wise's film as fictions that hide the town's hideousness. The hotel in which Stoker and his wife Julie stay is named Hotel Cozy, just as the Chinese restaurant next door is called 'Dreamland', an echo of Freud's 'uncanny' as the familiar American myth of 'paradise' in Paradise City takes place in world of penny arcades, cheap dives and ominous landscapes. Julie, for instance, takes a night-time journey through main street and encounters tawdry shops, sleazy bars, street hustlers, glittering dance venues. These are both extension of the boxing arena and an attempt to disguise its real brutality. The fighters are there for the raw entertainment of the crowd who respond to them as though they were pit bulls in a dog fight or the black boys in Ellison's 'Battle Royal' in *Invisible Man* (1952). As in Ellison's novel, the boxing ring is a setting for a slave auction.

Wise highlights the racial themes in March's poem in two ways: through the depiction of the boxing fans as a lynching mob and through Stoker who is portrayed as a fugitive slave in his flight from the 'owners' who feel that he has double-crossed them. The crowd as a mob appears as faces howling for blood: delighted, angry, amused, even sexually aroused by the action. The film focuses on three individuals who are comically sinister in their emotional obsessions: a glutton who wolfs down hot dogs, ice cream bars and beers, and laughs at the suffering of those on stage; a woman who claims she abhors violence but when it erupts in the ring howls 'kill him, kill him'. The last figure is perhaps the most bizarre, a blind man who depends upon a friend to describe the suffering in the ring, feeding upon it as the glutton feeds upon hot dogs. When told that one of Stoker's eyes is closed, he shouts, 'close the other one!' The more the boxers suffer, the more the blind man wants to hear, his opaque eyes becoming a metaphor for the blind fates that mark their lives.

Wise choreographed the boxing scenes with the Ashcan School of painting in mind, especially George Bellow's *Stag Night At Sharkey's* (1909). In Bellow's painting, the violence of the mob mirrors the violence in the ring, yet the locker room scenes in the film reflect a kind of entropy, a world in which the energy within the ring is replaced by anxiety, fear or despair. The locker room is a microcosm of the working class. One character in particular, Gunboat Johnson (David Clarke), foreshadows what Stoker's life might become. The demented Gunboat fantasises that he could be another Frankie Manila who lost twenty-one fights only to become a world champion. Yet Gunboat loses not only this fight but perhaps his life. Wise gives us a panning shot of faces staring down on him as he lies comatose on a table. They recognise their future in him. But this does not dim the optimism of Luther Hawkins (James Edwards), a young Pansy Jones, on his way to stardom, or so he thinks. The usually taciturn Stoker treats this young black boxer as though he were his son. The doubling contributes to the film's veiled theme because as Gunboat foreshadows Stoker's future so Stoker foreshadows Luther's.

The plot revolves around Stoker's win over Tiger Nelson (Hal Fieberling), a flashy youth groomed by a small time mobster, aptly named Little Boy (Alan Baxter). Elegantly dressed, Little Boy echoes one of Wilbur Cash's ersatz

Figure 8.3   Stoker (Robert Ryan) cornered like a rat in *The Set-Up*.

Southern aristocrats in *The Mind of the South* (1941), only a few notches removed from the rednecks he now despises. He considers himself a man of 'honour', as long as no one crosses him. On some level he knows Stoker is telling the truth, that he didn't know about the fix, but Little Boy needs a fall guy, as white Southerners needed black scapegoats to make the slaves stand in fear. Little Boy knows that if he doesn't make Stoker an example, he will lose his street cred as a man among men.

Wise highlights the identification of Stoker with an escaped slave when Stoker tries to leave the arena undetected by Big Boy and his goons. The boxing arena now empty, Stoker rushes from door to door trying to find a way out; all the while the boxing ring, like a slave auction block, is always present in the background (deep focus). He finds a door open, only to be cornered like a rat in alley.

Little Boy orders his hand broken so he won't fight again, but of course what we see is a castration, something emphasised in the film's ironic ending when Julie, who has not seen Stoker suffer and win, says that 'we both won tonight'. What she means is that she has won, that he will not fight again, something she thinks will save their marriage. Now he can have that 'tobacco stand' that he said he always wanted.

But the paradox of the film's ending is that Stoker is like Othello with his occupation gone, a man deprived of his identity because he is deprived of his 'work'. Earlier he tells Julie, when she complains about the beatings he's taken, 'if you're a fighter, you have to fight'. However, he is trapped within a metaphorical arena in which there are fights but no winners. In this world, the fix is always in, the cards are already marked. The real loser in the film is work that has no meaning or dignity, a theme often repeated in Frederick Douglass's slave *Narrative* (1845).

The film's ironic ending, Julie claiming victory, mirrors the ending of Fritz

Lang's *You Only Live Once*, an ending that at twelve years old James Baldwin saw as false. As the two fugitive lovers are dying, Eddie Taylor (Henry Fonda) hears the priest saying, as if in a dream, 'the gates are open'. In *The Devil Finds Work* (1976), his book of film criticism, Baldwin said that even at twelve, 'I knew damn well that the gates were *not* open, and, by this time, in any case, the lovers were dead'.[53] Growing up in Harlem, in a world of shrinking expectations, Baldwin identified with the white Eddie, the fugitive on the run with no place to hide. He would add, in the same essay, that 'in a way, we were all niggers in the thirties', that the 'genuine indignation which informs this film is a quality which was very shortly to disappear out of the American cinema'. I have argued that this 'quality' remained in film noir, that more than one black writer would identify with noir heroes even though they were white. Do not Richard Wright's Bigger Thomas, Ellison's invisible man and Toni Morrison's Sethe owe something to these cinematic fugitives? While we may disapprove of the racist stereotypes within these old films, as does African-American author Wanda Coleman, we should take her love of these films as her final word. 'Nothing cinematic,' she says, 'excites me more than film noir'.[54]

Notes

1. James Baldwin, 'The devil finds work', in James Baldwin, *Collected Essays* (New York: Library of America, 1998), p. 495.
2. Paul Schrader, 'Notes on film noir', in *Film Noir Reader*, in Alain Silver and James Ursini (eds) (New York: Limelight Editions, 1996), p. 53.
3. Gunnar Myrdal, *An American Dilemma*, vol. 1 (New York: Harper & Row, 1962), p. lxxxii.
4. Eric Lott, 'The whiteness of film noir', in Mike Hill (ed.), *Whiteness: A Critical Reader* (New York: New York University Press, 1997), p. 85.
5. Manthia Diawara, 'Noirs by noirs: Toward a new realism in black cinema', in Joan Copjec (ed.), *Shades of Noir* (London: Verso, 1993), p. 263.
6. E. Ann Kaplan, 'The dark continent of film noir: Race, displacement and metaphor in Tourneur's *Cat People* (1942) and Welles' *The Lady from Shanghai* (1948)', in E. Ann Kaplan (ed.), *Women in Film Noir* (London: British Film Institute, 1999), p. 185.
7. Julian Murphet, 'Film noir and the racial unconscious', *Screen* 39 (spring 1998), 27.
8. Paul Rabinowitz, *Black & White & Noir: America's Pulp Modernism* (New York: Columbia University Press, 2002), p. 61.
9. Curtis Bernhardt, dir. *Dark Passage*, Warner Bros., 1947; Mervyn LeRoy, dir. *I Am a Fugitive from a Chain Gang*, Warner Bros., 1932; Fritz Lang, dir. *You Only Live Once*, Walter Wanger Productions, 1937; Raoul Walsh, dir. *High Sierra*, Warner Bros., 1941; Jacques Tourneur, dir. *Out of the Past*, RKO, 1947.
10. Fritz Lang, dir. *Fury*, MGM, 1936.
11. Louis D. Rubin, Jr., 'Introduction', in Louis D. Rubin, Jr., *I'll Take My Stand: The South and the Agrarian Tradition* (Baton Rouge, LA: Louisiana State University Press, 1977), p. xxiv.
12. Sidney Lumet, dir. *The Fugitive Kind*, United Artists, 1959.
13. Phil Karlson, dir. *The Phenix City Story*, Universal, 1955.

14. Sigmund Freud, 'The uncanny', in Sigmund Freud, *Standard Edition of the Complete Psychological Works* (London: Hogarth Press, 1953–64), vol. 4, pp. 371–7.
15. Anthony Vidler, *The Architectural Uncanny: Essays in the Modern Unhomely* (Cambridge: MIT Press, 1996), p. 7.
16. James Baldwin, 'The devil finds work', p. 497.
17. John Irwin, *Unless the Threat of Death is Behind Them: Hard-Boiled Fiction and Film Noir* (Baltimore, MD: The Johns Hopkins University Press, 2006), p. 263.
18. Foster Hirsch, *The Dark Side of the Screen: Film Noir* (Cambridge, MA: Da Capo Press, 2002), p. 126.
19. Brian McCuskey, 'Not at Home: Servants, Scholars, and the Uncanny', *PMLA* 126 (March 2006), 425.
20. James Oakes, *The Ruling Race: A History of American Slaveholders* (New York: Vintage Books, 1983), pp. 153–91.
21. Toni Morrison, *Playing in the Dark: Whiteness and the Literary Imagination* (Cambridge, MA: Harvard University Press, 1992), p. 66.
22. Albert LaValley (ed.) *Mildred Pierce* (Madison, WI: University of Wisconsin Press, 1980), p. 35.
23. Roy Hoopes, *Cain* (New York: Holt, Rinehart and Winston, 1982), p. 350.
24. James M. Cain, *Mildred Pierce* (New York: Vintage Books, 1989), p. 298 [1941]. Michael Curtiz, dir. *Mildred Pierce*, Warner Bros., 1945.
25. Cain, *Mildred Pierce*, p. 131.
26. Eric Lott, 'The whiteness of film noir', p. 98.
27. LaValley (ed.), *Mildred Pierce*, p. 128.
28. Michael Rogin, *Black Face, White Noise: Jewish Immigrants in the Hollywood Melting Pot* (Berkeley, CA: University of California Press, 1996), pp. 73–120.
29. Donald Bogle, *Toms, Coons, Mulattoes, Mammies, & Bucks: An Interpretive History of Blacks in American Films* (New York: Continuum Publishing, 1989), p. 93.
30. Peter Stallybrass and Allon White, *The Politics and Poetics of Transgression* (Ithaca, NY: Cornell University Press, 1986), p. 164.
31. LaValley (ed.), *Mildred Pierce*, p. 127. As *Mildred Pierce* was being made, McQueen issued an ultimatum that the role of Lottie was the last cinematic fool she was going to play, yet it was her presence in *Mildred Pierce* that turned out to be more subversive than her ultimatum. See Marshall Fishwick, *Parameters of Popular Culture* (Bowling Green, OH: Bowling Green University Popular Press, 1974), pp. 149–50.
32. Joyce Nelson, '*Mildred Pierce* reconsidered', *Film Reader* 2 (January 1977), 70.
33. Ibid., p. 67.
34. Bonnie Thornton Dill, *Across the Boundaries of Race and Class: An Exploration of Work and Family among Black Female Domestic Servants* (New York: Garland Publishing, 1994), p. 15.
35. David M. Katzman, *Seven Days A Week: Women and Domestic Service in Industrializing America* (New York: Oxford University Press, 1978), p. 72.
36. Jacqueline Jones, *Labor of Love, Labor of Sorrow: Black Women, Work and the Family, From Slavery to the Present* (New York: Vintage Books), p. 127.
37. Phyllis Palmer, *Domesticity and Dirt: Housewives and Domestic Servants in the United States, 1920–1945* (Philadelphia, PA: Temple University Press, 1991), p. 73; Elizabeth Clark-Lewis, *Living In, Living Out: African American Domestics and the Great Migration* (New York: Kodansha International, 1996), p. 107.
38. Eric Lott, 'The whiteness of film noir', *American Literary History* 9 (Fall 1997), 546.

39. Billy Wilder, dir. *Double Indemnity*, Paramount Pictures, 1944.
40. Billy Wilder and Raymond Chandler, *Double Indemnity: The Complete Screenplay* (Berkeley, CA: University of California Press, 2000), pp. 86, 85, 100, 112, 25.
41. James M. Cain, *Double Indemnity* (New York: Vintage Books, 1992), p. 23 [1936].
42. Wilder and Chandler, *Double Indemnity*, pp. 36–7.
43. Ibid., p. 22.
44. Eric Lott, 'The whiteness of film noir', in *Whiteness: A Critical Reader*, pp. 85–6.
45. James Naremore, *More Than Night: Film Noir in its Contexts* (Berkeley, CA: University of California Press, 1998), p. 92.
46. Alan Spiegel, 'Seeing triple: Cain, Chandler, and Wilder on *Double Indemnity*', *Mosaic* 16 (winter–spring 1983), 98.
47. Wilder and Chandler, *Double Indemnity*, p. 82.
48. Richard C. Keenan, *The Films of Robert Wise* (Lanham, MD: Scarecrow Press, 2007), p. 48. Robert Wise, dir., *The Set-Up*, RKO, 1949, DVD, Warnervideo. Robert Wise, dir. *Odds Against Tomorrow*, HarBel Productions/United Artists, 1959.
49. Martin Scorsese, *The Set-Up*, DVD, Warnervideo. Gerald Early, 'Three notes toward a cultural definition of the Harlem Renaissance', *Callaloo* 14 (winter 1991), 139–42. Joseph Moncure March, *The Wild Party, The Set-Up: A Certain Wildness* (Porter's Landing, Freeport, ME: Bond Wheelwright Co., 1968), pp. 52–3.
50. March, *The Wild Party, The Set Up: A Certain Wildness*, pp. 41, 174.
51. Ibid., pp. 174–5.
52. T. S. Eliot, *The Waste Land and Other Poems*, ed. Frank Kermode (New York: Penguin Books, 1998), p. 57, l. 63.
53. James Baldwin, 'The devil finds work', p. 497. A similar ironic ending occurs in Raoul Walsh's *High Sierra* (1941) in which Marie (Ida Lupino) asks a cynical reporter what it means when a man 'crashes out'. The reporter responds, 'It means he's free', and Marie takes this to mean that her dead lover, 'Mad Dog' Roy Earle (Humphrey Bogart) is now free – and not, as the audience (and Marie) has just seen, gunned down like a dog.
54. Wanda Coleman, *Native in a Strange Land: Trials & Tremors* (Santa Rosa, CA: Black Sparrow Press, 1996), p. 160.

9. POSTSCRIPT: A HISTORY OF OUR WRITING ABOUT FILM NOIR

Alain Silver and James Ursini

DEFINING THE SUBJECT

Our involvement in noir criticism goes back to the 1970s. While enrolled in the film school at the University of California, Los Angeles, we collaborated on two books: an auteur study of David Lean and a genre study of the vampire film. In 1974 Alain Silver queried the Indiana University Press and was offered a contract to produce a volume on film noir for the Cinema One Series. When two collaborators dropped out of that project, the offer lost a lot of its lustre. Shortly thereafter, an excerpt from Alain's book-length study of the samurai film appeared in *Film Comment*. This, in turn, prompted a query from Peter Mayer at The Overlook Press, who was unaware that his book *The Samurai Film* had been pre-sold to another publisher. Undeterred Peter asked what other subjects we might be considering. When film noir was mentioned, the idea for an encyclopedia was his.

In retrospect, it should have been clear that such an undertaking at a time when very few of the titles of the classic period were available on demand – and then only via rentals of 16mm prints – would have to rely too heavily on the memories of the editors and contributors. When the deal was struck in the Santa Monica living room of Elizabeth Ward, who became the editor in charge of research, no one realised how monumental a task it would be. Before it was finished, the index cards that Elizabeth used to compile filmographic, bibliographic and other details numbered 16,000. The typescript of the book's index alone was over 300 pages long. The main text was almost ten times as many pages, created by diverse hands, few of whom had access to IBM Selectrics, with a melange of Pica and Elite fonts and mostly triple-spaced to permit room for revisions and redactions that were so heavy in places, it was remarkable that a typesetter could decipher them.

None of this is to say the time was not right for this endeavour. Aside from Durgnat's 'family tree', Schrader's 'notes' and a chapter called 'Black Cinema' in Higham and Greenberg's *Hollywood in the Forties*,[1] there was nothing in English attempting to define the film noir movement (or genre, as some have always characterised it). Back then the term was still in italics and noir had not become a catchall adjective for a dark spin applied to any art form. Back then Borde and Chaumeton's book was decades away from translation into English and the seminal articles in French were only available as low-contrast photocopies on milky paper. There had been two dissertations on the subject. One was by Robert Porfirio, whom Elizabeth Ward knew from time enrolled at California State University Fullerton. So after Bob and his student assistant Carl Macek became associate editors and the original contributors were recruited, mostly from the corps of UCLA graduate students in film, we relied on collective memory, the odd retrospective and often setting an alarm for 3am to catch a television screening. To augment notes and recollections, there were the trade reviews clipped and filed by the staffers at the AMPAS library. From all this we created the filmographic details, synopses and analyses for the 300 original entries.

After fourteen months of work, the result was painfully uneven. Plots and other particulars were misremembered. As our contributors had competed for assignment of the key titles and championed their favourite, obscure noirs, many important pictures ended up with short shrift. Many B titles, few of which had been seen by anyone except Bob or Carl or Alain, were marginalised or entirely absent. Present, on the other hand, were many 1970s movies such as *The Long Goodbye*, *Chinatown* and *Taxi Driver*. Before the boundaries of the classic period had been defined and before our colleague Todd Erickson coined the term neo-noir, it made sense to include pictures that were well known and easier to access.

For Alain, who had begun working long hours in the film industry in late 1975 and had little time for entry writing, the key to the volume was the introduction. At one point, when Overlook wanted to extend the Roman numerals of the front matter through the Introduction, he argued vehemently until they reconsidered. So on Arabic numeral page 1 of that original introduction, the positions of Schrader and Durgnat were recapped and adopted as we espoused the belief that noir is not a genre but a movement or cycle, limited in duration and defined as much by common style as it is by content. In 1979 Alain wrote:

> Film noir is grounded neither in personal creation nor in translation of another tradition into cinematic terms. Rather it is a self-contained

reflection of American cultural preoccupations in film form. In short, it is the unique example of a wholly American film style ... That may seem a substantial claim to make for a group of films whose plots frequently turn on deadly violence or sexual obsession, whose catalogue of characters includes numbers of down-and-out private eyes, desperate women, and petty criminals. Nor does the visceral unease felt by a viewer who watches a shadowy form move across a lonely street or who hears the sound of car tires creeping over wet asphalt automatically translate into sociological assertions about paranoia or guilt. At the same time, it is clear that the emergence of film noir coincides with these and other popular sentiments at large in America during World War II and at the start of a cold war dominated by fear of the atomic bomb.

Even as the introduction embraced and expanded the concept that film noir was a movement, limited resources compelled another compromise: the main entries only included 'urban noir', while appendices surveyed the stylistic impact on genres from westerns to comedies.

Despite all this and its awkward sub-title, *An Encyclopedic Reference to the American Style*, the first edition of *Film Noir* far outstripped the expectations of the publisher. As neo-noir proliferated in Hollywood, the thick volume became a pre-internet movie database for many writers, producers and directors who wished to refresh their recollections of classics and to steal ideas for new pictures. It even made a cameo appearance in *The McGuffin*, a 1986 BBC movie of the week where a fictional movie critic, who is also a transvestite and voyeur, pulls it from his bookshelf for a consultation. After such an enshrinement in the pantheon of film books that became film props, how could we have any thought of revisiting the subject?

In fact, for quite a while we stopped producing books altogether. When we came back to writing about film in the 1990s, it began with a second edition of *David Lean and his Films* and then an updating of *The Vampire Film*, our first collaboration with publisher Mel Zerman at Limelight Editions. From that, events came together to precipitate the initial *Film Noir Reader*. First, in 1992, Overlook had requested a second edition of the encyclopedia, but Alain, who was producing a sci-fi movie, could only cobble together a new essay on neo-noir and address the most egregious typos and errors of fact on Overlook's short deadline. In the process, he revisited the garage-shelf archive that housed 400 stills and frame enlargements and those milky copies of early articles.

Second, against our advice Mel Zerman insisted that our auteur study *What Ever Happened to Robert Aldrich?* (which still remains our worst-selling book) be printed in hardcover. Mel also quite properly vetoed our plan to reprint Alain's *Film Comment* piece entitled 'Kiss me deadly: Evidence of a style', as it was out of balance with the other Aldrich-book chapters. Lastly,

Bob Porfirio was approached about turning his dissertation into a series of essays, a project for which he had neither time nor inclination. The lightbulb appeared over our heads and flicked on.

Because of the poor showing of the Aldrich book, we offered *Film Noir Reader* to Limelight. We still had to convince a once-bitten Mel Zerman that it was a better bet than vampire films. *The Vampire Film* is now in the second printing of its 4th edition and has sold quite well, as had the encyclopedia; but despite being put together hastily and including some marginal pieces, within twenty-four months of its publication in 1996, in terms of units sold, *Film Noir Reader* had eclipsed all of our other work combined. So naturally, a sequel, *Reader 2* (1999), was undertaken shortly on its heels with many more important reprints not included in the first volume, most notably the earliest piece in English, Lloyd Shearer's 1945 disparagement of the movement for the *New York Times*.

The less successful *Film Noir Reader 3* (2002), co-edited with Bob Porfirio, was the first publication of interviews with classic period directors, writers, composers and actors that he had conducted while researching his dissertation more than two decades earlier. We added excerpts from oral histories of our own to fill out the volume. The series officially ended with mostly original case studies and essays on seminal movies in 2004 with *Film Noir Reader 4* but enjoyed a de facto resurrection in the larger format and unofficial number 5, *Film Noir the Directors* in 2012. Along the way through that series, we accepted a commission from Taschen for their 2004 film noir volume, expanded the neo-noir and other essays in a third edition of the Overlook encyclopedia and photographed a lot of local landmarks for *L.A. Noir: The City as Character* (2005).

Appearing when it did, as online resources were only beginning to proliferate, the original *Film Noir Reader* was also one of the first books designed by Alain Silver. He included scores of scene stills collected years earlier for the encyclopedia but not used in that volume. The first *Film Noir Reader* also replicated the many frame enlargements from the *Film Comment* pieces on noir's visual style and *Kiss Me Deadly* and first excerpted a detailed visual analysis from Bob Porfirio's dissertation, including frame captures he had made in the 1970s. With this extensive use of images adding to its appeal, when *Film Noir Reader* became a major seller for a minor trade house, Limelight made sure it kept getting out onto retail shelves. Most importantly it also coincided with an ongoing and growing interest in noir as a course subject in many colleges and universities for which the *Reader*'s compilation of key early writing became essential reading.

Seventeen years after the noir encyclopedia, this introduction opened with a recap and unintentional understatement:

Forty years after Raymond Borde and Étienne Chaumeton defined the challenge, critical commentators on film noir continue to grapple with it. Ironically, American writers did not immediately take up consideration of this indigenous phenomenon and the question of its 'essential traits'. Only gradually in a frequently cross-referenced series of essays in the 1970s did they begin to express themselves. There are now a dozen full-length books in English concerning film noir and undoubtedly more to follow.

Refining the Approach

So many noir studies have been written since our earliest work that their total has grown difficult to reckon. Unlike screenwriter Barry Gifford's breezy survey, *The Devil Thumbs a Ride*, most of the studies have academic origins. From the first we have tried to find a middle ground in our critical approach. Underlying it is the belief that it only takes a few days of actual work in motion picture production to realise that its collaborative nature trumps auteurist belief and makes it quite difficult to isolate or identify a single intentionality responsible for the creation of most movies.

Although those who have not worked in production may sometimes make inaccurate assumptions about the process and the objects that it produces, throughout the world in over more than a century of film history 99 per cent of narrative movies have a single director. The gaps across time and space in artistic vision and creative control for directors such as Herbert Brennon, Robert Bresson and Martin Brest are more than just a few letters in a last name. Issues of world-view, visual style or any other aesthetic questions aside, any method of grouping of directors – chronologically, alphabetically, geographically – begins with names whose common trait is credit as directors on finished films. Consequently, even from our first auteur study, our core assumption is always that the objects are paramount, particularly with a fluid and changing movement such a film noir. Certainly the diverse filmmakers behind noir films, the industrial and social contexts in which they were created, their antecedents and analogues in other media, all these are important considerations; but not more than the texts themselves.

In the years between the encyclopedia and the reader, many critics had questioned not just the nature of noir, movement versus genre, style versus content, but its very existence. Despite this, many new observers of the noir movement questioned whether it existed at all except as an invention of critical commentators. The introduction to *Film Noir Reader* responded on several levels (and sometimes quite sardonically) to those who in all seriousness (it's still hard not to be sardonic) actually asserted that the classic period's filmmakers had no idea what they were doing. On page 10 was our simplest and most palpable reply: we reproduced a picture of director Robert Aldrich standing on a set in 1956 and holding a copy of *Panorama du Film Noir*. Of course, we also cited cinematographer John Alton's description of noir mood from *Painting with Light*. Again turning to the objects themselves, we reiterated our detailed list and invited readers to

> consider a random selection of motion pictures released over an eighteen-month period such as *The Big Clock* (Paramount, 1948), *Brute Force* (Universal, 1947), *Cry of the City* (20th Century-Fox, 1948), *Force of Evil* (MGM, 1948), *Framed* (Columbia, 1947), *Out of the Past* (RKO, 1947), *The Pitfall* (United Artists, 1948), and *The Unsuspected* (Warner Bros., 1947) and discover that eight different directors, cinematographers, and screenwriters adapted different original stories for different stars at eight different studios. These people of great and small technical reputations created eight otherwise unrelated motion pictures with one cohesive style.

Next to be challenged were those who would pigeonhole film noir, some like David Bordwell, who regarded it as a 'strange case' (when at its core film noir is constructed almost entirely from mainstream Hollywood techniques), others who went so far as to deem the entire movement an imaginary moment in film history, not a creation by filmmakers but a post hoc invention by critical commentators.

Bordwell was cited to the effect that 'critics have not succeeded in defining specifically noir visual techniques ... or narrative structure. The problem resembles one in art history, that of defining "non-classical" styles'. Underlying this for Bordwell and Kristin Thompson is the 'fact' that 'the concept of film noir was constructed by French critics and imported to the US by Paul Schrader'.[2]

Aside from Alton and Aldrich our response to that has been the example, reiterated over several different books, of Impressionism, the term: how art historians have never taken the fact that an epithet created by a critic who intended to denigrate the work of a group of painters came to be adopted as a name for their movement and used it to suggest that the movement was defined by the term rather than by its objects. In our most recent study, *Film Noir Graphics: Where Danger Lives* we do consider how film noir, the concept and not the term, was externally isolated and defined by the marketing of its movies, how the graphics and catchphrases from its posters established a continuity of style during the classic period and used audience expectation from past releases to generate new ticket sales.

It is certainly valid to consider such factors as marketing has always influenced how movies get made or, as we wrote in *Film Noir Reader*:

> Irrefutably film noir does recruit the ethical and philosophical values of the culture as freely as it recruits visual conventions, iconic notations, and character types. This process both enriches and dislocates the noir cycle as a phenomenon so that it resists facile explanation.

We continued:

> At first glance there is nothing to dispute in Bordwell's remark. The tautological nature of his position is clearer in a more recent expression by a reviewer: 'Genres are invented by critics. When the first film noir – whatever you might consider that to be – was released, nobody yelled, "Hey, let's go on down to the Bijou! The first film noir is out!" What is at first innovation or anomaly only becomes a genre through repetition and eventual critical classification'. [Andy Klein, 'Shady characters, a fortnight of noir nihilism', *Los Angeles Reader*, V. 17, n. 16 (27 January, 1995), 15.] If nothing else, this is certainly a more cogent expression of the obvious than either Vernet or Bordwell make.

Even now the casual assertion that a concept defined by a body of films was 'constructed by French critics' or anyone other than the makers of the works does seem both facile and demeaning, which is what nineteenth-century art reviewer Louis Leroy meant to be when he extrapolated Impressionism from a Monet title or what Lloyd Shearer intended in 1945 without creating a term. While that may not be the intent of those championing post hoc invention of any film movement, from German Expressionism to the New Wave, it has scant utility for understanding any movement's dynamics.

More pernicious was the Eurocentric bias of French critic Marc Vernet and his 'solipsistic arrogance that can presume to "correct" anomalies which it does not understand and can generate the offhanded observation that film noir is "the triumph of European artists even as it presents American actors"'.[3] The anti-Vernet polemic in *Film Noir Reader*'s Introduction strove to refocus the discussion, to resound Paul Schrader's warning against 'overemphasizing the German influence in Hollywood' and to scrutinise and debunk 'recent attempts both to break down the "myth" of film noir and to relocate its origins'. 'As Borde and Chaumeton realised from the first, there is no easy answer. The noir cycle is an event garmented in the uneasy synthesis of social upheaval and Hollywood'.

One of the key reprints in the original *Film Noir Reader* was 'Some visual motifs in film noir' by Janey Place and Lowell Peterson. It seemed to us that no one had taken up the issues raised in this groundbreaking piece and portions of Bob Porfirio's dissertation: how visual style was essential to the definition of film noir. Among the possible texts considered for the *Film Noir Reader* were sections of cinematographer John Alton's 1947 *Painting with Light*. Although it was quoted in the Introduction, there was not enough material for an excerpt. Now we went back to that first edition (which has been a gift from Lowell Peterson) for help in formulating an outline for a new book, *The Noir Style*. We realised that the only way we could convince a publisher to let us write extensively about visual style in film noir was to insert our analyses discreetly inside a coffee-table book. The Overlook Press enthusiastically agreed, at least about the coffee-table part.

Despite the fact that we were restricted by what images were available and had to use production stills rather than high-resolution frame captures now made possible by Blu-ray prints, over the course of almost forty years of thinking and writing about the movement, we consider *The Noir Style* as our most important work. While it derived from the first steps taken with the encyclopedia and the refinements in approach of the first *Readers*, it was our initial opportunity to explore the heart of darkness that is film noir, an exploration that can never be complete. We are grateful to have had many opportunities to continue directly highlighting visual in the twenty audio commentaries that we have done for DVD releases of classic period titles.[4] Additional work in print with extensive illustrations includes the essay 'The gangster and film noir, themes and style', in *Gangster Film Reader* (2007), and the sidebar on long takes in *Where Danger Lives* in the 4th edition of the *Film Noir Encyclopedia* (2010).

As we have noted, underlying every book, essay and commentary, whether on noir or about unrelated directors or genres, it has been and remains our belief that nothing we can do or say can substitute for the unfiltered viewing of the movies themselves. It was firmly from that perspective that we undertook and wrote in *The Noir Style*:

> Because it is an evanescent thing and because it is subject to various readings, the survey of the *noir* style which follows makes no critical argument and follows no preconceived progression . . . We would hope that one could just leaf through this book, ignoring our comments entirely, and still come away with a clear sense of what the *noir* style is all about. Place and Peterson asked 'without the film before us . . . how can we discuss style'? As commentators, we must allow for some extrapolation, must as needed fill in the dramatic context of a motion picture for a reader who has only a single image as a referent. Within that single image lies only part of the story and part of the style. Ultimately, our hope is that viewers/readers of this book find inspiration to become viewers, again or for the first time, of the classic *noir* films themselves.

Recap of our Writing on Film Noir

Books in Progress

Jigsaw: A Critical History of Writing about Film Noir (Pendragon, 2015)
American Neo-Noir: The Movie Never Ends (Applause, 2015)

Books Published

Film Noir the Directors, Editors (New York: Limelight Editions, 2012)
Film Noir Graphics: Where Danger Lives (Santa Monica, CA: Pendragon Books, 2012)
The Film Noir Encyclopedia, Editors (4th edition, New York: The Overlook Press, 2010)
L.A. Noir (Santa Monica, CA: Santa Monica Press, 2005)
Film Noir (London and Cologne: Taschen Film Series, 2004)
Film Noir Reader 4, Editors (New York: Limelight Editions, 2004)
Film Noir Reader 3, Editors (New York: Limelight Editions, 2002)
The Noir Style (New York: The Overlook Press, 1999)
Film Noir Reader 2, Editors (New York: Limelight Editions, 1999)
Film Noir Reader, Editors (New York, Limelight Editions, 1996)
Film Noir: An Encyclopedia Reference To The American Style (1st, 2nd and 3rd editions), Editors (New York: The Overlook Press/Viking Press, 1979, 1987 and 1993)

Other Essays and Articles

'American neo-noir: 1990 and beyond' (essay) in Roberto Cueto and Antonio Santamarina (eds), *American Way of Death: American Film Noir 1990–2010* (San Sebastian: Donostia Zinemaldia, 2011)
'Crime and the mass media' (essay), in Charles Rzepka and Lee Horsley (eds), *A Companion to Crime Fiction* (Hoboken, NJ: Wiley-Blackwell, 2010)

Alain Silver only

'The gangster and film noir: Themes and style' (essay), in Alain Silver and James Ursini, *Gangster Film Reader* (Pompton Plains, NJ: Limelight Editions, 2007)
'Ride the pink horse: Money, mischance, murder, and the monads of film noir' (essay), in Mark T. Conard (ed.), *The Philosophy of Film Noir* (Lexington, KY: University of Kentucky Press, 2006).
'So what's with the ending of *Kiss Me Deadly*', *Images Film Journal* No. 2 Addendum (spring 1996), online at www.imagesjournal.com/issue02/infocus/kissdead.htm
'Son of noir' (article), *DGA Magazine* 17(3) (June–July 1992).
'Dark films to match a dark mood' (article), *The Los Angeles Times Calendar Magazine* (7 December 1980).
'Kiss me deadly: Nine elements of visual style' (article), *Film Comment* (March–April 1975).

Notes

1. Charles Higham asked that the title be changed to *Noir Cinema* when he gave permission for a reprint in the first *Film Noir Reader*.

2. Kristin Thompson and David Bordwell, 'Observations on film art', 3 April 2009, online at www.davidbordwell.net/blog/2009/04/03/love-isnt-all-you-need.
3. Alain Silver and James Ursini (eds), *The Film Noir Reader*, New York: Limelight Editions, 1996.
4. The DVD releases (in reverse chronological order): *Kiss Me Deadly* (United Artists/Criterion), *The Lodger* (Twentieth Century-Fox), *Tension, Mystery Street, Where Danger Lives* (Warner Bros.), *Brute Force* (Universal/Criterion), *The River's Edge* (Twentieth Century-Fox), *The Lady in the Lake* (Warner Bros.), *Boomerang, Kiss of Death, The Dark Corner, Street with No Name, Nightmare Alley, House of Bamboo* (Twentieth Century-Fox), *Crossfire* (Warner Bros.), *Thieves' Highway* (Twentieth Century-Fox/Criterion), *Panic in the Streets, Call Northside 777* (Twentieth Century-Fox), *Murder, My Sweet* (Warner Bros.), *Out of the Past* (RKO/Warner Bros.).

SELECTED BOOK CHAPTERS ON FILM NOIR

Arthur, Paul (1996), 'The gun in the briefcase: Or, the inscription of class in film noir', in David E. James and Rick Berg (eds), *The Hidden Foundation: Cinema and the Question of Class*, Minneapolis, MN: University of Minnesota Press, pp. 90–113.

Boozer, Jack (2002), 'Entrepreneurial femmes fatales in the film noir tradition', in Jack Boozer, *Career Movies: American Business and the Success Mystique*, Austin, TX: University of Texas Press.

Britton, Wesley A. (2005), 'McCarthy, television, and film noir', in Wesley A. Britton, *Beyond Bond: Spies in Fiction and Film*, Westport, CN: Praeger, pp. 71–98.

Bronfen, Elisabeth (2008), 'Femme fatale: Negotiations of tragic desire', in Rita Felski (ed.), *Rethinking Tragedy*, Baltimore, MD: The Johns Hopkins University Press, pp. 287–301.

Buhle, Paul (2002), 'Politics and mythology of film art: The noir era', in Paul Buhle and Dave Wagner (eds), *Radical Hollywood: The Untold Story Behind America's Favorite Movies*, New York: New Press.

Conley, Tom (2000), 'Noir in the red and the nineties in the black', in Wheeler Winston Dixon (ed.), *Film Genre 2000: New Critical Essays*, Albany, NY: State University of New York Press, pp. 193–210.

Davidson, Michael (2010), 'Phantom limbs: Film noir and the disabled body', in Sally Chivers and Nicole Markotic (eds), *The Problem Body: Projecting Disability on Film*, Columbus, OH: Ohio State University Press.

Davis, Blair (2004), 'Horror meets noir: The evolution of cinematic style, 1931–1958', in Steffen Hantke (ed.), *Horror Film: Creating and Marketing Fear*, Jackson, MS: University Press of Mississippi, pp. 191–212.

Desser, David (1993), 'The wartime films of John Huston: Film noir and the emergence of the therapeutic', in Gaylyn Studlar and David Desser (eds), *Reflections in a Male Eye: John Huston and the American Experience*, Washington, DC: Smithsonian Institution Press.

Dixon, Wheeler Winston (2006), 'The endless embrace of hell: Hopelessness and betrayal in film noir', in Murray Pomerance (ed.), *Cinema and Modernity*, New Brunswick, NJ: Rutgers University Press, pp. 38–56.

——. (2008), 'House of strangers: The family in film noir', in Murray Pomerance (ed.), *A Family Affair: Cinema Calls Home*, New York: Wallflower, pp. 13–28.

Dyer, Richard (2002), 'Homosexuality and film noir – Victim: hegemonic project', in Richard Dyer, *The Matter of Images: Essays on Representation*, 2nd edition, London: Routledge.

Ehrlich, Matthew C. (2004), 'News in a noir world', in Matthew C. Ehrlich, *Journalism in the Movies*, Urbana, IL: University of Illinois Press.

Flory, Dan (2002), 'The epistemology of race and Black American film noir: Spike Lee's *Summer of Sam* as lynching parable', in Kevin L. Stoehr (ed.), *Film and Knowledge: Essays on the Integration of Images and Ideas*, Jefferson, NC: McFarland, pp. 174–90.

Fotsch, Paul Mason (2007), 'Film noir and the hidden violence of transportation in Los Angeles', in Paul Mason Fotsch, *Watching the Traffic Go By: Transportation and Isolation in Urban America*, Austin, TX: University of Texas Press.

Freedman, Carl (2009), 'Marxism, cinema and some dialects of science fiction and film noir', in Mark Bould and China Miéville (eds), *Red Planets: Marxism and Science Fiction*, Middletown, CN: Wesleyan University Press.

Garrett, Roberta (2007), 'Neo-noir and noir-lite: Masculinity and postmodernist aesthetics in recent noir', in Roberta Garrett (ed.), *Postmodern Chick Flicks: The Return of the Woman's Film*, New York: Palgrave Macmillan.

Gates, Philippa (2011), 'The maritorious melodrama: The female detective in 1940s film noir', in Philippa Gates, *Detecting Women: Gender and the Hollywood Detective Film*, Albany, NY: State University of New York Press.

Hanson, Philip (2008), 'The arc of national confidence and the birth of film noir, 1929–41', in Philip Hanson, *This Side of Despair: How the Movies and American Life Intersected During the Great Depression*, Madison, NJ: Fairleigh Dickinson University Press.

Harvey, Sylvia (1996), 'Woman's place: The absent family of film noir', in John Belton (ed.), *Movies and Mass Culture*, New Brunswick, NJ: Rutgers University Press, pp. 171–82.

Hockley, Luke (2001), 'Film noir: Archetypes or stereotypes?', in Christopher Hauke and Ian Alister (eds), *Jung & Film: Post-Jungian Takes on the Moving*, New York: Brunner-Routledge, pp. 177–93.

Kennedy, Barbara (1999), 'Post-feminist futures in film noir', in Michelle Aaron (ed.), *The Body's Perilous Pleasures: Dangerous Desires and Contemporary Culture*, Edinburgh: Edinburgh University Press, pp. 126–42.

Krutnik, Frank (1997), 'Something more than night: Tales of the noir city', in David B. Clarke (ed.), *The Cinematic City*, London and New York: Routledge, pp. 87–112.

Levy, Emanuel (1999), 'The resurrection of noir', in Emanuel Levy, *Cinema of Outsiders: The Rise of American Independent Film*, New York: New York University Press.

Lott, M. Ray (2006), 'Film noir, feminism and private heat', in M. Ray Lott, *Police on Screen: Hollywood Cops, Detectives, Marshals and Rangers*, Jefferson, NC: McFarland.

Martin, Nina K. (2007), 'The subject of passion, the object of murder: Soft-core's refashioning of the gothic and film noir genres', in Nina K. Martin, *Sexy Thrills: Undressing the Erotic Thriller*, Urbana, IL: University of Illinois Press.

May, Lary (2000), '"Outside the groove of history": Film noir and the birth of a counterculture', in Lary May, *The Big Tomorrow: Hollywood and the Politics of the American Way*, Chicago, IL: University of Chicago Press.

Miller, Laurence (2001), 'Juvenile delinquency in films during the era of film noir: 1940–1959', in Michael A. Oliker and Walter P. Krolikowski (eds), *Images of Youth: Popular Culture as Educational Ideology*, New York: P. Lang.

Mosher, Jerry (2008), 'Hard boiled and soft bellied: The fat heavy in film noir', in Krin Gabbard and William Luhr (eds), *Screening Genders*, New Brunswick, NJ: Rutgers University Press, pp. 141–54.

Munby, Jonathan (1999), 'The un-American film art: Robert Siodmak, Fritz Lang, and the significance of film noir's German connection', in Jonathan Munby, *Public Enemies, Public Heroes: Screening the Gangster from Little Caesar to Touch of Evil*, Chicago, IL: University of Chicago Press.

Naremore, James (1999), 'Hitchcock at the margins of noir', in Richard Allen and S. Ishii-Gonzales (eds), *Alfred Hitchcock: Centenary Essays*, London: British Film Institute, pp. 263–77.

Neale, Stephen (2000), 'Film noir', in Stephen Neale, *Genre and Contemporary Hollywood*, New York: Routledge, pp. 142–67.

Neve, Brian (1992), 'Film noir and society', in Brian Neve, *Film and Politics in America: A Social Tradition*, London and New York: Routledge.

Orr, John (2005), 'Inside out: Hitchcock, film noir and David Lynch', in John Orr, *Hitchcock and Twentieth-century Cinema*, New York: Wallflower.

Palmer, R. Barton (2004), 'The sociological turn of adaptation studies: The example of film noir', in Robert Stam and Alessandra Raengo (eds), *A Companion to Literature and Film*, Oxford: Blackwell, pp. 258–77.

Pells, Richard H. (2011), 'Night and fog: From German expressionism to film noir', in Richard H. Pells, *Modernist America: Art, Music, Movies, and the Globalization of American Culture*, New Haven, CT: Yale University Press.

Place, Janey (1990), 'Women in film noir', in Tony Bennett (ed.), *Popular Fiction: Technology, Ideology, Production, Reading*, London and New York: Routledge.

Place, J. A. and L. S. Peterson (1976), 'Some visual motifs of film noir', in Bill Nichols (ed.), *Movies and Methods: An Anthology*, Berkeley, CA: University of California Press, pp. 325–38.

Pratt, Ray (2001), 'The dark vision of film noir', in Ray Pratt, *Projecting Paranoia: Conspiratorial Visions in American Film*, Lawrence, KS: University Press of Kansas.

Ray, Robert Beverley (1985), 'The discrepancy between intent and effect: Film noir, youth rebellion pictures, musicals, and westerns', in Robert Beverley Ray, *A Certain Tendency of the Hollywood Cinema, 1930–1980*, Princeton, NJ: Princeton University Press.

Richardson, Michael (2010), 'Otherness in the night: Film noir', in Michael Richardson, *Otherness in Hollywood Cinema*, New York: Continuum.

Rosenberg, Norman (1996), 'Law noir', in John Denvir (ed.), *Legal Reelism: Movies as Legal Texts*, Urbana, IL: University of Illinois Press, pp. 280–302.

Sarris, Andrew (1998), 'The film noir', in Andrew Sarris, *'You Ain't Heard Nothin' Yet': The American Talking Film, History & Memory, 1927–1949*, New York: Oxford University Press.

Schrader, Paul (1995), 'Notes on film noir', in Barry Keith Grant (ed.), *Film Genre Reader III*, Austin, TX: University of Texas Press, pp. 229–42.

Simpson, Philip (2010), 'Noir and the psycho-thriller', in Charles J. Rzepka and Lee Horsley (eds), *A Companion to Crime Fiction*, Chichester and Malden, MA: Wiley-Blackwell, pp. 187–97.

Sobchack, Vivian (1998), 'Lounge time: Postwar crises and the chronotope of film noir', in Nick Browne (ed.), *Refiguring American Film Genres: History and Theory*, Berkeley, CA: University of California Press, pp. 129–70.

Staiger, Janet (2008), 'Film noir as male melodrama: The politics of film genre labeling', in Lincoln Geraghty and Mark Jancovich (eds), *The Shifting Definitions of Genre: Essays on Labeling Films, Television Shows and Media*, Jefferson, NC: McFarland, pp. 71–91.

Stanfield, Peter (2002), '"Film noir like you've never seen": Jim Thompson adaptations and cycles of neo-noir', in Steve Neale (ed.), *Genre and Contemporary Hollywood*, London: British Film Institute.

Stevens, Jason W. (2010), 'McCarthyism through sentimental melodrama and film noir', in Jason W. Stevens, *God-fearing and Free: A Spiritual History of America's Cold War*, Cambridge, MA: Harvard University Press.

Tasker, Yvonne (1998), 'New Hollywood, new film noir and the femme fatale', in Yvonne Tasker, *Working Girls: Gender and Sexuality in Popular Cinema*, London and New York: Routledge.

Telotte, J. P. (1992), 'Film noir at Columbia: Fashion and innovation', in Bernard F. Dick (ed.), *Columbia Pictures: Portrait of a Studio*, Lexington, KY: University Press of Kentucky.

——. (1997), 'The woman in the door: Framing presence in film noir', in Gary R. Edgerton (ed.), *In the Eye of the Beholder: Critical Perspectives in Popular Film and Television*, Bowling Green, OH: Bowling Green State University Popular Press.

——. (2001), 'Noir narration', in John Orr and Olga Taxidou (eds), *Post-war Cinema and Modernity: A Film Reader*, New York: New York University Press.

Žižek, Slavoj (1993), '"The thing that thinks": The Kantian background of the noir subject', in Joan Copjec (ed.), *Shades of Noir: A Reader*, London and New York: Verso, pp. 199–226.

SELECTED FILM NOIR BOOKS

Abbott, Megan E. (2002), *The Street was Mine: White Masculinity in Hardboiled Fiction and Film Noir*, New York: Palgrave Macmillan.
Alloway, Lawrence (1971), *Violent America: The Movies, 1946–1964*, New York: Museum of Modern Art.
Auerbach, Jonathan (2011), *Dark Borders: Film Noir and American Citizenship*, Durham, NC: Duke University Press.
Ballinger, Alexander (2007), *The Rough Guide to Film Noir*, London and New York: Rough Guides.
Bassoff, Lawrence (1997), *Crime Scenes: Movie Poster Art of the Film Noir: The Classic Period, 1941–1959*, Beverly Hills, CA: L. Bassoff Collection.
Biesen, Sheri Chinen (2005), *Blackout: World War II and the Origins of Film Noir*, Baltimore, MD: The Johns Hopkins University Press.
Borde, Raymond and Étienne Chaumeton (1955; 1988), *Panorama du film noir américain, 1941–1953*, Paris: Flammarion.
——. (2002), *Panorama of American Film Noir, 1941–1953*, trans. Paul Hammond, San Francisco: City Lights Books.
Bould, Mark (2005), *Film Noir: From Berlin to Sin City*, New York: Wallflower.
Broe, Dennis (2009), *Film Noir, American Workers, and Postwar Hollywood*, Gainesville, FL: University Press of Florida.
Brook, Vincent (2009), *Driven to Darkness: Jewish Émigré Directors and the Rise of Film Noir*, New Brunswick, NJ: Rutgers University Press.
Butler, David (2002), *Jazz Noir: Listening to Music from Phantom Lady to The Last Seduction*, Westport, CN: Praeger.
Cameron, Ian (ed.) (1993), *The Book of Film Noir*, New York: Continuum.
Chopra-Gant, Mike (2006), *Hollywood Genres and Postwar America: Masculinity, Family and Nation in Popular Movies and Film Noir*, New York: I. B. Tauris.
Christopher, Nicholas (1997), *Somewhere in the Night: Film Noir and the American City*, New York: Free Press.

Cochran, David (2000), *America Noir: Underground Writers and Filmmakers of the Postwar Era*, Washington, DC: Smithsonian Institution Press.
Conard, Mark T. (2006), *The Philosophy of Film Noir*, Lexington, KY: University Press of Kentucky.
Copjec, Joan (ed.) (1993), *Shades of Noir: A Reader*, London and New York: Verso.
Crowther, Bruce (1988), *Film Noir: Reflections in a Dark Mirror*, New York: Continuum.
Dickos, Andrew (2002), *Street with no Name: A History of the Classic American Film Noir*, Lexington, KY: University Press of Kentucky.
Dimendberg, Edward (2004), *Film Noir and the Spaces of Modernity*, Cambridge, MA: Harvard University Press.
Dixon, Wheeler Winston (2009), *Film Noir and the Cinema of Paranoia*, New Brunswick, NJ: Rutgers University Press.
Dussere, Erik (2013), *America is Elsewhere: The Noir Tradition in the Age of Consumer Culture*, Oxford: Oxford University Press.
Faison, Stephen E. (2008), *Existentialism, Film Noir, and Hard-boiled Fiction*, Amherst, NY: Cambria Press.
Fay, Jennifer (2010), *Film Noir: Hard-boiled Modernity and the Cultures of Globalization*, London and New York: Routledge.
Flory, Dan (2008), *Philosophy, Black Film, Film Noir*, University Park, PA: Pennsylvania State University Press.
Gifford, Barry (1988), *The Devil Thumbs a Ride, and Other Unforgettable Films*, New York: Grove Press.
——. (2001), *Out of the Past: Adventures in Film Noir*, Jackson, MS: University Press of Mississippi.
Grossman, Julie (2009), *Rethinking the Femme Fatale in Film Noir: Ready for her Close-up*, New York: Palgrave Macmillan.
Hannsberry, Karen Burroughs (1998), *Femme Noir: Bad Girls of Film*, Jefferson, NC: McFarland.
——. (2003), *Bad Boys: The Actors of Film Noir*, Jefferson, NC: McFarland.
Hanson, Helen (2007), *Hollywood Heroines: Women in Film Noir and the Female Gothic Film*, London and New York: I. B. Tauris.
Hanson, Helen and Catherine O'Rawe (eds) (2010), *The Femme Fatale: Images, Histories, Contexts*, New York: Palgrave Macmillan.
Hare, William (2003), *Early Film Noir: Greed, Lust and Murder Hollywood Style*, Jefferson, NC: McFarland.
——. (2004), *L.A. Noir: Nine Dark Visions of the City of Angels*, Jefferson, NC: McFarland.
Hibbs, Thomas S. (2008), *Arts of Darkness: American Noir and the Quest for Redemption*, Dallas, TX: Spence Publishing.
Hirsch, Foster (1983), *The Dark Side of the Screen: Film Noir*, New York: Da Capo Press.
Horsley, Lee (2001), *The Noir Thriller*, New York: Palgrave Macmillan.
Irwin, John T. (2006), *Unless the Threat of Death is Behind Them: Hard-boiled Fiction and Film Noir*, Baltimore, MD: The Johns Hopkins University Press.
Johnson, Kevin (2007), *The Dark Page: Books that Inspired American Film Noir, 1940–1949*, New Castle, DE: Oak Knoll Press.
Kaplan, E. Ann (ed.) (1998), *Women in Film Noir*, London: British Film Institute.
Keaney, Michael F. (2003), *Film Noir Guide: 745 Films of the Classic Era, 1940–1959*, Jefferson, NC: McFarland.
Keating, Patrick (2010), *Hollywood Lighting from the Silent Era to Film Noir*, New York: Columbia University Press.

Krutnik, Frank (1991), *In a Lonely Street: Film Noir, Genre, Masculinity*, London and New York: Routledge.
Luhr, William (1991), *Raymond Chandler and Film*, Tallahassee, FL: Florida State University Press.
Lyons, Arthur (2000), *Death on the Cheap: The Lost B Movies of Film Noir*, New York: Da Capo Press.
Marling, William (1995), *The American Roman Noir, Hammett, Cain, Chandler*, Athens, GA: University of Georgia Press.
Martin, Richard (1997), *Mean Streets and Raging Bulls: The Legacy of Film Noir in Contemporary American Cinema*, Lanham, MD: Scarecrow Press.
Maxfield, James F. (1996), *The Fatal Woman: Sources of Male Anxiety in American Film Noir, 1941–1991*, Madison, NJ: Fairleigh Dickinson University Press.
Mayer, Geoff (2007), *Encyclopedia of Film Noir*, Westport, CN: Greenwood Press.
McCann, Sean (2000), *Gunshoe America: Hard-boiled Crime Fiction and the Rise and Fall of New Deal Liberalism*, Durham, NC: Duke University Press.
Meehan, Paul (2011), *Horror Noir: Where Cinema's Dark Sisters Meet*, Jefferson, NC: McFarland.
——. (2008), *Tech-noir: The Fusion of Science Fiction and Film Noir*, Jefferson, NC: McFarland.
Miklitsch, Robert (2011), *Siren City: Sound and Music in Classic American Noir*, New Brunswick, NJ: Rutgers University Press.
Muller, Eddie (2002), *The Art of Noir: The Posters and Graphics from the Classic Era of Film Noir*, Woodstock, NY: The Overlook Press.
——. (2001), *Dark City Dames: The Wicked Women of Film Noir*, New York: Regan Books.
——. (1998), *Dark City: The Lost World of Film Noir*, New York: St. Martin's Griffin.
Naremore, James (2008), *More Than Night: Film Noir in its Contexts*, Berkeley, CA: University of California Press.
Oliver, Kelly and Benigno Trigo (2003), *Noir Anxiety*, Minneapolis, MN: University of Minnesota Press.
Orr, Stanley (2010), *Darkly Perfect World: Colonial Adventure, Postmodernism, and American Noir*, Columbus, OH: Ohio State University Press.
Osteen, Mark (2013), *Nightmare Alley: Film Noir and the American Dream*, Baltimore, MD: The Johns Hopkins University Press.
Ottoson, Robert (1981), *A Reference Guide to the American Film Noir, 1940–1958*, Metuchen, NJ: Scarecrow Press.
Palmer, R. Barton (1994), *Hollywood's Dark Cinema: The American Film Noir*, New York: Twayne.
——. (ed.) (1996), *Perspectives on Film Noir*, London: Prentice Hall.
Park, William (2011), *What is Film Noir?*, Lewisburg, PA: Bucknell University Press.
Phillips, Gene D. (2000), *Creatures of Darkness: Raymond Chandler, Detective Fiction, and Film Noir*, Lexington, KY: University Press of Kentucky.
——. (2012), *Out of the Shadows: Expanding the Canon of Classic Film Noir*, Lanham, MD: Scarecrow Press.
Pippin, Robert B. (2012), *Fatalism in American Film Noir: Some Cinematic Philosophy*, Charlottesville, VA: University of Virginia Press.
Porfirio, Robert, Alain Silver and James Ursini (2002), *Film Noir Reader 3: Interviews with Filmmakers of the Classic Noir Period*, New York: Limelight.
Rabinowitz, Paula (2002), *Black & White & Noir: America's Pulp Modernism*, New York: Columbia University Press.

Renzi, Thomas C. (2006), *Cornell Woolrich: From Pulp Noir to Film Noir*, Jefferson, NC: McFarland.
Rich, Nathaniel (2005), *San Francisco Noir: The City in Film Noir from 1940 to the Present*, New York: Little Bookroom.
Richardson, Carl (1992), *Autopsy: An Element of Realism in Film Noir*, Metuchen, NJ: Scarecrow Press.
Rosow, Eugene (1978), *Born to Lose: The Gangster Film in America*, New York: Oxford University Press.
Sanders, Steven M. and Aeon J. Skoble (eds) (2008), *The Philosophy of TV Noir*, Lexington, KY: University Press of Kentucky.
Schwarz, Ronald (2001), *Noir, Now and Then: Film Noir Originals and Remakes, 1944–1999*, Westport, CT: Greenwood Press.
Selby, Spencer (1984), *Dark City: The Film Noir*, Jefferson, NC: McFarland.
Shadoian, Jack (1977), *Dreams and Dead Ends: The American Gangster/Crime Film*, Cambridge, MA: MIT Press.
Silver, Alain and James Ursini (1996), *Film Noir Reader*, New York: Limelight.
——. (1999), *Film Noir Reader 2*, New York: Limelight.
——. (1999), *The Noir Style*, Woodstock, NY: The Overlook Press.
——. (2004), *Film Noir Reader 4*, New York: Limelight.
——. (2005), *L.A. Noir: The City as Character*, Santa Monica, CA: Santa Monica Press.
——. (2012), *Film Noir: The Directors*, New York: Limelight.
Silver, Alain and Elizabeth Ward (eds) (1992), *Film Noir: An Encyclopedic Reference to the American Style*, Woodstock, NY: The Overlook Press.
Smith, Imogen Sara (2011), *In Lonely Places: Film Noir Beyond the City*, Jefferson, NC: McFarland.
Spicer, Andrew (2002), *Film Noir*, New York: Longman/Pearson.
——. (2010), *Historical Dictionary of Film Noir*, Lanham, MD: Scarecrow Press.
Spicer, Andrew and Helen Hanson (eds) (2013), *Companion to Film Noir*, Chichester: Blackwell.
Stephens, Michael L. (1995), *Film Noir: A Comprehensive, Illustrated Reference to Movies, Terms, and Persons*, Jefferson, NC: McFarland.
Telotte, J. P. (1989), *Voices in the Dark: The Narrative Patterns of Film Noir*, Urbana, IL: University of Illinois Press.
Tuska, John (1984), *Dark Cinema: American Film Noir in Cultural Perspective*, Westport, CN: Greenwood Press.
Wager, Jans B. (2005), *Dames in the Driver's Seat: Rereading Film Noir*, Austin, TX: University of Texas Press.
——. (1999), *Dangerous Dames: Women and Representation in the Weimar Street Film and Film Noir*, Athens, OH: Ohio University Press.

SELECTED GUIDE TO FILM NOIR

The project of amassing lists of films noirs, including films that influenced noir, is daunting. Still, we have essayed to present an historical and somewhat thorough list of films noirs from the silent era to the 1970s. For a list of noirs representing global cinema, readers should consult our *International Noir* volume from Edinburgh University Press.

Pre-World War I Noir-influencing Films

Fantômas (Louis Feuillade, serial, 1913)
Judex (Louis Feuillade, serial, 1916)
Les Vampires (Louis Feuillade, serial, 1915)
Lucille Love (Francis Ford, 1914)
The Musketeers of Pig Alley (D. W. Griffith, 1912)

German Expressionism

Algol [*Algol – Tragödie der Macht*] (Hans Werckmeister, 1920)
Destiny [*Der Müde Tod*] (Fritz Lang, 1921)
Dr. Mabuse: the Gambler [*Dr. Mabuse, der Spieler*] (Fritz Lang, 1922)
Earth Spirit [*Erdgeist*] (Leopold Jessner, 1923)
From Morning to Midnight [*Von Morgens bis Mitternacht*] (Karl Heinz Martin, 1920)
Genuine [*Genuine, die Tragödie eines seltsamen Hauses*] (Robert Wiene, 1920)
M (Fritz Lang, 1931)
Metropolis (Fritz Lang, 1927)
Nerves [*Nerven*] (Robert Reinert, 1919)
Nosferatu [*Nosferatu – eine Symphonie des Grauens*] (F. W. Murnau, 1922)
Phantom (F. W. Murnau, 1922)

SELECTED GUIDE TO FILM NOIR

The Cabinet of Dr. Caligari [*Das Cabinet des Dr. Caligari*] (Robert Wiene, 1920)
The City without Jews [*Die Stadt ohne Juden*] (H. K. Breslauer, 1924)
The Golem: How he Came into the World [*Der Golem, wie er in die Welt kam*] (Carl Boese, Paul Wegener, 1920)
The Hands of Orlac [*Orlac Hände*] (Robert Wiene, 1925)
The Last Laugh [*Der Letzte Mann*] (F. W. Murnau, 1924)
The Street [*Die Strasse*] (Karl Grune, 1923)
The Student of Prague [*Der Student von Prag*] (Henrik Galeen, 1926)
The Testament of Dr. Mabuse [*Das Testament des Dr. Mabuse*] (Fritz Lang, 1933)
Vampyr (Carl Theodor Dreyer, 1932)
Vanina [*Vanian oder die Galgenhochzeit*] (Arthur von Gerlach, 1922)
Warning Shadows: A Nocturnal Hallucination [*Schatten – eine Nächtliche Halluzination*] (Arthur Robison, 1923)
Waxworks [*Das Wachsfigurekabinet*] (Paul Leni, Leo Birinsky, 1924)

Proto-noirs

Alibi (Roland West, 1929)
Asphalt (Erich Pommer, 1929)
Blackmail (Alfred Hitchcock, 1929)
Dr. Mabuse, der Spieler (Fritz Lang, 1922)
The Docks of New York (Josef von Sternberg, 1928)
The Lodger: A Story of the London Fog (Alfred Hitchcock, 1927)
The Racket (Lewis Milestone, 1928)
Thunderbolt (Josef von Sternberg, 1929)
Underworld (Josef von Sternberg, 1927)
Woman Trap (William Wellman, 1929)

1930s

Baby Face (Alfred E. Green, 1933)
Beast of the City (Charles Brabin, 1932)
City Streets (Rouben Mamoulian, 1931)
Das Testament des Dr. Mabuse (Fritz Lang, 1933)
Fury (Fritz Lang, 1936)
Heat Lightning (Mervyn LeRoy, 1934)
Hell's Highway (Rowland Brown, 1932)
Hôtel du Nord (Marcel Carné, 1938)
I am a Fugitive from a Chain Gang (Mervyn LeRoy, 1932)
King of the Underworld (Lewis Seller, 1939)
La Bête humaine (Jean Renoir, 1938)
Le Jour se lève (Marcel Carné, 1939)
Le Quai des Brumes (Marcel Carné, 1938)
Little Caesar (Mervyn LeRoy, 1931)
M (Fritz Lang, 1931)
Midnight (Chester Erskine, 1934)
Night World (Hobart Henley, 1932)
Paid (Sam Wood, 1930)
Pépé Le Moko (Julien Duvivier, 1937)
Safe in Hell (William Wellman, 1931)
Satan Met a Lady (William Dieterle, 1936)
Scarface (Howard Hawks, 1932)

The Maltese Falcon (Roy Del Ruth, 1931)
The Man Who Knew Too Much (Alfred Hitchcock, 1934)
The Mindreader (Roy Del Ruth, 1933)
The Mouthpiece (James Flood, Elliott Nugent, 1932)
The Petrified Forest (Archie Mayo, 1936)
The Testament of Dr. Mabuse (Fritz Lang, 1933)
The 39 Steps (Alfred Hitchcock, 1935)
3 on a Match (Mervyn LeRoy, 1932)
You Only Live Once (Fritz Lang, 1937)

Mystery Serials and Film Series

Bulldog Drummond (silent, starring Carlyle Blackwell, 1922; Jack Buchanan, 1925; first sound, Ronald Colman, 1929, then 1934; Kenneth MacKenna, 1930; Ralph Richardson, 1934; John Howard, 1937–9; Ray Milland, 1937; Ron Randell, 1947; Tom Conway, 1948; Walter Pidgeon, 1951)
Charlie Chan (*House without a Key*, silent, George Kuwa, 1926)
Charlie Chan (starring Warner Oland, 1931–7)
Charlie Chan (starring Sidney Toler, 1938–46)
Charlie Chan (starring Roland Winters, 1948–9)
Hildegarde Withers (starring Edna May Oliver, 1932–4; Helen Broderick, 1936; ZaSu Pitts, 1936–7)
Michael Shayne Mysteries (starring Lloyd Nolan, 1940–2)
Michael Shayne Mysteries (starring Hugh Beaumont, 1945–6)
Mr. Moto (starring Peter Lorre, 1937–9)
Mystery of the Double Cross (starring Léon Bary and Mollie King, 1917)
Nick Carter (starring Pierre Bressol, 1908; Walter Pidgeon, 1939–40)
Office 444 (starring Ben F. Wilson, 1926)
Perry Mason (starring Warren William, 1934–6; Ricardo Cortez, 1936; Donald Woods, 1937)
Philo Vance (starring William Powell, 1929–34; Basil Rathbone, 1930; Warren William, 1934, 1939; Paul Lukas, 1936; Edmund Lowe, 1936; William Wright, 1947; Alan Curtis, 1947)
Radio Detective (starring Jack Dougherty, 1926)
The Falcon (starring George Saunders, 1941–2)
The Falcon (starring Tom Conway, 1943–6)
The Falcon (starring John Calvert, 1948–9)
The Mystery of 13 (starring John B. Clymer, 1919)
The Saint (starring George Saunders, 1939–41)
The Saint (starring Hugh Sinclair, 1941)
The Thin Man (starring William Powell and Myrna Loy, 1936–47)

European (Foreign Language) Noirs of the 1940s

Le Corbeau (Henri-Georges Clouzot, 1943)
Ossessione (Luchino Visconti, 1943)
Quai des Orfèvres (Henri-Georges Clouzot, 1947)

1940s

A Dangerous Profession (Ted Tetzlaff, 1949)
A Double Life (George Cukor, 1948)

SELECTED GUIDE TO FILM NOIR

A Woman's Face (George Cukor, 1941)
A Woman's Secret (Nicholas Ray, 1949)
Abandoned (Joseph M. Newman, 1949)
Act of Violence (Fred Zinnemann, 1949)
Among the Living (Stuart Heisler, 1941)
Angels over Broadway (Ben Hecht, Lee Garmes, 1940)
Apology for Murder (Sam Newfield, 1945)
Assigned to Danger (Budd Boetticher, 1948)
Background to Danger (Raoul Walsh, 1943)
Backlash (Eugene Forde, 1947)
Behind Locked Doors (Oscar Budd Boetticher, 1948)
Behind the Green Light (Otto Brower, 1946)
Berlin Express (Jacques Tourneur, 1948)
Betrayed (William Castle, 1944)
Bewitched (Arch Oboler, 1945)
Beyond the Forest (King Vidor, 1949)
Black Angel (Roy William Neill, 1946)
Blackmail (Lesley Selander, 1947)
Blonde Ice (Jack Bernhard, 1948)
Blues in the Night (Anatole Litvak, 1941)
Body and Soul (Robert Rossen, 1947)
Bodyguard (Richard Fleischer, 1948)
Boomerang! (Elia Kazan, 1947)
Border Incident (Anthony Mann, 1949)
Born to Kill (Robert Wise, 1947)
Brighton Rock (John Boulting, 1947)
Brute Force (Jules Dassin, 1947)
Bury Me Dead (Bernard Vorhaus, 1947)
Calcutta (John Farrow, 1947)
Call Northside 777 (Henry Hathaway, 1948)
Canon City (Crane Wilbur, 1948)
Caught (Max Ophuls, 1949)
Champion (Mark Robson, 1949)
Chicago Deadline (Lewis Allen, 1949)
Christmas Holiday (Robert Siodmak, 1944)
Circumstantial Evidence (John Larkin, 1945)
City across the River (Maxwell Shane, 1949)
Cloak and Dagger (Fritz Lang, 1946)
C-Man (Joseph Lerner, 1949)
Conflict (Curtis Bernhardt, 1945)
Contraband (Michael Powell, 1940)
Convicted (Henry Levin, 1950)
Cornered (Edward Dmytryk, 1945)
Crack-Up (Irving Ross, 1946)
Crime, Inc. (Lew Landers, 1945)
Criss Cross (Robert Siodmak, 1949)
Crossfire (Edward Dmytryk, 1947)
Cry of the City (Robert Siodmak, 1948)
Daisy Kenyon (Otto Preminger, 1947)
Danger Signal (Robert Florey, 1945)
Dark Passage (Delmar Daves, 1947)
Dark Waters (André De Toth, 1944)

Dead Reckoning (John Cromwell, 1947)
Deadline at Dawn (Harold Clurman, 1946)
Deception (Irving Rapper, 1946)
Decoy (Jack Bernhard, 1946)
Deep Valley (Jean Negulesco, 1947)
Desert Fury (Lewis Allen, 1947)
Desperate (Anthony Mann, 1947)
Destiny (Reginald LeBorg, Julien Duvivier, 1944)
Detour (Edgar G. Ulmer, 1945)
Dillinger (Max Nosseck, 1945)
Don't Gamble with Strangers (William Beaudine, 1946)
Double Indemnity (Billy Wilder, 1944)
Escape (Joseph L. Mankiewicz, 1948)
Escape in the Fog (Budd Boetticher, 1945)
Fall Guy (Reginald LeBorg, 1947)
Fallen Angel (Otto Preminger, 1946)
Fear (Alfred Zeisler, 1946)
Fear in the Night (Maxwell Shane, 1947)
Flamingo Road (Michael Curtiz, 1949)
Flaxy Martin (Robert L. Bare, 1949)
Follow Me Quietly (Richard Fleischer, 1949)
For You I Die (John Reinhardt, 1947)
Force of Evil (Abraham Polonsky, 1948)
Framed (Richard Wallace, 1947)
Gilda (Charles Vidor, 1946)
Grand Central Murder (S. Sylvan Simon, 1942)
Guest in the House (John Brahm, 1944)
Hangmen Also Die (Fritz Lang, 1943)
Hangover Square (John Brahm, 1945)
He Walked By Night (Alfred Werker, 1949)
Her Kind of Man (Frederick de Cordova, 1946)
High Sierra (Raoul Walsh, 1941)
High Tide (John Reinhardt, 1947)
High Wall (Curtis Bernhardt, 1947)
Hollow Triumph (Steve Sekely, 1948)
Homicide (Felix Jacoves, 1949)
House of Strangers (Joseph L. Mankiewicz, 1949)
House on 92nd Street (Henry Hathaway, 1945)
I Love Trouble (S. Sylvan Simon, 1948)
I Wake Up Screaming (H. Bruce Humberstone, 1942)
I Walk Alone (Byron Haskin, 1948)
I Wouldn't Be in Your Shoes (William Nigh, 1948)
Impact (Arthur Lubin, 1949)
It Always Rains on Sunday (Robert Hamer, 1947)
Jealousy (Gustav Machaty, 1945)
Jigsaw (Fletcher Markle, 1949)
Johnny Allegro (Ted Tetzlaff, 1949)
Johnny Angel (Edwin L. Marin, 1945)
Johnny Eager (Mervyn LeRoy, 1942)
Johnny O'Clock (Robert Rossen, 1947)
Johnny Stool Pigeon (William Castle, 1949)
Journey into Fear (Norman Foster, 1943)

SELECTED GUIDE TO FILM NOIR

Key Largo (John Huston, 1948)
Key Witness (D. Ross Lederman, 1947)
Kiss of Death (Henry Hathaway, 1947)
Kiss the Blood off My Hands (Norman Foster, 1948)
Knock on any Door (Nicholas Ray, 1949)
Ladies in Retirement (Charles Vidor, 1941)
Lady Gangster (Robert Florey, 1942)
Lady in the Lake (Robert Montgomery, 1947)
Lady on a Train (Charles David, 1945)
Laura (Otto Preminger, 1944)
Leave Her to Heaven (John M. Stahl, 1945)
Lured (Douglas Sirk, 1947)
Manhandled (Lewis R. Foster, 1949)
Mildred Pierce (Michael Curtiz, 1945)
Ministry of Fear (Fritz Lang, 1945)
Money Madness (Sam Newfield, 1948)
Moonrise (Frank Borzage, 1949)
Moontide (Archie Mayo, Fritz Lang, 1942)
Murder, My Sweet (Edward Dmytryk, 1944)
My Name is Julia Ross (Joseph H. Lewis, 1945)
Night Editor (Henry Levin, 1946)
Night Has a Thousand Eyes (John Farrow, 1948)
Nightmare Alley (Edmund Goulding, 1947)
Nobody Lives Forever (Jean Negulesco, 1946)
Nocturne (Edwin L. Marin, 1946)
Nora Prentiss (Vincent Sherman, 1947)
Notorious (Alfred Hitchcock, 1946)
Obsession (Edward Dmytryk, 1949)
Odd Man Out (Carol Reed, 1947)
Out of the Fog (Anatole Litvak, 1941)
Out of the Past (Jacques Tourneur, 1947)
Phantom Lady (Robert Siodmak, 1944)
Pitfall (André De Toth, 1948)
Port of New York (Laszlo Benedek, 1949)
Possessed (Curtis Bernhardt, 1947)
Race City (Edwin L. Marin, 1948)
Rage in Heaven (W. S. Van Dyke, 1941)
Railroaded (Anthony Mann, 1947)
Raw Deal (Anthony Mann, 1948)
Rebecca (Alfred Hitchcock, 1940)
Red Light (Roy Del Ruth, 1949)
Ride the Pink Horse (Robert Montgomery, 1947)
Road House (Jean Negulesco, 1948)
Rope of Sand (William Dieterle, 1949)
Ruthless (Edgar G. Ulmer, 1948)
Saboteur (Alfred Hitchcock, 1942)
Scarlet Street (Fritz Lang, 1945)
Scene of the Crime (Roy Rowland, 1949)
Secret Beyond the Door (Fritz Lang, 1948)
Shadow of a Doubt (Alfred Hitchcock, 1943)
Shadow of a Woman (Joseph Santley, 1946)
Shed No Tears (Jean Yarbrough, 1948)

Shock (Alfred L. Werker, 1946)
Shockproof (Douglas Sirk, 1949)
Shoot to Kill (William Berke, 1947)
Sign of the Ram (John Sturges, 1948)
Singapore (John Brahm, 1947)
Sleep, My Love (Douglas Sirk, 1948)
So Dark the Night (Joseph H. Lewis, 1946)
Somewhere in the Night (Joseph L. Mankiewicz, 1946)
Sorry, Wrong Number (Anatole Litvak, 1948)
Specter of the Rose (Ben Hecht, 1946)
Spellbound (Alfred Hitchcock, 1945)
Strange Illusion (Edgar G. Ulmer, 1945)
Strange Impersonation (Anthony Mann, 1946)
Strange Triangle (Ray McCarey, 1946)
Stranger Woman (Edgar G. Ulmer, 1946)
Strangers in the Night (Anthony Mann, 1944)
Street of Chance (Jack Hively, 1942)
Suspense (Frank Tuttle, 1946)
Take One False Step (Chester Erskine, 1949)
Temptation (Irving Pichel, 1946)
Tension (John Berry, 1949)
The Accused (William Dieterle, 1949)
The Amazing Mr. X (Bernard Vorhaus, 1948)
The Arnelo Affair (Arch Oboler, 1947)
The Big Clock (John Farrow, 1948)
The Big Sleep (Howard Hawks, 1946)
The Big Steal (Don Siegel, 1949)
The Black Book (aka *Reign of Terror*) (Anthony Mann, 1949)
The Blue Dahlia (George Marshall, 1946)
The Brasher Doubloon (John Brahm, 1947)
The Bribe (Robert Z. Leonard, 1949)
The Chase (Arthur Ripley, 1946)
The Clay Pigeon (Richard Fleischer, 1949)
The Crooked Way (Robert Florey, 1949)
The Dark Corner (Henry Hathaway, 1946)
The Dark Mirror (Robert Siodmak, 1946)
The Dark Past (Rudolph Maté, 1948)
The Devil Thumbs a Ride (Felix E. Feist, 1947)
The Fallen Sparrow (Richard Wallace, 1943)
The Flame (John H. Auer, 1947)
The Gangster (Gordon Wiles, 1947)
The Glass Alibi (W. Lee Wilder, 1946)
The Glass Key (Stuart Heisler, 1942)
The Great Flamarion (Anthony Mann, 1945)
The Guilty (John Reinhardt, 1947)
The House Across the Street (Richard Bare, 1949)
The Hunted (Jack Bernhard, 1948)
The Killers (Robert Siodmak, 1946)
The Lady Confesses (Sam Newfield, 1945)
The Lady from Shanghai (Orson Welles, 1948)
The Lady Gambles (Michael Gordon, 1949)
The Letter (William Wyler, 1940)

SELECTED GUIDE TO FILM NOIR

The Locket (John Brahm, 1947)
The Long Night (Anatole Litvak, 1947)
The Maltese Falcon (John Huston, 1941)
The Man I Love (Raoul Walsh, 1947)
The Mark of the Whistler (William Castle, 1944)
The Mask of Demitrios (Jean Negulesco, 1944)
The Naked City (Jules Dassin, 1948)
The Postman Always Rings Twice (Tay Garnett, 1946)
The Pretender (W. Lee Wilder, 1947)
The Reckless Moment (Max Ophuls, 1949)
The Red House (Delmer Daves, 1947)
The Set-Up (Robert Wise, 1949)
The Seventh Victim (Mark Robson, 1943)
The Shanghai Gesture (Josef von Sternberg, 1941)
The Small Back Room (Michael Powell, Emeric Pressburger, 1949)
The Spider (Robert D. Webb, 1945)
The Spiral Staircase (Robert Siodmak, 1946)
The Strange Affair of Uncle Harry (Robert Siodmak, 1945)
The Strange Loves of Martha Ivers (Lewis Milestone, 1946)
The Stranger (Orson Welles, 1946)
The Stranger on the Third Floor (Boris Ingster, 1940)
The Street with No Name (William Keighley, 1948)
The Strip (Laszlo Kardos, 1951)
The Suspect (Robert Siodmak, 1944)
The Third Man (Carol Reed, 1949)
The Threat (Felix E. Feist, 1949)
The Two Mrs. Carrolls (Peter Godfrey, 1947)
The Undercover Man (Joseph H. Lewis, 1949)
The Unfaithful (Vincent Sherman, 1947)
The Unsuspected (Michael Curtiz, 1947)
The Verdict (Don Siegel, 1946)
The Voice of the Whistler (William Castle, 1945)
The Web (Michael Gordon, 1947)
The Whistler (William Castle, 1944)
The Window (Ted Tetzlaff, 1949)
The Woman in the Window (Fritz Lang, 1945)
The Woman on the Beach (Jean Renoir, 1947)
They Don't Believe Me (Irving Pichel, 1947)
They Drive by Night (Raoul Walsh, 1940)
They Live By Night (Nicholas Ray, 1948)
They Made Me a Fugitive (Alberto Cavalcanti, 1947)
They Won't Believe Me (Irving Pichel, 1947)
Thieves' Highway (Jules Dassin, 1949)
This Gun for Hire (Frank Tuttle, 1942)
Three Strangers (Jean Negulesco, 1946)
T-Men (Anthony Mann, 1945)
To the Ends of the Earth (Robert Stevenson, 1948)
Too Late for Tears (Byron Haskin, 1949)
Trapped (Richard Fleischer, 1949)
Two O'clock Courage (Anthony Mann, 1945)
Undercurrent (Vincente Minnelli, 1946)
Violence (Jack Bernhardt, 1947)

Voice in the Wind (Arthur Ripley, 1944)
Walk a Crooked Mile (Gordon Douglas, 1948)
When Strangers Meet (William Castle, 1944)
Whiplash (Lewis Seller, 1948)
Whirlpool (Otto Preminger, 1949)
Whispering City (Fedor Ozep, 1947)
Whispering Footsteps (Howard Bretherton, 1943)
Whistle Stop (Leonide Moguy, 1946)
White Heat (Raoul Walsh, 1949)
Wife Wanted (Phil Karlson, 1946)
Without Honor (Irving Pichel, 1949)

EUROPEAN (FOREIGN LANGUAGE) *NOIRS* OF THE 1950S

L'Ascenseur pour l'échafaud (Louis Malle, 1958)
Bob le flambeur (Jean-Pierre Melville, 1956)
Les Diaboliques (Henri-Georges Clouzot, 1955)
Du rififi chez les hommes (Jules Dassin, 1955)
Touchez pas au grisbi (Jean Becker, 1954)

1950S

A Blueprint for Murder (Andrew L. Stone, 1953)
A Bullet for Joey (Lewis Allen, 1955)
A Cry in the Night (Frank Tuttle, 1956)
A Kiss Before Dying (Gerd Oswald, 1956)
A Lady without a Passport (Joseph H. Lewis, 1950)
A Life at Stake (Paul Guilfoyle (1954)
A Stolen Face (Terence Fisher, 1952)
A Woman's Devotion (Paul Henried, 1956)
Accused of Murder (Joseph Kane, 1956)
Affair in Havana (Laslo Benedek, 1957)
Affair in Trinidad (Vincent Sherman, 1952)
Angel Face (Otto Preminger, 1953)
Another Man's Poison (Irving Rapper, 1951)
Appointment with a Shadow (Richard Carlson, 1952)
Appointment with Danger (Lewis Allen, 1951)
Armored Car Robbery (Richard Fleischer, 1950)
Baby Face Nelson (Don Siegel, 1957)
Backfire (Vincent Sherman, 1950)
Bad Blonde (Reginald Le Borg, 1953)
Bad for Each Other (Irving Rapper, 1953)
Between Midnight and Dawn (Gordon Douglas, 1950)
Beware, My Lovely (Harry Horner, 1952)
Beyond a Reasonable Doubt (Fritz Lang, 1956)
Black Tuesday (Hugo Fregonese, 1954)
Black Widow (Nunnally Johnson, 1954)
Born to be Bad (Nicholas Ray, 1950)
Breakdown (Edmond Angelo, 1952)
Caged (John Cromwell, 1950)
Cause for Alarm! (Tay Garnett, 1951)
Chicago Calling! (John Reinhardt, 1951)

SELECTED GUIDE TO FILM NOIR

Chicago Confidential (Sidney Salkow, 1957)
City of Fear (Irving Lerner, 1958)
City that Never Sleeps (John H. Auer, 1953)
Clash by Night (Fritz Lang, 1952)
Code Two (Fred M. Wilcox, 1953)
Convicted (Henry Levin, 1950)
Cop Hater (William Berke, 1957)
Crashout (Lewis R. Foster, 1955)
Crime in the Streets (Don Siegel, 1957)
Crime of Passion (Gerd Oswald, 1957)
Crime Wave (André De Toth, 1954)
Cry Danger (Robert Parrish, 1951)
Cry of the Hunted (Joseph H. Lewis, 1953)
Cry Terror! (Andrew L. Stone, 1958)
Cry Vengeance (Mark Stevens, 1954)
Dangerous Crossing (Joseph M. Newman, 1953)
Dark City (William Dieterle, 1951)
Deadly Game (Daniel Britt, 1954)
Death in Small Doses (Joseph Newman, 1957)
Death of a Scoundrel (Charles Martin, 1956)
Dementia (John Parker, 1955)
Destination Murder (Edward L. Cahn, 1950)
Detective Story (William Wyler, 1951)
Dial 119 (Gerald Mayer, 1950)
D.O.A. (Rudolph Maté, 1950)
Don't Bother to Knock (Roy Ward Baker, 1952)
Down 3 Dark Streets (Arnold Laven, 1954)
Drive a Crooked Road (Richard Quine, 1954)
Duffy of San Quentin (Walter Doniger, 1954)
Edge of Doom (Mark Robson, 1950)
FBI Girl (William Burke, 1951)
Female Jungle (Bruno VeSota, 1954)
Female on the Beach (Joseph Pevney, 1955)
Fingerprints Don't Lie (Sam Newfield, 1951)
5 Against the House (Phil Karlson, 1955)
Footsteps in the Night (Jean Yarbrough, 1957)
Fourteen Hours (Henry Hathaway, 1951)
Gambling House (Ted Tetzlaff, 1951)
Guilty Bystander (Joseph Lerner, 1950)
Gun Crazy (Joseph H. Lewis, 1950)
He Ran All the Way (John Berry, 1951)
Heat Wave (Ken Hughes, 1954)
Hell on Frisco Bay (Frank Tuttle, 1955)
Hell's Half Acre (John H. Auer, 1954)
Hell's Island (Phil Karlson, 1955)
Highway 301 (Andrew L. Stone, 1950)
Highway Dragnet (Nathan Juran, 1954)
His Kind of Woman (John Farrow, 1951)
Hit and Run (Hugo Haas, 1957)
Hoodlum Empire (Joseph Kane, 1952)
House by the River (Fritz Lang, 1950)
House of Bamboo (Samuel Fuller, 1955)

House of Numbers (Russell Rouse, 1957)
House on Telegraph Hill (Robert Wise, 1951)
Human Desire (Fritz Lang, 1954)
Hunt the Man Down (George Archainbaud, 1950)
I Confess (Alfred Hitchcock, 1953)
I Died a Thousand Times (Stuart Heisler, 1955)
I Want to Live! (Robert Wise, 1958)
I Was a Communist for the F.B.I. (Gordon Douglas, 1951)
I, the Jury (Harry Essex, 1953)
I'll Get You (Seymour Friedman, 1952)
Illegal (Lewis Allen, 1955)
In a Lonely Place (Nicholas Ray, 1950)
Inferno (Roy Ward Baker, 1953)
Jeopardy (John Sturges, 1953)
Julie (Andrew L. Stone, 1956)
Kansas City Confidential (Rhil Karlson, 1952)
Killer's Kiss (Stanley Kubrick, 1955)
Kiss Me Deadly (Robert Aldrich, 1955)
Kiss Tomorrow Goodbye (Gordon Douglas, 1950)
Lightning Strikes Twice (King Vidor, 1951)
Loan Shark (Seymour Friedman, 1952)
Lonelyhearts (Vincent J. Donehue, 1958)
Loophole (Hard Schuster, 1954)
M (Joseph Losey, 1951)
Macao (Josef von Sternberg, 1952)
Make Haste to Live (William A. Seiter, 1954)
Man Bait (Terence Fisher, 1952)
Man in the Attic (Hugo Fregonese, 1953)
Mask of the Dragon (Sam Newfield, 1951)
Murder by Contract (Irving Lerner, 1958)
Murder is My Beat (Edgar G. Ulmer, 1955)
My Gun is Quick (George A. White, Phil Victor, 1957)
Mystery Street (John Sturges, 1950)
New York Confidential (Russell Rouse, 1955)
Niagara (Henry Hathaway, 1953)
Night and the City (Jules Dassin, 1950)
Night Without Sleep (Roy Ward Baker, 1952)
Nightfall (Jacques Tourneur, 1957)
Nightmare (Maxwell Shane, 1956)
99 River Street (Phil Karlson, 1953)
No Man of Her Own (Mitchell Leisen, 1950)
No Questions Asked (Harold F. Kress, 1951)
No Way Out (Joseph L. Mankiewicz, 1950)
Odds Against Tomorrow (Robert Wise, 1959)
On Dangerous Ground (Nicholas Ray, 1952)
One Girl's Confession (Hugo Haas, 1953)
One Way Street (Hugo Fregonese, 1950)
Outside the Wall (Crane Wilbur, 1950)
Over-Exposed (Lewis Seller, 1956)
Panic in the Streets (Elia Kazan, 1950)
Party Girl (Nicholas Ray, 1958)
Pickup (Hugo Haas, 1951)

SELECTED GUIDE TO FILM NOIR

Pickup on South Street (Samuel Fuller, 1953)
Playgirl (Joseph Pevney, 1954)
Please Murder Me (Peter Godfrey, 1956)
Plunder Road (Hubert Cornfield, 1957)
Private Hell 36 (Don Siegel, 1954)
Pushover (Richard Quine, 1954)
Queen Bee (Ranald MacDougall, 1955)
Quicksand (Irving Pichel, 1950)
Red Light (Roy Del Ruth, 1950)
Riot in Cell Block 11 (Don Siegel, 1954)
Roadblock (Harold Daniels, 1951)
Rogue Cop (Roy Rowland, 1954)
Ruby Gentry (King Vidor, 1952)
Saint Louis Bank Robbery (Charles Guggenheim, 1959)
Scandal Sheet (Phil Karlson, 1952)
711 Ocean Drive (Joseph M. Newman, 1950)
Shack out on 101 (Edward Dein, 1955)
Shakedown (Joe Pevney, 1950)
Shield for Murder (Edmond O'Brien, Howard W. Koch, 1954)
Short Cut to Hell (James Cagney, 1957)
Side Street (Anthony Mann, 1950)
Sirocco (Curtis Bernhardt, 1951)
Slaughter on Tenth Avenue (Arnold Laven, 1957)
Slightly Scarlet (Allan Dwan, 1956)
Southside 1-1000 (Boris Ingster, 1950)
Split Second (Dick Powell, 1953)
Step down to Terror (Harry Keller, 1959)
Storm Fear (Cornel Wilde, 1956)
Storm Warning (Stuart Heisler, 1951)
Strange Fascination (Hugh Haas, 1952)
Strangers on a Train (Alfred Hitchcock, 1951)
Sudden Fear (David Miller, 1952)
Suddenly (Lewis Allen, 1954)
Sunset Boulevard (Billy Wilder, 1950)
Sweet Smell of Success (Alexander MacKendrick, 1957)
Talk About a Stranger (David Bradley, 1952)
Tension (John Berry, 1950)
The Asphalt Jungle (John Huston, 1950)
The Basketball Fix (Felix E. Feist, 1951)
The Big Bluff (W. Lee Wilder, 1955)
The Big Carnival [Ace in the Hole] (Billy Wilder, 1951)
The Big Combo (Joseph Lewis, 1955)
The Big Heat (Fritz Lang, 1953)
The Big Knife (Robert Aldrich, 1955)
The Big Night (Joseph Losey, 1951)
The Black Glove (Terence Fisher, 1953)
The Blue Gardenia (Fritz Lang, 1953)
The Breaking Point (Michael Curtiz, 1950)
The Brothers Ricco (Phil Karlson, 1957)
The Burglar (Paul Wendkos, 1957)
The Captive City (Robert Wise, 1952)
The Capture (John Sturges, 1950)

The Case Against Brooklyn (Paul Wendkos, 1958)
The Cobweb (Vincente Minnelli, 1955)
The Crimson Kimono (Samuel Fuller, 1959)
The Damned Don't Cry (Vincent Sherman, 1950)
The Desperate Hours (William Wyler, 1955)
The Edge of the City (Martin Ritt, 1957)
The Enforcer [*Murder, Inc.*] (Bretaigne Windust, 1951)
The File on Thelma Jordan (Robert Siodmak, 1950)
The Garment Jungle (Vincent Sherman, 1957)
The Glass Tomb (Montgomery Tull, 1955)
The Glass Wall (Maxwell Shane, 1953)
The Glass Web (Jack Arnold, 1953)
The Harder They Fall (Mark Robson, 1956)
The Hitch-Hiker (Ida Lupino, 1953)
The Hoodlum (Max Nosseck, 1951)
The Human Jungle (Joseph M. Newman, 1954)
The Killer Is Loose (Budd Boetticher, 1956)
The Killer that Stalked New York (Earl McEvoy, 1951)
The Killing (Stanley Kubrick, 1956)
The Las Vegas Story (Robert Stevenson, 1952)
The Lawless (Joseph Losey, 1950)
The Limping Man (Charles de LaTour, 1953)
The Lineup (Don Siegel, 1958)
The Long Dark Hall (Reginald Beck, 1951)
The Long Wait (Victor Saville, 1954)
The Man from Cairo (Ray Enright, 1953)
The Man in the Net (Michael Curtiz, 1959)
The Man who Cheated Himself (Felix E. Feist, 1950)
The Man with My Face (Edward J. Montagne, 1951)
The Mob (Robert Parrish, 1951)
The Naked Alibi (Jerry Hopper, 1954)
The Naked Street (Maxwell Shane, 1955)
The Narrow Margin (Richard Fleischer, 1952)
The Night Holds Terror (Andrew Stone, 1955)
The Night of the Hunter (Charles Laughton, 1955)
The Night Runner (Abner Biberman, 1957)
The Other Woman (Hugo Hass, 1954)
The People Against O'Hara (John Sturges, 1951)
The Phenix City Story (Phil Karlson, 1955)
The Price of Fear (Abner Biberman, 1956)
The Prowler (Joseph Losey, 1951)
The Racket (John Cromwell, 1951)
The Raging Tide (George Sherman, 1951)
The Second Woman (James V. Kern, 1950)
The Secret Fury (Mel Ferrer, 1950)
The Sellout (Gerald Mayer, 1952)
The Shadow on the Window (William Asher, 1957)
The Sleeping City (George Sherman, 1950)
The Sniper (Edward Dmytryk, 1952)
The Steel Trap (Andrew L. Stone, 1952)
The Strip (Leslie Kardos, 1951)
The System (Lewis Seller, 1953)

The Tall Target (Anthony Mann, 1951)
The Tattered Dress (Jack Arnold, 1957)
The Tattooed Stranger (Edward J. Montagne, 1950)
The Thief (Russell Rouse, 1952)
The 13th Letter (Otto Preminger, 1951)
The Trap (Norman Panama, 1959)
The Turning Point (William Dieterle, 1952)
The Underworld Story (Cy Endfield, 1950)
The Unholy Wife (John Farrow, 1957)
The Unknown Man (Richard Thorpe, 1951)
The Well (Russell Rouse, 1951)
The Woman on Pier 13 (Robert Stevenson, 1950)
The Wrong Man (Alfred Hitchcock, 1956)
This Side of the Law (Richard Bare, 1950)
Tight Spot (Phil Karlson, 1955)
Timetable (Mark Stevens, 1956)
Tomorrow Is Another Day (Felix Feist, 1951)
Touch of Evil (Orson Welles, 1958)
Try and Get Me (Cyril Endfield, 1950)
Two of a Kind (Henry Levin, 1951)
Union Station (Rudolph Maté, 1950)
Vicki (Harry Horner, 1953)
Violent Saturday (Richard Fleischer, 1955)
Walk East on Beacon! (Alfred L. Werker, 1952)
Walk Softly Stranger (Robert Stevenson, 1950)
Where Danger Lives (John Farrow, 1950)
Where the Sidewalk Ends (Otto Preminger, 1950)
While the City Sleeps (Fritz Lang, 1956)
Wicked Woman (Russell Rouse, 1953)
Wings of Danger (Terence Fisher, 1952)
Without Warning! (Arnold Laven, 1952)
Witness to Murder (Roy Rowland, 1954)
Woman in Hiding (Michael Gordon, 1950)
Woman on the Run (Norman Foster, 1950)
Women's Prison (Lewis Seller, 1955)
World for Ransom (Robert Aldrich, 1954)

1960s

Blast of Silence (Allen Baron, 1963)
Brainstorm (William Conrad, 1965)
Cape Fear (J. Lee Thompson, 1962)
Experiment in Terror (Blake Edwards, 1962)
FBI Code 98 (Leslie H. Martinson, 1962)
Girl of the Night (Joseph Cates, 1960)
Harper (Jack Smight, 1966)
In Cold Blood (Richard Brooks, 1967)
In the Heat of the Night (Norman Jewison, 1967)
Madigan (Don Siegel, 1968)
Marlowe (Paul Bogart, 1969)
Mirage (Edward Dmytryk, 1965)
Mister Buddwing (Delbert Mann, 1966)

Murder, Inc. (Burt Balaban, Stuart Rosenberg, 1960)
Point Blank (John Boorman, 1967)
Pressure Point (Hubert Cornfield, 1962)
Psycho (Alfred Hitchcock, 1960)
Seconds (John Frankenheimer, 1966)
Shock Corridor (Samuel Fuller, 1963)
Something Wild (Jack Garfein, 1961)
The Hustler (Robert Rossen, 1961)
The Killers (Don Siegel, 1964)
The Manchurian Candidate (John Frankenheimer, 1962)
The Money Trap (Burt Kennedy, 1965)
The Naked Kiss (Samuel Fuller, 1964)
The Pawnbroker (Sidney Lumet, 1964)
Underworld U.S.A. (Samuel Fuller, 1961)
Walk on the Wild Side (Edward Dmytryk, 1962)
Whatever Happened to Baby Jane? (Robert Aldrich, 1962)

1970S

Chandler (Paul Magwood, 1971)
Charley Varrick (Don Siegel, 1973)
Chinatown (Roman Polanski, 1974)
Dirty Harry (Don Siegel, 1971)
Farewell, My Lovely (Dick Richards, 1975)
Fat City (John Huston, 1972)
French Connection II (John Frankenheimer, 1975)
Klute (Alan J. Pakula, 1971)
Night Moves (Arthur Penn, 1975)
Taxi Driver (Martin Scorsese, 1976)
The Conversation (Francis Ford Coppola, 1974)
The Drowning Pool (Stuart Rosenberg, 1975)
The French Connection (William Friedkin, 1971)
The Friends of Eddie Coyle (Peter Yates, 1973)
The Long Goodbye (Robert Altman, 1973)

NOIR WESTERNS

Bad Day at Black Rock (John Sturges, 1955)
Blood on the Moon (Robert Wise, 1948)
Colorado Territory (Raoul Walsh, 1949)
Day of the Outlaw (André De Toth, 1959)
Devil's Doorway (Anthony Mann, 1950)
Duel in the Sun (King Vidor, 1946)
Forty Guns (Samuel Fuller, 1957)
I Shot Jesse James (Samuel Fuller, 1949)
Johnny Guitar (Nicholas Ray, 1954)
Jubal (Delmer Daves, 1956)
Little Big Horn (Charles Marquis Warren, 1951)
Man from Del Rio (Harry Horner, 1956)
Man with a Gun (Richard Wilson, 1955)
Pursued (Raoul Walsh, 1947)
Ramrod (André De Toth, 1947)

SELECTED GUIDE TO FILM NOIR

Rancho Notorious (Fritz Lang, 1952)
Rawhide (Henry Hathaway, 1951)
7 Men from Now (Budd Boetticher, 1956)
Silver Lode (Allan Dwan, 1954)
Station West (Sidney Lanfield, 1948)
The Badlanders (Delmer Daves, 1958)
The Furies (Anthony Mann, 1950)
The Gunfighter (Henry King, 1950)
The Man Who Shot Liberty Valence (John Ford, 1962)
The Naked Spur (Anthony Mann, 1953)
The Ox-Bow Incident (William Wellman, 1943)
The Ride Back (Allen H. Milner, Oscar Rudolph, 1957)
The Tall T (Budd Boetticher, 1957)
The Violent Men (Rudolph Maté, 1955)
3:10 to Yuma (Delmer Daves, 1957)
Tin Star (Anthony Mann, 1957)
Two Flags West (Robert Wise, 1950)
Valerie (Gerd Oswald, 1957)
Winchester '73 (Anthony Mann, 1950)
Yellow Sky (William Wellman, 1948)

INDEX

Abbott and Costello Meet Captain Kidd (1952, Charles Lamont), 105
Abschied (1930, Robert Siodmak), 122, 140
Act of Violence (1948, Fred Zinnemann), 152–4, 156–7, 162, 203
Aldrich, Robert, 94, 119, 184–5, 187, 210–11, 213–14
Alighieri, Dante, 176
Allen, Woody, 121
Alpi, Deborah Lazaroff, 122, 139–40
Altman, Georges, 2, 14
Altman, Robert, 103–4, 106, 114–18, 120–1, 140, 214
Alton, John, 39, 48, 187, 189
American Civil Liberties Union, 100
American Expeditionary Force, 62, 77
American Individualism (1922), 61
Andrew, Dudley, 22, 35, 37, 55
Andrews, Dana, 89, 99, 104
Angel Face (1952, Otto Preminger), 50, 208
Anthony, Ray, 105
Appy, Christian G., 101
Arizona Memorial, 98
Arness, James, 97
Around the World in Eighty Days (1956, Michael Anderson), 104
Arthur, Paul, 192
Asphalt Jungle, The (1950, John Huston), 59, 142, 211
Astor, Mary, 32, 61, 65–6, 144–5
Atomic City, The (1952, Jerry Hopper), 94–5
Axman, Hanne, 92

Baby Face (1933, Alfred E. Green), 29, 35, 201, 208

Baldwin, James, 164–5, 179–81
Balzac, Honoré de, 1, 6, 7–9, 14–15
Barnet, Charles, 105
Barnett, Griff, 131
Barr, Byron, 173
Barron, Stephanie, 55
Barry, Gene, 95
Baruch, Bernard, 88
Baudelaire, Charles, 3
Baxter, Alan, 177
Baxter, Anne, 104, 111
Beckmann, Max, 41
Belafonte, Harry, 119, 175
Bellow, George, 177
Bennett, Bruce, 171
Bennett, Joan, 51
Bergstrom, Janet, 38, 113, 121
Berigan, Bunny, 105
Berkeley, Busby, 115
Berlin, 40–1, 46, 56, 86, 177, 196, 203
Bernhardt, Curtis, 39, 179, 203–6, 211
Bête humaine, La (1938, Jean Renoir), 21, 23, 35, 201
Bick, Jerry, 115
Bickford, Charles, 90
Big Clock, The (1948, John Farrow), 187, 206
Big Combo, The (1955, Joseph H. Lewis), 48–9, 211
Big Heat, The (1953, Fritz Lang), 59, 154, 156–7, 162, 211
Big Jim McLain (1953, Edward Ludwig), 97–8
Big Sleep, The (1946, Howard Hawks), 59, 114–15, 121, 143, 162, 206
Billy the Kid Versus Dracula (1966, William Beaudine), 105
Biskind, Peter, 101

Black Mask (Magazine), 60, 65
Blaue Reiter, Der (Blue Rider), 40
Blaue Reiter Almanac, 40
Bleyl, Fritz, 40
Blue Gardenia, The (1953, Fritz Lang), 103–5, 111–14, 117–21, 211
'Blue Gardenia' (song), 105, 111–14
Blyth, Ann, 169
Bogart, Humphrey, 60, 65, 114, 121, 143–6, 159, 162, 181, 213
Bomba and the Jungle Girl (1952, Ford Beebe), 105
Bonanova, Fortunio, 173
Bond, Ward, 65
Boozer, Jack, 192
Borde, Raymond, 130, 142, 183–4, 186, 188
Border Incident (1949, Anthony Mann), 48, 203
Bordwell, David, 19, 35–6, 187, 188, 191
Bouton, Jim, 105, 115
Boyer, Paul, 101
Brahm, John, 39, 105, 204, 206–7
Brando, Jocelyn, 155
Brando, Marlon, 166
Breakfast at Tiffany's (1961, Blake Edwards), 106
Brennon, Herbert, 186
Bresson, Robert, 186
Brest, Martin, 186
Britton, Wesley A., 192
Brodie, Steve, 106
Brody, Jo Ann, 116
Broken Blossoms (1919, D. W. Griffith), 22, 35
Bronfen, Elisabeth, 143, 162–3, 192
Brook, Vincent, 35–6, 196
Brooks, Louise, 47
Brooks, Peter, 6–7, 15
Brücke, Die (Bridge), 40
Brute Force (1947, Jules Dassin), 142, 187, 191, 203
Budapest, 90
Budd, Norman, 92
Buhle, Paul, 192
Bullock, Chick, 105
Burr, Raymond, 96, 99, 104, 111

Cabinet of Dr. Caligari, The (1919, Robert Wiene), 38, 43–5, 54–5, 201
Cain, James M., 58–60, 73, 77, 79, 168, 170, 173, 180–1, 198
California Split (1974, Robert Altman), 114
Callahan, Vicki, 16, 35–7
Capra, Frank, 82
Captive City, The (1952, Robert Wise), 93, 211
Carson, Jack, 169
Carter, Janis, 98
Caspary, Vera, 120
Cassuto, Leonard, 65, 78
Cat People (1943, Jacques Tourneur), 105, 109, 179
Caute, David, 101
Cavell, Stanley, 150, 162–3
Centre Georges Pompidou, 46, 56
Ceplair, Larry, 101
Chandler, Raymond, 8, 15, 58–60, 66–8, 70–3, 77–9, 114–15, 121, 181, 198
Chase, The (1946, Arthur Ripley), 123, 140, 206
Chaumeton, Étienne, 130, 142, 183, 186, 188, 196
Chinatown (1974, Roman Polanski), 183, 214
Chion, Michael, 127, 141
Christensen, Terry, 101
Christmas Holiday (1944, Robert Siodmak), 122, 137, 140, 203
Churchill, Winston, 83
Cinema One, 182
Citizen Kane (1941, Orson Welles), 71, 122–3, 130, 140–1
City of Fear (1959, Irving Lerner), 94, 209
Civil Rights, 121, 172
Clark, T. J., 6, 15
Clarke, David, 177, 193
Coen, Joel and Ethan, 16, 35, 37
Cohen, Leonard, 116
Cold War, 2, 12, 80–9, 91, 93–5, 97–102, 184, 195
Cole, Nat King, 105, 111–13, 119
Coleman, Wanda, 179, 181
Collette, Buddy, 105
Columbia Pictures, 72, 78, 94–5, 162, 187, 195
Comédie humaine, La, 1
Condon, Richard, 100
Conley, Tom, 192
Conte, Richard, 104, 111
Cooke, Mervyn, 120

Cooper, Maxine, 94
Copjec, Joan, 35–7, 55, 121, 147, 162–3, 179, 195, 197
Corkin, Stanley, 9, 15
Cortez, Ricardo, 63, 202
Crane, Stephen, 176
Crawford, Joan, 168–9
Cripps, Thomas, 118, 121
Criss-Cross (1949, Robert Siodmak), 51–2, 122–42, 203
Crossfire (1947, Edward Dmytryk), 5, 105, 191, 203
Crowther, Bosley, 82, 92, 102
Cry of the City (1948, Robert Siodmak), 122, 187, 203
Cukor, George, 91, 202–3
Cummins, Peggy, 49
Currie, Finlay, 86
Curtis, Tony, 134
Curtiz, Michael, 118, 146, 180, 204–5, 207, 211–12

Dall, John, 49
Dall'Asta, Monica, 26, 35, 37
Danger Signal (1945, Robert Florey), 59, 203
Daniels, Bebe, 63, 211
Dante's Inferno, 176
Dark City (1950, William Dieterle), 59, 209
Dark Mirror, The (1946, Robert Siodmak), 122, 197, 206
Dark Passage (1947, Delmer Daves), 59, 165, 179, 203
Daumier, Honoré, 1–6, 8–9, 14–15
Davidson, Michael, 192
Davis, Bette, 66, 107
Davis, Blair, 192
Davis, Johnny 'Scat', 117
Davis Jr, Sammy, 119
de Balzac, Honoré, 1, 8, 15
De Carlo, Yvonne, 51–2, 134–9
Del Ruth, Roy, 63, 202, 205, 211
DeMille, Cecil B., 17, 160–1
de Rochemont, Louis, 86
Derr, Richard, 90
Desser, David, 192
Detour (1945, Edgar G. Ulmer), 21, 23, 30, 32, 34–5, 49, 51, 204
Diawara, Manthia, 164–5, 179
Dieterle, William, 39, 66, 201, 205–6, 209, 213

Dimendberg, Edmund, 20, 35, 37, 47–8, 57, 197
Diplomatic Courier (1952, Henry Hathaway), 91
Disasters of War, The, 3
Dix, Otto, 41–2
Dixon, Wheeler Winston, 192, 197
Dmytryk, Edward, 1–2, 4–10, 14–15, 35, 68–72, 105, 203, 205, 212–14
D.O.A. (1950, Rudolph Maté), 165, 209
Doane, Mary Ann, 143, 162
Doherty, Thomas, 101
Donnell, Jeff, 111
'Do Nothin' Till You Hear from Me' (song), 105
'Don't Get Around Much Anymore' (song), 105
Dorgan, Tad, 62, 77
Double Indemnity (1944, Billy Wilder), 21–2, 29, 31, 35, 37, 39, 48–9, 58, 72–4, 79, 81, 84–5, 137, 142, 158–60, 162, 164, 168, 172, 181, 204
Douglas, Gordon, 95–6, 208, 210
Douglas, Kirk, 106, 147
Douglass, Frederick, 178
Dreiser, Theodore, 176
Dresden, 40
Dr. Mabuse, the Gambler (1922, Fritz Lang), 42–3, 46, 200
Durgnat, Raymond, 183
Duryea, Dan, 52

Eagle-Lion Films, 90
Eastern Europe, 83, 90–1, 96
East Germany, 91
Edwards, Blake, 106, 213
Edwards, James, 177
Ehrlich, Matthew C., 193
Eisner, Lotte H., 45–6, 56
Eliot, T. S., 176, 181
Ellington, Duke, 105
Ellis, Seger, 105
Ellison, Ralph, 177, 179
Elsaesser, Thomas, 47, 55
Engelhardt, Tom, 101
Englund, Steven, 101
Erdman, Richard, 111
Evans, Charles, 95

Fallen Angel (1945, Otto Preminger), 59, 204

INDEX

Fantomas (1913, Louis Feuillade), 18–20, 23–30, 33–5, 200
Farewell, My Lovely (book), 8, 15, 67, 70–1, 78
Farmer, Francis, 105
Fat City (1972, John Huston), 175, 214
Faulkner, William, 71, 115, 168
Fearmakers, The (1958, Jacques Tourneur), 99
Feist, Felix, 90, 206–7, 211–13
Felixmuller, Conrad, 41
Fenneker, Josef, 46, 56
Feuillade, Louis, 16–20, 22–3, 28–30, 32–7, 200
Fieberling, Hal, 177
Fifth Amendment, 97
File on Thelma Jordan, The (1950, Robert Siodmak), 122, 212
Film Comment, 55, 57, 182, 184–5, 190
Fine, David M., 73, 79
'First Time I Saw You, The' (song), 105–12, 117
Flory, Dan, 193, 197
Flowers, Tiger, 175
Foran, Dick, 99
Force of Evil (1948, Abraham Polonsky), 187, 204
Ford, Glenn, 100, 155
Foster, Norman, 105, 140, 204–5, 213
Fotsch, Paul Mason, 193
Framed (1947, Richard Wallace), 187, 204
Francis, Anne, 11
Frankenheimer, John, 100, 214
Freedman, Carl, 193
Freud, Sigmund, 15, 55, 133, 167, 177, 180
Freund, Karl, 39, 44, 55
From Morning to Midnight (1920, Karlheinz Martin), 45
Fuchs, Daniel, 130–2, 136, 139
Fugitive Kind, The (1959, Sidney Lumet), 165–6, 179
Fugitive Slave Law (1793), 165
Fuller, Barbra, 92
Fuller, Samuel, 7, 49, 94, 209, 211–12, 214
Fury (1936, Fritz Lang), 165, 179, 201
Futurism, 40–1

Gabbard, Krin, 103, 121, 194
Gabin, Jean, 21, 23
Gaddis, John Lewis, 101
Gaines, Richard, 174
Gardner, Ava, 48, 51, 130
Gargantua, 4–5
Garrett, Roberta, 193
Gaslight (1944, George Cukor), 91
Gates, Philippa, 193
Genuine (1920, Robert Wiene), 45, 200
German Expressionism, 16–17, 36, 38–57, 176, 188, 194, 200
Germany, 38, 40–1, 47, 55–6, 81–2, 84, 91, 122
G. I. Bill of Rights, The, 92
Gifford, Barry, 186, 197
Girl of the Night (1960, Joseph Cates), 11, 213
Golem, The (1920, Paul Wegener), 44, 201
Goodman, Benny, 117
Gomez, Thomas, 98
Gorbman, Claudia, 108, 112, 118, 120–1, 141
Gould, Elliott, 105, 115–16
Goux, Jean-Joseph, 10, 15
Goya, Francisco, 3
Graham, Gloria, 156
Grant, Barry Keith, 56, 194
Granville, Bonita, 90
Graves, Ernest, 86
Great Depression, 59–60, 73, 78, 82, 193
Greb, Harry, 175
Green, Dorothy, 155
Greenberg, Joel, 183
Greenstreet, Sydney, 146, 162
Greer, Jane, 31, 49, 104, 110, 147, 165
Griffith, D. W., 9, 17, 22, 35, 200
Grosz, George, 41–2
Groundhog Day (1993, Harold Ramis), 105
Grusin Trio, 116–17
Guilty of Treason (1950, Felix Feist), 90, 98
Gun Crazy (1950, Joseph H. Lewis), 49, 59, 209
Gunning, Tom, 111, 113, 120–1

Haas, Peter J., 101
Hammett, Dashiell, 58–66, 77, 143, 198
Hanson, Philip, 193
Harris, Theresa, 107, 119, 165–6
Hart, Dorothy, 96
Harvey, Laurence, 100

Harvey, Sylvia, 146, 162, 193
Hathaway, Henry, 91, 203–6, 209–10, 215
Haut, Woody, 101
Hayden, Sterling, 104
Haynes, John E., 102
Hays Office, The 34, 108, 165, 169
Hayward, Louis, 95
Hayworth, Rita, 30, 54
Hazard of New Fortunes, A, 9
Heather, Joan, 173
Heckel, Erich, 40
Heflin, Van, 153
Helton, Percy, 133
He Walked By Night (1948, Alfred Werker & Anthony Mann), 48, 204
Hewison, Robert, 102
Higham, Charles, 183, 190
High Noon (1953, Fred Zinnemann), 104
High Sierra (1941, Raoul Walsh), 165, 179, 181, 204
Hinterteppe (Backstairs, 1921, Leopold Jessner & Paul Muni), 46
Hirsch, Foster, 167, 180, 197
Hitchcock, Alfred, 91, 122, 194, 201–2, 205–6, 210–11, 213–14
Hitler, Adolph, 6, 38, 57, 90, 102, 174
Hixson, Walter L., 102
Hockley, Luke, 193
Holden, William, 51, 135, 159
Holland, Edna, 133
Hollywood, 6, 15, 17, 20, 22, 28, 34, 36–9, 47–8, 56–7, 68, 72, 74, 78, 80–2, 87–9, 91, 93, 97–8, 101–5, 107, 109, 114–15, 123, 130, 132, 139–42, 146, 159–60, 162–3, 165, 167, 172, 180, 183–4, 187–8, 192–8
Hollywood Hotel (1938, Busby Berkeley), 115, 117
Hoover, Herbert, 61
Hoover, J. Edgar, 84
Hopper, Jerry, 94, 212
House, Billy, 125
House on the Moon/Haus zum mond (1920, Karlheinz Martin), 45, 56
House Un-American Activities Committee (HUAC), 5–6, 72, 81, 93, 97–8
Howell, William Dean, 9
Hungary, 90–1
Huston, John, 7, 35, 63, 77, 143, 145–6, 162, 164, 175, 192, 205, 207, 211, 214
Huston, Virginia, 106

I Am a Fugitive from a Chain Gang (1932, Mervyn Le Roy), 165, 179, 201
I Led Three Lives (TV Series), 97
'I'll Remember April' (song), 137
Images (1972, Robert Altman), 116
I Married a Communist (1953, Robert Stevenson), 98
Indiana University, 120, 182
Ingster, Boris, 11, 81, 207, 211
Invasion of the Body Snatchers (1956, Don Siegel), 167
Invisible Man (1952), 177, 179
Iron Curtain, 83, 88, 90–2
Iron Curtain, The (1948, William Wellman), 88–90, 93, 98
Island of Lost Women (1959, Frank Tuttle), 105
It's a Wonderful Life (1946, Frank Capra), 82, 102
I Walked With a Zombie (1943, Jacques Tourneur), 107, 109
I Was a Communist for the FBI (1951, Gordon Douglas), 96–7

James, Harry, 117
James, Henry, 2, 14
Jazz Singer, The (1927, Alan Crosland), 169
Jessner, Leopold, 46, 200
Jezebel (1938, William Wyler), 107
Johnson, Jack, 175
Jolson, Al, 169
Journey into Fear (1943, Norman Foster), 105, 204
Jour se lève, Le (1939, Marcel Carne), 2, 14, 21–3, 35, 201
Jowett, Corson J., 123
Joyless Street (1925, G. W. Pabst), 47, 49, 56
Judex (1917, Louis Feuillade), 28–30, 34–7, 200

Kai-Shek, Chiang, 83
Kampf um Rom (1968, Robert Siodmak), 130
Kandinsky, Wassily, 40
Kaper, Bronislau, 123

Kaplan, Amy, 9, 15
Kaplan, E. Ann, 162, 164–5, 179, 197
Kasten, Jürgen, 45, 56
Kastner, Elliott, 115
Katzman, David M., 171, 180
Kazan, Elia, 94, 203, 210
Kefauver, Estes, 93
Kelly, David, 90–1
Kennan, George F., 87–9, 91, 102
Kennedy, Barbara, 193
Kerr, John, 11
Keynes, John Maynard, 59, 77
Killers, The (1946, Robert Siodmak), 48–9, 51–2, 54, 122, 130, 133, 137, 139–40, 165, 206
King, Clydie, 116
King Kong (1933, Ernest B. Schoedsack & Merian C. Cooper), 71
Kirchner, Ernst Ludwig, 40
Kiss Me Deadly (1955, Robert Aldrich), 94, 119, 163, 185, 190–1, 210
Kiss the Blood Off My Hands (1948, Norman Foster), 123, 140, 205
Knight, Arthur, 140
Kobe, Hanns, 45
Kokoschka, Oscar, 42
Korean War, 88, 99
Kortner, Fritz, 47
Kracauer, Sigfried, 47, 49, 57
Krapp, George Philip, 62
Kraushaar, Raoul, 105, 112–13
Kroeger, Berry, 89
Krutnik, Frank, 15, 78, 109, 120, 142–3, 162, 193, 198
Kubrick, Stanley, 7, 210, 212
Kurer, Vilma, 87
Kurtz, Rudolf, 44–5, 56
Kuznick, Peter J., 102

Lady from Shanghai, The (1947, Orson Welles), 22–3, 30, 35, 54, 123, 130, 140, 179, 206
Lally, William J., 92
Lang, Fritz, 7, 39, 42, 45–6, 51, 56, 81, 103, 113, 119–21, 154–5, 162, 164–6, 179, 194, 200–5, 207–11, 213, 215
Langford, Frances, 117
Last Laugh, The (1924, F. W. Murnau), 44, 201
Laura (1944, Otto Preminger), 104, 120, 163, 205

'Laura' (song), 104
Lawson, John Howard, 6
Lee, Canada, 175
Lee, Lester, 105
Lee, Rowland V., 105
Leigh, Janet, 153
Lend-Lease, 93
Leni, Paul, 45–6, 201
Leopard Man, The (1943, Jacques Tourneur), 109
Lerner, Irving, 94, 209–10
LeRoy, Mervyn, 179, 201–2, 204
Levy, Emanuel, 193
Lewis, Joseph H., 7, 48–9, 205–9, 211
Lippmann, Walter, 88
Litvak, Anatole, 39, 203, 205–7
Locket, The (1946, John Brahm), 105, 207
Long, Richard, 126, 133
Long Goodbye, The (1973, Robert Altman), 103–4, 106, 114–18, 120–1, 183, 214
Long Telegram, 87, 102
Lorre, Peter, 60, 146, 162, 202
Los Alamos, 95
Los Angeles, 5, 67–8, 71, 73–5, 78–9, 94, 111, 113, 120, 131, 133, 135, 148, 153, 182, 193
Los Angeles County Museum of Art, 41
Los Angeles County Regional Planning Commission, 75
Lott, Eric, 164–5, 169, 172, 179–81
Love is a Many-Splendored Thing (1955, Henry King), 104
Lovejoy, Frank, 96
Ludwig, Edward, 97
Luhr, William, 77, 107, 110, 119–20, 194, 198
Lumet, Sidney, 166, 179, 214
Lunceford, Jimmy, 105

M (1931, Fitz Lang), 46
Macek, Carl, 140, 183
MacMurray, Fred, 48, 72, 85, 102, 137, 158, 172
Magnani, Anna, 166
Mainwaring, Daniel, 167
Maltese Falcon, The (1941, John Huston), 19, 21, 32–3, 35, 58–9, 61, 64–6, 77–8, 143, 145–7, 150, 157, 162–4, 202, 207

Manchurian Candidate, The (1962, John Frankenheimer), 100–1, 214
Mancini, Henry, 106, 120
Mann, Anthony, 7, 48, 203–7, 211, 213–15
Mann der seinen Mörder sucht, Der (1931, Robert Siodmak), 122
Manning, Jack, 86
Man Who Wasn't There, The (2001, Joel Coen), 16, 35, 37
Marc, Franz, 40
March, Joseph Moncure, 175, 181
Marlowe, Jo Anne, 169
Martin, Karlheinz, 45
Martin, Nina K., 193
Marvin, Lee, 156
Marxist-Leninism, 87
M*A*S*H (1970, Robert Altman), 114
Maté, Rudolph, 39, 206, 209, 213, 215
May, Alan Nunn, 89
May, Lary, 102, 193
Mayer, Louis B., 72
Mayer, Peter, 182
McCarthy, Joseph, 100, 192
McCarthyism, 5, 101, 195
McCuskey, Brian, 167, 180
McGuffin, The (1986, Colin Bucksey), 184
McNally, Stephen, 132
McQueen, Butterfly, 167–8, 170, 172, 180
Meeker, Ralph, 94, 119
Menken, Shepard, 92
Menzies, William Cameron, 99
Mercer, Johnny, 103–4, 106, 116, 120–1
Merchant of Venice, The, 64
Merivale, Philip, 126
Metro Goldwyn Mayer (MGM), 72, 91, 100, 162, 179, 187
Metropolis (1926, Fritz Lang), 44–5, 200
Mildred Pierce (book), 168, 180
Mildred Pierce (1945, Michael Curtiz), 59, 73, 118, 167–8, 170, 180, 205
Miller, Joan, 133
Miller, Laurence, 194
Millican, James, 96
Mind of the South, The (1941), 178
Mindszenty, Cardinal, 90
Miranda, Carmen, 169
Mitchum, Robert, 49–50, 104, 107, 109–10, 115, 121, 147, 165–6

'Moon River' (song), 106
Morales, Esy, 130–1, 134–5, 139, 142
Morrison, Toni, 168, 179–80
Moscow, 87, 99, 101
Mosher, Jerry, 194
Mr. Deeds Goes to Town (1936, Frank Capra), 82
Mrs. Miniver (1942, William Wyler), 151
Mr. Smith Goes to Washington (1939, Frank Capra), 82
Munby, Jonathan, 194
Murder, Hope of Women (play), 42
Murder, My Sweet (1944, Edward Dmytryk), 4–6, 8, 10, 15, 22, 35, 39, 58, 68–72, 78, 121, 191, 205
Murder on Acker Street (1916), 42
Murphet, Julian, 164–5, 179
Murphy, George, 6, 86
Musuraca, Nicholas, 106, 108, 112
Myrdal, Gunnar, 164, 179

Nadel, Alan, 102
Naked City (photographs), 48, 57
Napier, Alan, 98
Naremore, James, 17, 20, 36–7, 55, 102, 107, 120, 130, 139–41, 174, 181, 194, 198
Narrative (1845), 178
Nashville (1975, Robert Altman), 114
Neal, Tom, 49
Neale, Stephen, 15, 78, 142, 194–5
Neff, Hildegarde, 91
Nelson, Joyce, 171, 180
Neue Sächlichkeit (New Objectivity), 41
Neve, Brian, 15, 78, 142, 194
New Deal, 59–60, 72–3, 77, 82, 84, 198
New Mexico, 95
New Orleans, 94, 166
New York Times, 82, 92, 102, 121, 185
Nolan, Jeanette. 155
Nolan, Lloyd, 11, 202
Nolde, Emil, 40
Norris, Frank, 176
Norvo, Red, 105

Oakes, James, 167, 180
O'Brien, Edmond, 139, 211
Odds Against Tomorrow (1959, Robert Wise), 11, 119, 175, 181, 210
Office of War Information, The, 93
O'Keefe, Dennis, 95
Olson, Nancy, 97, 160

Ophuls, Max, 39, 203, 207
Orpheus Descending (play), 166
Orr, John, 194–5
O'Ryan, John F., 62
Osterloh, Robert, 138
Out of the Past (1947, Jacques Tourneur), 19, 23, 31, 35, 49–51, 59, 103–7, 109–12, 114–15, 117–20, 139, 147, 149–53, 155, 158, 160, 162, 165–6, 179, 187, 191, 197, 205
Overlook Press, The, 182, 189–90, 198–9

Pabst, G. W., 46, 49
Palmer, Christopher, 105, 120
Palmer, R. Barton, 80, 139, 141–2, 194, 198
Pandora's Box (1928, G. W. Pabst), 46
Panic in the Streets (1950, Elia Kazan), 94, 191, 210
Paramount Pictures, 23, 72, 160–2, 181, 186–7
Patrick, Lee, 60
Pechstein, Max, 40–1
Pells, Richard H., 194
'Pennsylvania Polka' (song), 105
Père Goriot, 7, 15
Peterson, Caleb, 107
Peterson, Lowell, 36, 57, 188–9, 194
Petrified Forest, The (1936, Archie Mayo), 94, 202
Petro, Patrice, 47, 56, 92
Phantom Lady (1944, Robert Siodmak), 122, 137, 140, 196, 205
Phenix City Story, The (1955, Phil Karlson), 166, 179, 212
Philippe, Louis, 5
Phillips, Gene D., 123, 139–41, 198
Pickup on South Street (1953, Samuel Fuller), 94, 211
Pièges (1939, Robert Siodmak), 122, 140
Pitfall (1948, André de Toth), 187, 205
Place, Janey, 36, 162, 188–9, 194
Planer, Franz, 131, 133
Poetic Realism (France), 16–17, 22, 39–40, 55
Porfirio, Robert G., 39–40, 55, 183, 185, 188, 198
Porter, Edwin S., 9
Postman Always Rings Twice, The (1946, Tay Garnett), 21, 33–5, 73, 207
Powell, Dick, 4–5, 68, 70–1, 94, 211
Power, Tyrone, 91
Pratt, Ray, 194
Preminger, Otto, 39, 50, 104, 203–5, 208, 213

Quintet (1979, Robert Altman), 114

Rabinowitz, Paula, 164–5, 179, 199
Radosh, Ronald & Alan, 102
Rafferty, Terence, 115, 121
Raging Bull (1980, Martin Scorsese), 175
Railroaded (1947, Anthony Mann), 59, 205
Raksin, David, 104
Ramis, Harold, 105
Rand, Ayn, 93
Randall, Meg, 133
Raskolnikov (1922, Robert Wiene), 45
Raw Deal (1948, Anthony Mann), 48–9, 205
Ray, Robert B., 121
Reagan, Ronald, 6, 93
Realism, 7–9, 15, 199
Rebecca (1940, Alfred Hitchcock), 91, 205
Red Menace (1949, R. G. Springsteen), 92, 102, 164
Reid, Elliott, 99
Reinhardt, Max, 45–6, 56
Republic Pictures, 92
Richardson, Michael, 194
Riddle, Norman, 109
Riley, Jack, 116
RKO Radio Pictures, 68, 72, 78, 94, 98–9, 106, 162, 175, 179, 181, 187, 191–2
Robertson, Cliff, 49
Robinson, Edward G., 51, 74, 123, 158, 173
Rockwell, Robert, 92
Rogin, Michael, 169, 180
Rose, Lisle, 102
Rosenbaum, Jonathan, 117, 121
Rosenberg, Norman, 194
Roux, Tony, 119
Rózsa, Miklós, 130–3, 135, 138–9, 142
Rubin J., Louis D., 179
Rue Transnonain, 3–5, 14
Runciman, W. C., 12

Russell, Bob, 105
Ryan, Robert, 98, 153, 175, 178

Salt, Barry, 45, 56
Sarris, Andrew, 194
Satan Met a Lady (1936, William Dieterle), 66, 201
Savage, Ann, 51
Sayre, Nora, 102
Schatz, Thomas, 32, 36–7
Schmidt-Rottluff, Karl, 40
Schrader, Paul, 36, 39, 48, 55, 57, 164, 179, 183, 187, 188, 194
Schwarz, Richard A., 102
Scorsese, Martin, 114, 175, 181, 214
Scott, Adrian, 5–6, 72, 78
Scott, Zachary, 169
Scottsboro Boys, 96
Screen Guide for Americans, A, 93
Seabright, Paul, 58, 77
Sekula, Allan, 17, 36
Set-Up, The (1949, Robert Wise), 168, 175, 178, 181, 207
Sex Murderer: Self-Portrait (1920), 42
Shadoian, Jack, 139, 142, 199
Shaheen, Jack, 102
Shakespeare, William, 64, 162–3
Shayne, Konstantin, 123–4, 202
Shilkret, Nathaniel, 105–6
Silver, Alan, 36, 55, 57, 140, 179, 182, 185, 190–1, 198–9
Simmons, Jean, 50
'Simple Art of Murder, The', 66, 78
Simpson, Philip, 194
Sinatra, Frank, 100
Since You Went Away (1944, John Cromwell), 151
Siodmak, Robert, 7, 39, 41, 51, 122–3, 130–4, 136–40, 142, 194, 203, 205–7, 212
Sirk, Douglas, 39, 205–6
Sloane, Everett, 54
Smedley, Nick, 83–4, 102
Sobchack, Vivian, 151, 162–3, 194
Spielberg, Steven, 116
Spiral Staircase, The (1945, Robert Siodmak), 122, 207
Split Second (1953, Dick Powell), 94, 211
Springsteen, R. G., 92
Stag Night at Sharkey's (1909), 177
Staiger, Janet, 194

Stalin, Josef, 90, 92
Stallybrass, Peter, 170, 180
Stanfield, Peter, 15, 78, 142, 195
Stanwyck, Barbara, 29, 31, 48, 74–5, 85, 102, 137, 158–9, 173
Steiner, Max, 39, 118
Steinlen, Théophile Alexandre, 5
Št panek, Kárel, 86
Sterritt, David, 121
Stevens, Jason W., 195
Stevenson, Robert, 98, 207, 212–13
Stewart, Jimmy, 84
Sturm, Der (The Storm), 40–1
Sturme der Leidenschaft (1931, Robert Siodmak), 122, 140
Strange Affair of Uncle Harry, The (1945, Robert Siodmak), 122, 207
Strange Loves of Martha Ivers, The (1946, Lewis Milestone), 29, 35, 147, 207
Stranger, The (1946, Orson Welles), 122–41, 207
Stranger on the Third Floor (1940, Boris Ingster), 11, 71, 81, 207
Street, The (Die Strasse, 1923, Karl Grune), 49, 201
Stripling, Robert E., 5
Sugarland Express, The (1974, Steven Spielberg), 116
Sunset Boulevard (1950, Billy Wilder), 51, 135, 159–62, 211
Surrealism, 40
Suspect, The (1945, Robert Siodmak), 122, 207
Swanson, Gloria, 51, 159, 161

Taiwan, 83
Taschen (publication), 185, 190
Tasker, Yvonne, 195
Tatar, Maria, 41–2, 55
Taxi Driver (1976, Martin Scorsese), 183, 214
Taylor, Elisabeth, 91
Taylor, Robert, 91
Telotte, J. P., 195, 199
Testament of Dr. Mabuse, The (1932, Fritz Lang), 46, 55, 201–2
Thaxter, Phyllis, 154
They Live By Night (1948, Nicholas Ray), 48, 165, 207
Thieves' Highway (1949, Jules Dassin), 59, 191, 207

INDEX

Thieves Like Us (1971, Robert Altman), 114
Tierney, Gene, 89, 104
Tih Minh (1918, Louis Feuillade), 34–5
Toast of New York, The (1937, Rowland V. Lee), 105
Too Late for Tears (1949, Byron Haskin), 59, 207
Torgus (Hanns Kobe, 1921), 45
Touch of Evil (1958, Orson Welles), 103, 122–3, 140, 194, 213
Tourneur, Jacques, 35, 49, 99, 103, 105, 107, 109, 119, 134, 139, 147–8, 150, 152, 162, 165, 179, 203, 205, 210
Touzet, René, 134, 142
Tracy, Don, 130
Tracy, Spencer, 165
Trial, The (1955, Mark Robson), 100
Trieste, 91
Truman Doctrine, 83–4, 87–8
Trumbo, Dalton, 6
Twentieth-Century Fox, 57, 88, 91, 94, 187, 191

Ulmer, Edgar G., 35, 39, 49, 204–6, 210
Underworld U.S.A. (1961, Samuel Fuller), 49, 214
Union Station (1950, Rudolph Mate), 48, 213
United Artists, 72, 93–4, 99–100, 115, 179, 181, 187, 191
United Nation, 83
Universal Pictures, 72, 93–4, 131, 179, 187, 191
University of California (Los Angeles), 182
Unsuspected, The (1947, Michael Curtiz), 187, 207

Valentine, Paul, 106
Vampires, Les (1915, Louis Feuillade), 26, 34–5, 200
van Pallandt, Nina, 105
Variety (1924, E. A. Dupont), 44
Veidt, Conrad, 43
Venice Film Festival, 46
Vernet, Marc, 17, 36, 55, 188
Vidler, Anthony, 167, 180
Vidor, King, 93, 203, 210–11, 214
Vincendeau, Ginette, 17, 36
von Stroheim, Erich, 160

Walden, Herwarth, 40
Walk a Crooked Mile (1948, Gordon Douglas), 95–6, 208
Walk East on Beacon (1952, Alfred W. Werker), 86, 93, 213
Walker, Vernon L., 71
Ward, Elizabeth, 140, 182–3, 199
Warner Brothers, 96–7, 118, 162, 179–80, 187, 191
Washington, Dinah, 105
Waste Land, The (1922), 176, 181
Waxman, Franz, 39
Waxworks (1924, Paul Leni), 45, 201
Wayne, John, 93, 97
Webb, Roy, 105–6, 109–10
Webster, Daniel, 97–8
Weegee, 48, 57
Weimar Cinema, 38, 41, 43–9, 52, 54–6, 199
Weimar Republic, 38
Welles, Orson, 34, 54, 103, 122–5, 127, 129–30, 139–41, 179, 206–7, 213
Wellman, William, 88, 201, 215
Werker, Alfred W., 48, 86, 204, 206, 213
When It Was All Over, They Played Cards (1917), 42
Whip Hand, The (1951, William Cameron Menzies), 99
White, Allon, 170, 180
Whitfield, Stephen J., 102
Widmark, Richard, 94
Wiene, Robert, 45, 200–1
Wilder, Billy, 35, 39, 49, 51, 72, 75, 79, 81, 157–8, 160–2, 164, 173–4, 181, 204, 206–7, 211
Willard, Jess, 175
Willett, John, 40, 55
William, Warren, 66, 202
Williams, Duke, 92
Williams, John, 103–6, 116, 118, 120–1
Williams, Tennessee, 166
Wilmington, Michael 121
Wise, Robert, 11, 93, 119, 175, 181, 203, 207, 211, 214–15
Wojcik, Pamela Robertson, 140
Woman in the Window (1944, Fritz Lang), 51, 81, 207
Woman on Pier 13, The (1953, Robert Stevenson), 98–9, 213

World War II, 2, 14, 48–9, 82, 89, 91, 93, 121, 146, 151, 164–5, 184, 196
Wrubel, Allie, 105–6

Young, Loretta, 126–7
You Only Live Once (1937, Fritz Lang), 165, 179, 202

Zerman, Mel, 184–5
Zinnemann, Fred, 39, 152, 162, 203
Žižek, Slavoj, 195
Zola, Émile, 176
Zsigmond, Vilmos, 117

EU representative:
Easy Access System Europe
Mustamäe tee 50, 10621 Tallinn, Estonia
Gpsr.requests@easproject.com